Theresa Cheung was born into a family of psychics and spiritualists. Since leaving King's College, Cambridge University with a Masters in Theology and English, she has dedicated her life to the study of the unexplained and writing books to raise spiritual awareness of supernormal potential within ourselves and in the world around us, as well as the very real possibility of life after death. The author of numerous bestselling mind, body and spirit books, including two *Sunday Times* top 10 bestsellers, Theresa's books have also been translated into twenty-five different languages. She has never claimed to be psychic but sees the world around her with spiritual eyes and describes herself as an ordinary woman who has had extraordinary experiences.

Please visit her at her popular Theresa Cheung author page on Facebook or email her at angeltalk710@aol.com or via her website: www.theresacheung.com.

Heaven Called My Name

*Incredible True Stories of Heavenly
Encounters and the Afterlife*

THERESA CHEUNG

piatkus

PIATKUS

First published in Great Britain in 2016 by Piatkus

1 3 5 7 9 10 8 6 4 2

A CIP catalogue record for this book
is available from the British Library.

ISBN 978-0-349-41300-6

Typeset in Bembo by M Rules
Printed and bound in Great Britain by
Clays Ltd, St Ives plc

Papers used by Piatkus are from well-managed forests
and other responsible sources.

MIX
Paper from
responsible sources
FSC® C104740

Piatkus
An imprint of
Little, Brown Book Group
Carmelite House
50 Victoria Embankment
London EC4Y 0DZ

An Hachette UK Company
www.hachette.co.uk

www.improvementzone.co.uk

Just as a candle cannot burn without fire,
we cannot live without a spiritual life.

BUDDHA

For death is no more than a turning of us
over from time to eternity.

WILLIAM PENN

CONTENTS

ACKNOWLEDGEMENTS

When I got the news that the honour of writing a book about heaven for Piatkus was all mine, I looked heaven-wards and screamed with delight. I truly believe that each time another book about matters spiritual is presented by a mainstream publisher, it is a positive step forwards. In today's often materialistic and unforgiving age we urgently need to consider the needs of our hearts and spirits, and I sincerely hope this book will speak to and nourish the hearts and spirits of all those who read it. I am therefore deeply thankful to Claudia Connal, Zoe Bohm, Jillian Stewart and everyone at Piatkus involved in the decision to greenlight this book, for sensing the very real and urgent need for more literature of this kind.

As always, my heartfelt thanks go to all the inspiring people who contributed their incredible stories to the book. I want you to know you are making a real difference by sharing your words, hearts and spirits, and bringing comfort, hope and light in the darkness. I would also like to thank anyone who has ever got in touch with me over the years through my publisher, my angeltalk710@aol.com email and/or www.theresacheung.com, or more recently, my Theresa Cheung Author Facebook page. You may not know it, but you are a constant source of insight, inspiration and encouragement to me as we all work together to spread the life-changing message that heaven is real.

Thanks also go to Kim Nash, a remarkable lady with a passion for blogging about books (www.kimthebookworm. co.uk) and, as good fortune would have it, the afterlife. Kim got in touch with me last year and helped me to see the light by encouraging me to embrace social media as an essential way to promote spirit to large numbers of people. Kim, thank you for your inspiration and all the great work you do.

My sincerest gratitude goes to my wise and lovely agent, Lorella Belli, who works tirelessly and with great heart. I am blessed to have her representing me.

Finally, a massive and heartfelt thank you to Ray, Robert and Ruthie for their patience, understanding and love, while I poured my heart, mind and spirit into writing a book I truly felt called from above and within to write.

INTRODUCTION

OUT OF THIS WORLD

*If we find ourselves with a desire that nothing
else can satisfy, the most obvious explanation is
that we were made for another world.*

C.S. LEWIS

I believe in heaven. I know in my heart that we don't die, and that our loved ones watch over us from the other side and speak to us on Earth in countless miraculous ways. Yes, near-death experiences offer the closest thing we have to 'proof' of heaven, but I believe heaven can also call out to us through a vivid dream, gentle touch, heartfelt smile, lovely song, mysterious scent, flash of insight, glorious rainbow, white feather, passing cloud, singing bird, puff of air, shaft of sunlight, kind word or deed, stunning coincidence, or anyone or anything in this life that for a fleeting moment of bliss takes our spirits out of this world.

If you have ever experienced unexpected feelings of love, wonder, healing and joy, I believe this is heaven calling your name.

Things certainly haven't always had this clarity for me. Even though I was born into a family of psychics and spiritualists – and can't recall a time when I haven't been drawn to the invisible world – there have been many times in my life when I have longed to hear, see or feel the eternal spirit that exists within and around us, but have only been met with silence. I'm sure I'm not the only one to experience this. Perhaps you don't think you have ever heard heaven speak to you. Maybe you long to believe in heaven, but doubt often gets the upper hand. You may have experienced something you thought was magical at the time, but then in hindsight you start to second guess yourself until you aren't really sure of anything any more.

Few people have had near-death experiences, or direct personal confirmation of life after death through a full-blown afterlife encounter that leaves them in no doubt that heaven is real (and I'm not one of them), so where does that leave the rest of us? Where do we draw our certainty and comfort from? How can we know for sure if we are hearing the voice of heaven or not?

This book isn't only about the moments that have the 'wow' factor, or that are so out of this world that there is no doubt heaven is speaking loud and clear. It is also about the less obvious ways heaven can whisper when we feel misunderstood, unloved and alone. My great hope is that reading the pages that follow will open your mind and heart to spirit, and help you to recognise that heaven is calling out to you all the time in unseen ways. It is calling out to you right now as you read these words.

Open your mind

Of course, I can't offer you absolute proof, but I am going to try to open your mind to the very real possibility that heaven exists and there is life after death. Open your mind in this way and you may just find that your life transforms in miraculous ways.

I've had the privilege of writing about the spiritual life for many years now. During this time I have read thousands of stories about the afterlife and near-death experiences (or NDEs) from people of all ages, backgrounds, religions and walks of life. I have also interviewed some of the world's leading afterlife/spiritual experts, teachers, scientists and parapsychologists. In that time I have become entirely convinced that the afterlife is real, and have also come to understand that anyone, whoever they are and wherever they come from, can find their own unique way to communicate with heaven.

I have also noticed that even though the medium in which heaven chooses to express its soothing presence differs greatly in individual details and circumstances, all the stories remind us that what we actually see is not so very important. It is to the invisible that we need to look for meaning. It is the unseen that has total power, the unseen that is always in charge and the ultimate reality – whether we realise it or not.

Looking back on my life, this 'invisible in charge' theme was always present for me. I just wasn't aware of it at the time.

Head in the clouds

For most of my life I felt like an outsider. I did all I could to try to fit in and look cool. I wanted to be accepted. I worked hard and earnestly, but nothing truly worked. I never felt 'normal' or as though I belonged anywhere. I also had no idea why I was on this planet or what my purpose was.

Growing up in a borderline poor family of psychics and spiritualists didn't help much. I remember the whispers as my mother (who was Dutch Indonesian with a heavy accent so, I guess, rather an outsider in the UK of the 1960s) and my father (who was British but isolated from the mainstream because he was disabled and mildly autistic) dropped me off at the school gates. I remember the taunts and sometimes wishing I could just disappear.

Of course, school was torture. I was educated in the days when teachers still let class members choose sports teams, and guess who was usually picked last. Looking back I don't blame my classmates as I had absolutely no hand and eye coordination, as well as a tendency to daydream, so I would have been a liability for any team – sporting or otherwise.

The story of my isolation continued at Cambridge University. I was from a poor, mixed-race family and simply didn't have the articulation, financial means or confidence to fit in. Being a girl didn't help much either as Cambridge was pretty much male orientated at the time and I went to King's College, the destination of many an Etonian. I was too shy to eat in the splendid dining hall, and took to hiding in my room with a packet of crisps and library books. In seminars and lecture groups I did my best to blend into the background, as the eloquence of my peers terrified me. The only time I felt vaguely confident was in university shows, as I have always had a natural talent for dance.

Looking back I still can't believe I was offered a place at such a prestigious university, given my unusual family circumstances and home-education background. My entire time there felt surreal. Heaven must have played a hand in sending me there, though, as all the other universities I chose rejected my application. It was only Cambridge that took a leap of faith for me, and I am forever grateful to it for the priceless opportunity it gave me to study there.

Sadly, however, the confidence boost of getting into Cambridge didn't help me overcome the feelings of not being good enough that filtered through into my early adult life. After university I lost myself in relationships and jobs that were simply not right for me and lowered my self-esteem even further (if that were possible). I think you get the idea. I was like a fragile reed blown in the wind.

In hindsight, I can see now that my continuous feeling of not fitting in was actually a longing for spiritual meaning and true understanding of myself. I was searching for happiness, meaning and a sense of belonging, but looking in all the wrong places. I had no idea who I was on the inside, and what life was calling me to be or do. Of course, at the time I just felt out of this world – as though I didn't belong.

To make things worse, my thoughts and feelings always seemed so very different from those of my peer group. I was hyper-emotional and cried for very little reason – and I lost count of the number of times people told me I was too sensitive for my own good. Bright lights, crowds and noise overwhelmed me. My dreams were powerful and vivid, and time alone was as necessary to me as food and water. Like one of those Jane Austin heroines, if I didn't have plenty of space to reflect on the day's events in solitude each day, I would get stressed and uptight. The world in general felt like a very scary and threatening place. I needed regular time out to escape and regain my emotional strength.

It also seemed as though everybody else was content to focus on the everyday, but my mind was always somewhere in the clouds. I kept thinking, *Is this it? We are born, go to school, get a job, get married, have children and/or a career, then get old and die? Is that all that life is?* The world I was trying so hard to fit into valued money, romance, appearance and success, but my spiritual upbringing had always taught me that there is something more to this life outside ordinary thinking and the everyday. The trouble was that I couldn't find that 'something more', and the world I longed to be embraced and accepted by didn't seem to value or even notice the invisible side of things, so a battle raged endlessly in my heart and mind. I wanted to fit in so much, but couldn't relate to the world I was trying to fit into.

It didn't help that throughout my life I had only ever experienced fleeting encounters with the invisible world. My first memorable encounter with spirit began at around the age of sixteen, when I suffered from anorexia and was slowly killing myself with fear of my body, food, other people, the world, life, the universe – everything. One morning I struggled out of bed to close the curtains because the light was hurting my eyes, and as I did so a shaft of sunlight played over me and I was rooted to the spot. In that moment a surge of joy, love and unbelievable warmth catapulted through me. I knew then that I wanted to live and there was a better way; a path of light and love to replace fear and self-hate. In the months that followed, my anxiety about food began to disappear. I recovered gradually without hospitalisation or help from therapists, drawing inspiration from a feeling of growing love and light inside me. I still felt somewhat out of place and confused about my life, but this brief glimpse of warmth and security had given me something to hold on to, and the hope that there was indeed another way.

At the time I didn't share my experience outside my family, because I knew no one would believe me. I kept my encounter with the spiritual side of life hidden within me, buried myself in the business of trying to come to terms with daily life, and took the road well travelled of fear, competition and the everyday. I thought being as normal as possible would cure my feelings of alienation – instead it made them worse and led me to car-crash relationships, exercise addiction and other deeply unhealthy, unhappy, co-dependent, self-harming scenarios. My life took an even darker turn when my mother died. I was in my late twenties at the time and longed for her to send me a sign, but I felt nothing. Without any sense of spiritual connection to my mother, I lost faith in the existence of an afterlife and plunged into full-blown depression.

Luckily, throughout it all my hunger for spiritual meaning never vanished completely, and it always somehow managed to pull me from the edge of disaster in the nick of time. Gentle nudges from above through dreams, coincidences and flashes of intuition continued to guide or protect me. I simply didn't recognise them at the time for the divine inspiration they were. Everything changed, however, when I hit my early thirties and heaven sent me a sign that was impossible for me to fully explain away or dismiss. Even though my doubts didn't completely subside, that sign gave me a spiritual foundation and a sense of purpose I had been lacking before. I'll share the story of that life-changing afterlife encounter in Chapter 1, so you can understand why I now feel called to spread the word that the afterlife is real. For now, though, let's focus firmly on what is important here – you.

Let's talk about you

It doesn't matter whether you've had a near-death experience, afterlife encounter or dramatic wake-up call from heaven or not. The fact that you feel drawn to matters spiritual and are reading this book says everything I need to know about you.

Think of this book as spirit calling out to you and connecting you with the piece of heaven inside your heart and the presence of the divine all around you. I know you must be longing for that sense of connection. Perhaps, like me, you have always felt a little out of this world. Perhaps you are deeply grieving the loss of a loved one, or going through a traumatic relationship break-up or job loss. Maybe you are trying to deal with stress, addiction, depression, low self-esteem or body issues. There may not even be any issues or conflicts – you could merely be at a point when you long to find a deeper meaning to things.

Where you are right now is totally normal, as most of us get separated from love many times in our lives. We have fleeting glimpses of meaning when we sense a more beautiful way, perhaps through relationships, the beauty of nature, kindness or moments of unexplained euphoria, but we don't actually trust such feelings and they slip away. For some reason we tend to have more trust in fear than in love, but there is always a voice inside us reminding us that there is something better – that love is more powerful – and it is this voice that drew you to this book. It is the voice that longs to reconnect you to heaven.

So many times in my life I have chosen fear over love, and lost faith in heaven and myself in the process. However, the older I get – and especially now I have entered my fifth decade – the more deeply I feel the presence of heaven and departed loved ones, and this gives me heart and courage, especially during darker days. I have had personal experiences, and read countless stories that should give me all the so-called 'proof' I need, but my afterlife experiences and decades of afterlife research are *not* the true incentive for me to believe in heaven. I believe because I have finally learned to trust the supreme power of my heart to connect me to the afterlife. It is through my heart and the love that lives there that heaven calls to me now.

Let's talk about heaven

The traditional image of heaven features white clouds, harps, spirits of departed loved ones, and angels with wings and halos, but glimpsing heaven in this obvious way is extremely rare. From my experience and research, the form heaven takes on Earth can vary widely, and each person experiences it in their own unique way. It can be visible and invisible. The possibilities for eternal love and goodness to manifest in this world are endless, and you can read about some of them in this book. As you read you may feel that some stories have logical or psychological explanations, but to those who experienced them no amount of rational or sceptical explanation will ever match the power of their personal belief that heaven spoke to them, or that they heard the voices of departed loved ones. The definition of faith is, after all, belief – or better still, trust – without the need for absolute proof.

For me, the only convincing conclusion given the large amount of trustworthy witness statements on offer is that heaven is real, and that it exists all around us and within us. There is spirit (consciousness) within us, and an invisible spiritual realm all around us that intermingles with the physical world. In this way heaven is more a state of mind or eternal consciousness than a place. People do not experience heaven because they are religious or because they believe in it, or even because they long or need to see it, but because the time is right for them to awaken spiritually.

I'm living proof that religion, belief in the afterlife, or the desire to see and talk to spirit are not essential requirements for afterlife encounters. I was taught from an early age to believe in heaven, longed fiercely to talk to the other side and on many occasions could really have done with a divine boost. I didn't get one – all I got was silence. I tried so very hard and experimented with a variety of religions and belief systems, but made little progress. You can imagine how disillusioned with myself I felt growing up in a family of psychics whose gifts I hadn't inherited.

Today, I have made significant progress spiritually, but it took me a good four decades to achieve a breakthrough and I still would not say I am psychic. I simply say that I am an ordinary person who has had glimpses of something extraordinary – but not having a full-blown afterlife encounter, or seeing and hearing heaven in the clear way a medium or psychic can, matters less and less to me now. Age and life experience have taught me that heaven speaks to me in ways that are unique and highly personal to me, and the subtlety of these ways does not make them any less profound.

It seems that I am not alone in my gradual and individual awakening to spirit. The thousands of afterlife-encounter stories sent to me over the years show that increasing numbers of people are conquering their fears and reservations, and looking heavenwards. It seems that spirit is revealing itself today as never before. There are countless books, websites, magazines, blogs and an escalating number of films and documentaries – not to mention cutting-edge research by scientists and doctors – tentatively confirming the survival of consciousness after death.

I'm honest and I won't ever claim to know the answers to the big 'why' questions, but I do know that we need this chorus of belief in heaven and life after death right now more than ever before. In an increasingly conflicted world of religious difference and unfair wealth distribution, never has it been more crucial for us to believe in the power of love and goodness that exists within and around us. Never has it been more important for us to trust that compassion, light and eternal life will always be stronger than the forces of hate, darkness and death. Never has the time been more right than for the publication of a book like this, dedicated to the reality of heaven.

Heavenly voices

In these pages you'll find many amazing afterlife stories sent to me by my readers, punctuated with my own spiritual experiences and insights. I want you to understand where I'm coming from, so Chapter 1 tells the story of my quest to hear the voice of heaven, about how my life was saved by the voice of spirit, and how this became the catalyst for my career as a spiritual writer, researching and gathering afterlife stories from all over the world. Chapters 2–5 explore the four most common ways I have identified that heaven can reach out to us – through our hearing and sight, and our intuition and our emotions. Chapter 6 describes the mind-blowing world of near-death experiences. Chapter 7 gives advice on how to establish your own direct line of communication with the world of spirit, and Chapter 8 is devoted to the subject of afterlife signs or calling cards. Chapter 9 ends with a heartfelt message from above. There is also an appendix section that compliments certain passages in the book.

For the most part the stories I have been sent by various people have been left unchanged, but I have changed people's names – and, in some instances other details – to protect their identities. All the people who got in touch with me impressed me greatly with their honesty, and I have no reason to doubt them. Some told me that this was the first time they had shared their story with anyone. Others said that until heaven reached out to them they had not been particularly spiritual, or would have laughed at the idea of an afterlife. Some were religious but most were not. Like a lot of people today, they believed in something but were not sure what until heaven called and filled their life with meaning.

Just as I don't consider myself a psychic or medium, those whose accounts you will read here are ordinary people with ordinary lives, and they come from all walks of life, backgrounds and cultures. I hope their stories will give you a vibrant and vivid depiction of the many ways departed loved ones and the voice of heaven can call you, and inspire you to find your own spiritual path, or to continue on the path you are already on with renewed passion.

I hope, too, that you will be as inspired and moved by the stories as I never fail to be, and that if you have a spiritual experience, story or insight of your own to share you will write to me (for details, *see page 287*). The more of us who talk about heaven and share our experiences of it, the closer it becomes.

Tears and smiles

Today, heaven continues to call my name, and it is an honour and privilege to share with you my story and the remarkable stories of other people.

Many tears and smiles surged through me as I wrote this book and opened myself to my spiritual calling, and as answers to questions I have had all my life began to form. However, as you read please bear in mind that with any book, as in life, the greater message relates to your heart and spirit, and is therefore invisible. You can take this invisible message as a metaphor or a profound truth – it doesn't really matter. However, if you read carefully and listen keenly to your heart, you will find that there is so much for you to learn about yourself, especially when you know how to read what is hidden between the lines.

Finally, I'd like to express my gratitude to you for reading this book and strengthening the numbers of people around the world who long to hear the voice of spirit in their lives, and to connect with departed loved ones. I hope that as you read you will rediscover yourself and what matters to you in this life and the next. I hope you will learn a great deal about the world of spirit so that the next time it calls from above, or gently knocks from within your heart, you will instantly recognise that heaven is calling – that it is urging you to be more loving, deeper and so much more powerful than you ever thought you could be.

I hope you will wake up one day, breathe deeply, be still and hear heaven calling your name.

Heaven is calling this morning. Shhh, Listen.
Can you hear it? Will you answer the call?

ANON

CHAPTER ONE

HEAVEN CALLED
MY NAME

*The spiritual journey is individual, highly
personal. It can't be organised or regulated. It
isn't true that everyone should follow one path.
Listen to your own truth.*

RAM DASS

Growing up, as already mentioned, in a family of spiritualists and psychics, I longed to hear the voice of heaven. I wanted to be like the boy in the *Sixth Sense* film and 'see dead people'. I wasn't like him. I was a sensitive deep thinker who absolutely believed in heaven, but had no direct personal experience of communication with the other side. I simply couldn't see, hear or feel heaven.

In my late teens the longing to enter into an intimate dialogue with heaven was so strong that I was drawn to the contemplative life. I decided to spend a few weeks in a convent retreat to consider my options. I needed to make that spiritual journey to see if this was how the voice of heaven would actually speak to me.

Secrets of the sisterhood

During my retreat the gentle rhythm of the prayers, and the quiet and joyful companionship of the sisters, felt like a purification. According to Aristotle, 'Happiness in the highest sense is the contemplative life' and, at the time, I was profoundly influenced by his sound arguments that to achieve spiritual fulfilment contemplation is essential. The writings of my namesake Sister Teresa, in particular *Interior Castle*, which is a book about a life of prayer or continuous intimate dialogue with the divine, also appeared to be calling me to a life of contemplation. Another huge influence on my thinking was the work of Thomas Merton (d. 1966), who left a frantically busy life in New York to lead a monastic life. Merton's spiritual quest was to find awakening – insight into the nature of things – and he felt that he needed simplicity and silence to hear the voice of heaven speak to him. I thought that I needed that, too.

There is a lot of mystery surrounding life in a nunnery or monastery, but from my admittedly brief personal experience I can tell you that simplicity and openness are the key words, rather than mystery. Having said that, although the life of a nun is ordered and serene on the outside, inside there is often a tremendous complexity and even struggle. This was certainly the case for me, especially when it soon became abundantly clear that such a life wasn't my calling, and that heaven wasn't going to speak to me in this way. I did, however, learn some profound spiritual truths, and take the liberty of digressing a little here by sharing them with you, because in some ways heaven was speaking to me through what I learned from my time with the nuns. In hindsight, I can see I was being given the recipe for a spiritually fulfilled life.

I learned that only interior beauty should ever be used to judge someone's character and appearance. This is a particularly important message for our image-obsessed age. We all want to look our best, of course, but the way to truly glow or look radiant isn't by using make-up and having a designer wardrobe, but by achieving inner happiness. If someone is happy from the inside they radiate something extraordinarily lovely that can't be achieved with styling. That's why now that I have finally overcome my allergy to social media, and have surprised myself by somehow finding the courage to do video blogs, I do them without wearing make-up or having makeovers. This way, with my readers being able to see the real me, I feel free and able to speak from the heart.

Another thing I learned – and I feel this is of increasing importance today when we are all constantly plugged into our computers and phones – was the importance of silence. Back in the early 1980s all these technological innovations weren't in place yet, so there wasn't quite the same level of stress and distraction, but I do remember the absolute bliss of not speaking for days on end. I knew then that only by unplugging myself and having moments of quiet could I focus on who I was and what heaven was saying to me.

This need for regular quiet reflection has remained with me ever since.

Perhaps the most powerful lesson I learned was something I probably instinctively already knew but needed reminding of (and will always need to be reminded of), and this was that true happiness does not come from material things or stuff. I spent time with sisters who had given up everything they owned to lead a contemplative life and tend to the needs of the homeless. The joy on their faces as they lived and worked, and heard heaven call their names, was abundant.

How I wished I had felt that joy and heard that voice talking to me, too, but I didn't. I have nothing but admiration for people who give up everything to devote themselves to a life of contemplation, but I realised it was something I just couldn't do. I needed to find other ways to hear heaven without retiring from the world or joining an order. So I headed off to Cambridge University to read theology with a heart full of hope that I would soon find my way to hear heaven speak to me.

Eternal student

One day, while studying world religions in the old university library at Cambridge, it dawned on me (in a divine moment of illumination) that there is a difference between being religious and being spiritual. I could clearly see that all religions are a path to the divine, and that one religion does not have exclusive access. In other words, you don't necessarily need to be religious to hear the voice of heaven.

Freed from adherence to one specific religion, my instinct was to learn. I was going to become a spiritual expert. I was going to study all the esoteric arts, learn psychic or mediumistic techniques, and train myself to see and talk to heaven. There had to be a way to do it. I was going to find it.

The results of my energetic and determined quest for a direct experience of the afterlife were unspectacular, often misguided and sometimes ridiculous – as when I found myself attending psychic classes and pretending to see and hear spirits when I really couldn't, so keen was I to impress. Or when I attended a summer solstice celebration and watched the meditation leader fall asleep during a guided visualisation so monotonous that my eyelids were fighting sleep, too. I didn't realise it at the time, but in place of my adherence to Christianity I was simply replacing it with a 'New Age' identity, and copying gurus and psychics instead of finding what was right for me. Finding my vocation had become an act of will, not heart. Heaven wasn't going to speak to me until I tuned into and listened to the voice of my heart.

There is nothing wrong with imitation as a starting point, but there will always come a time when the individual (spirit) within you needs recognition, when you need to know who you are and not how you are defined by other people's expectations or belief systems. There will come a time when you need to trust yourself and move from the stage of belonging, or copying what works for others, to becoming. Of course, trying to copy what works for others is actually much less demanding than being your true self, because when you copy others all the thinking and planning has been done for you. Many of us find being ourselves so hard that we try to run away from it, but taking that easier path will never lead to true spiritual fulfilment. I think this wonderful quote by Rabbi Zusya sums things up so very well: 'In the coming world, they will not ask me, Why were you not Moses? They will ask me, Why were you not Zusya?'

During all those years spent trying so hard to find rituals, methods and techniques that would help me talk to heaven, I simply wasn't trusting myself or finding my own way to speak to heaven. It is hardly surprising that – having such a weak spiritual foundation to sustain me – when I reached my late twenties and my mother suddenly died my heart and life crumbled.

Lights in the darkness

I lost two years of my life to the black hole that is depression following the loss of my mother. Depression is terrifying for those who haven't experienced it. I can only compare the emotional pain to that of a hammer hitting a bruise over and over again. I longed to hear my mother speak to me in spirit, but her silence catapulted me even deeper into despair, if that were possible. I begged and pleaded for her to send me a sign from the other side, but there was nothing. I felt alone and directionless. The disillusionment I felt was deep and profound, especially as my mother had inspired my insatiable appetite for spiritual understanding. She had always taught me that heaven was real, so surely she should send me a sign. Why didn't she reach out to me? I lost my faith in heaven.

Mercifully, I somehow stumbled through my period of depression, and the passing of time eventually pulled me out of the black hole. As days passed into weeks and months passed into years, I gradually began to see life in colour again, rather than in black and white. I started to dream about my mother. The dreams were vivid and realistic, and in them my mother would do ordinary and everyday things, like tidying my bedroom or making a cup of tea. She never spoke to me in the dreams. I just watched her. The dreams felt so real that I would wake up from them with the feeling that she was still alive, but then within seconds the reality of her passing away would hit me like a brick. The disappointment on waking was harrowing. However, looking back I can see that each time I had a dream about my mother, in the days that followed there would be gentle progress. I would get the urge to do something positive for myself – something simple like having a haircut or going for a walk. Putting together all these simple steps started to make a real difference.

At the time I didn't think of the dreams as afterlife signs because they were so ordinary and my mother did nothing spectacular in them, and didn't directly communicate anything of significance, but looking back I can now see they were signs. I simply didn't recognise them as such because I expected something much more dramatic and spectacular.

The gift of becoming a mother when I was in my early thirties finally shifted my perspective and priorities from darkness to joy, and gradually my days became more about smiles than tears. As depression faded slowly into the background, I also began to lose my burning desire for a direct experience of afterlife communication. Although the search for spiritual meaning in life was still crucial to me, I finally accepted that talking to dead people wasn't my gift, and that I probably wasn't going to experience it. I put my passion into researching the phenomenon and, as is so often the case when you let go of something you want so much, it was then that I had the most dramatic and life-changing afterlife experience of my life to date.

Listen to me

My memory of the moment is crystal clear. Driving along in my car, I was heading to a busy junction and intending to turn left. I was getting a bit frustrated that I couldn't see the road ahead because I was stuck behind a large van for so long that I memorised its number plate. Then, just as I reached the junction, I heard the voice of my departed mother tell me to 'take the right path'.

My mother's disembodied voice came from outside my head rather than inside it, and it was so familiar and persuasive that I obeyed without question. It didn't make sense at all at the time, because heading in the wrong direction made me take a longer route to my destination than was necessary and I missed an appointment. I was frustrated with myself and didn't understand why I had taken the wrong turn, and wasted a morning driving to an appointment that I then missed. Later, when I switched on the news, I recognised the junction and the van I had been trailing behind for so long, and everything fell into place. The van had been involved in a fatal collision involving a pile-up of several vehicles a few moments after it turned left at the junction. Three people died that day, and one of them could very well have been me if the voice of my mother in spirit had not warned me.

After the shock of seeing the accident on the local news, I thought about the voice I had heard. I still didn't trust that I had heard heaven. My mother had told me countless times when I was growing up to always take the right path – in the sense that she wanted me to always do the right thing – and I dismissed what I had experienced as a latent memory resurfacing. The coincidence of that memory surfacing moments before the car crash was remarkable – as was the fact that I had blindly obeyed the warning voice – but I still couldn't bring myself to believe that this was an actual afterlife sign.

Instead, I felt confused, guilty and drained by the thought of all those people dying when it could so easily have been me. I hadn't actually seriously contemplated my own mortality until that point. Like many young people I had thought I was immortal, but narrowly escaping that accident shook me to the core. I realised for the first time that my life could have been over in seconds and I would never have seen my son again. The thought was terrifying. It all felt so random and meaningless. Why was I still alive while other people had died? Why were three lives snuffed out so senselessly? Why did horrible things happen to good people?

Feeling a headache coming on – as I often did and still do when I ponder the big 'why' questions in life – I went to bed, but my sleep was restless and fitful. I woke in the early hours of the morning to find my bedclothes and sheets pulled onto the floor. This was very unusual, as I like to be warm and tucked in at night and it was a cold night. Feeling a chill, I reached for my bedclothes. As I did so a range of emotions clashed inside my heart, ranging from gratitude and guilt to anxiety, about where the people who had died were now and whether they had found peace.

It was then that I heard a voice of a woman. It wasn't my own voice, or that of my mother or of anyone I knew. I wasn't afraid, merely curious to discover the source, so I sat up and looked around, but there was nobody there. I was just about to get up to look outside my window to see if there were people outside when I heard the voice again, and it was much louder and clearer. I can't remember all the words exactly, but it told me that I should not be afraid and that my mother was all right. The last thing the voice said, and I remember it word for word, was, 'Everything is all right for us three and everything will be all right for you, too.'

Then the voice was gone. It was just a few moments of heaven but it changed my life forever. A feeling of deep knowing and peace filled me. It was a feeling I have never had before or since, and I can only compare it to being wrapped in a warm, soft blanket on a cold winter's day. Heaven had spoken to me.

I jumped out of bed and pinched myself. I was most definitely awake, and had heard the voice. I had not been dreaming. Turning on the light, I sat at the end of the bed luxuriating in the feeling of peace – the comfort of knowing that everything made sense and was going to be all right. I still don't know why my life had been spared that day, but I have dedicated my life ever since to making my mother, in spirit, and those three people who died that day, proud.

The way ahead

In the years after the above event, many doubts and fears about whether the voice I had heard was actually from spirit have returned to haunt me, especially when life has dealt me personal blows, but nothing has ever been completely the same again for me from that moment onwards. It was as if heaven had poured a little of itself into me. I was given an understanding beyond words. I knew in my heart that there is an afterlife and that there was a reason why everything happens, even pain and loss. We just can't understand the 'whys' in this life.

Believe me, even though I have had my personal 'proof' of heaven, I continue to find injustice and suffering intolerable. I often find myself questioning heaven when I see unexplained cruelty, loss and pain. However, I have come to understand that it is important that we don't know the reasons why bad things happen to good people in this life, or why loved ones die before we are ready to say goodbye to them. Think about it. We know why a woman screams in pain during childbirth, and are not too concerned because we know her pain will soon give way to the miracle of new life. Just imagine if we knew the reason for all the suffering in the world. We would simply accept it as natural and normal, and would be less likely to offer kindness and empathy, or to go out of our way to find a way to alleviate the suffering of others. That is a world I certainly would not want to live in, so perhaps it is best that we don't fully understand. Perhaps it is best that the 'why do bad things happen to good people?' question remains unanswered.

The way I tend to think about and deal with the problem of suffering now is with the metaphor of a tapestry. This life is the underside, and nothing but messy ends and confusion, but then in heaven you turn it over and see the bigger picture where everything makes sense. Narnia author C.S. Lewis compared suffering to the blows of a hammer when creating a sculpture. The blows hurt but are necessary to create something perfect. These metaphors aren't perfect or completely satisfactory answers to the problem of suffering and the pain of grief, but they may provide some peace of mind.

As well as helping me to see the light about pain and suffering, my encounter gave me a clear sense of direction. I knew then that my mission was to spread the word that the afterlife is real, and that it is possible to hear heaven speak, but in a way uniquely personal to you, not necessarily in the way you would expect. I decided to use my experience as a starting point to encourage as many ordinary people as possible to get in touch with me and share their afterlife stories, so I could then in turn share them with a wider readership in my books. In this way all our stories would become the message that the world needed to hear. Together, we could show that heaven is real and can reveal itself in ordinary but extraordinary ways through ordinary but extraordinary people.

Between the lines

Over the years, as I researched and gathered together thousands of incredible afterlife stories sent to me by my readers, some of which you will read in this book, I gradually began to uncover perhaps the most personally reassuring and transforming revelation of all. The majority of the people writing to me and sending their stories and insights shared similar personality traits with me.

Many longed to find a connection to loved ones who had died, or to the afterlife. They were also extremely emotional and deeply sympathetic to the feelings of others, and had frequently been told that they needed to 'toughen up'. Often they 'just knew' things without knowing how they knew. For instance, they could walk into a room and instantly become aware of the mood or atmosphere. Bright lights, loud noises, crowds, busy streets, strong odours and other everyday stresses unsettled them greatly. Violence of any kind repulsed them, and they felt most at peace when with nature, animals, art and beauty. Some said that seeing or reading about cruelty of any kind online, in the newspapers or on TV affected them deeply as they had great empathy for the suffering of others. Many felt a calling to help or be kind to others and heal the world in some way, but they didn't know how to translate that compassion into reality.

Reading deeper between the lines it became abundantly clear to me that I was reading episodes of my own spiritual journey in the stories of these people. It was like peering into my own spirit. I was not the only one who experienced life in this deeper way, or who felt somehow outside of everything, including themselves, and that there had to be more to this life than meets the eye. For the first time ever, I felt as though I was understood and a part of something. It was like coming home. It gave me a fresh perspective on myself and my life. Due to this, I regard everyone who has ever contacted me about their afterlife experiences as an angel calling my name.

Perhaps you can relate to the above? Perhaps you have often felt a bit outside this world? If that's the case you may be someone with highly sensitive personality traits (in Appendix 6 you can read more about these traits), but if that description doesn't fit you, or if you don't consider yourself to be particularly sensitive, this book is also for you. Like increasing numbers of people these days, you may have grown disillusioned or dissatisfied with religion or New Age alternatives but still believe in something higher – but have no idea what that 'higher' is and how to find it. I'm convinced that the stories and insights in this book will provide you with much-needed spiritual comfort, guidance and illumination.

True spirit

After years of gathering together afterlife stories I now find deep joy and peace in the work that I do. Leading a life in spirit means something totally different to me now than it did all those years ago, when I started on this quest to hear the voice of heaven. I have come to understand that afterlife communication is not a goal but a gift to be received. When heaven calls my name today it is not through a voice 'out there' urging me to follow or copy others, or to become something I am not. It does so through the voice inside me calling me to be the person I was born to be – and that person is Theresa. When heaven calls my name today it is not through blinding lights and angel sightings, but through ordinary things illuminated by spiritual or eternal meaning.

My spiritual journey from fear and doubt to love and meaning may appear dramatic, but that is simply because I have been given the privilege to share it with you here in book form. My story isn't actually special at all, and your story would probably be far more compelling. I have shared my tears with you simply to show you that uncertainty, grief, pain, doubt and necessity made me cry out to heaven for my sense of purpose, and out of love heaven showed me the light by helping me discover eternal love within and all around me.

The grace I have been offered is summed up in a single word – spirit. It is a magic word, and a word that has become the heart of my life. It is the word heaven wants us all to discover, because when you discover your true spirit you will know deep in your heart that you are a spiritual being experiencing life on Earth. You will know that heaven is real, that loved ones do not die and that from this moment on you are being called to live a life of profound and endless meaning.

In short, you don't need to go on a retreat, join a convent or monastery, follow gurus or spiritual teachers, mediate for hours, visit a psychic or medium, do endless exercises and rituals, or have a dramatic afterlife vision to hear heaven talk to you. You merely need to follow the promptings of your heart, and trust and believe that when the time is right for you heaven will find its way to speak.

Let me count the ways

Understanding the different ways heaven tries to reach out is the first step for making divine connections. From my decades of research and reading countless afterlife stories, I have found that most people make contact with spirit through one of the following channels: hearing, thinking, seeing or feeling. The next four chapters focus on one of these categories of afterlife communication respectively.

To find out which method is preferable for you, observe yourself in the days ahead. Are you a good listener, or do you rely on your intuition? Do you think in pictures or words, or just sense or feel things deeply? It doesn't matter at this stage if you aren't sure which way is you, if you think they all apply to you to some degree, or if so far in your life you have struggled to pick up heaven's voice in any of them. I'm hoping that by the end of this book, as you begin to watch yourself more closely, things will become clearer and fall naturally into place – and that you will notice a primary channel for heaven to initiate communication with you.

The most important thing, though, is not to force anything. Trust me – trying to force or make afterlife communication happen to you is a recipe for disaster as it just causes tension, competitiveness and frustration, which will shut the door to heaven. I've made that mistake too many times in my life, and it may well explain why it took me close to four decades to actually recognise what genuine spiritual experiences were. The best state of mind for spiritual growth is one of calmness, trust and awe. Indeed, the more you connect with feelings of wonder and awe within yourself and in the world around you, the more likely it is that you will hear heaven speaking.

Take your time to savour what you read from now on. Let it sink in on both a conscious and an unconscious or invisible level. Remember, everyone's experience of the afterlife will be unique to them. There is no right or wrong way to hear, see or feel spirit. I hope that what you read will help you connect with departed loved ones and discover your own soothing, magical ways to feel their presence all around and within you, and to talk to heaven.

We talk about heaven being so far away. It is within speaking distance to those who belong there.

DWIGHT MOODY

CHAPTER TWO

CLEAR HEARING

The song of the voice is sweet, but the song of
the heart is the pure voice of heaven.

KHALIL GIBRAN

I must admit that when I was growing up and there was talk of actually hearing voices from the other side, a part of me felt that this was verging on the crazy. Now, however, I'm convinced that heavenly voices are the most truthful and sane sounds a person can ever hear. They have absolutely nothing to do with crazy, and everything to do with divine inspiration.

Hearing divine voices is called clairaudience, or clear hearing. It is the ability to tune into spirit through the medium of sound, and to hear voices or words inside your head, or just outside your head as if someone is standing close by. If this is all new to you I expect you will be wondering if this is getting just a bit too far out. My aim here is to normalise afterlife experiences and show how the extraordinary frequently manifests in the ordinary. Read the list below and you may be surprised to discover that some of the situations described are remarkably ordinary, and have probably already occurred in your life, but you dismissed them as inconsequential at the time because you didn't recognise them for what they truly were – the voice of spirit.

- You hear a disembodied voice say something profound or life changing to you. The voice may also give you directions or tell you where to find a lost item. Typically, the voice is familiar because it belongs to a deceased relative or loved one, and you hear it in your head, in your dreams or on rare occasions outside your head. Sometimes the voice is your own and sometimes it is not familiar but simply clear and decisive.

- You wake up and before you open your eyes you hear someone calling your name, but no one actually did so. You may also experience this name calling in a crowd of people or when walking in the street, but when you turn or look around for the source there isn't one.

- You turn on the TV or radio or go online and hear exactly the thing you need to be hearing. Similarly, you may overhear a conversation other people are having, and what they say speaks directly to your heart and spirit.

- You can't get a song or piece of music out of your head, and when you turn on the radio or TV or go online you hear it again.
- You hear snatches of beautiful music you haven't heard before that have no detectible source.
- You can sometimes hear the whispers of departed loved ones or the voice of heaven in the sound of birdsong, waves lapping on the shore, the howling of the wind or the sighing of the breeze.
- Your doorbell or phone rings but when you respond you find there is no one there – you just know it is a loved one in spirit calling out to you. You may also receive a text or phone call that you can't explain.
- You may hear sounds typically associated with a departed loved one, for example coins jangling in a pocket or heels tapping on the floor.
- You experience a sharp, high-pitched ringing sound in your ear for a few moments. This is not the same as the long-term harsh noise associated with tinnitus. Some psychic experts believe this gentle ringing comes from the other side, as if heaven is downloading information for your soul. If this happens, take a moment to let the divine wisdom sink in and work its magic on an unconscious level.

As already described, twenty or so years ago I believe I heard the voice of my mother in spirit call out to me when I was at a busy junction, urging me to take the right path when I intended to turn left, and listening to that voice saved my life. At the time I thought I was remembering her voice from the past or imagining it, so I kept quiet about my experience. However, in the years that followed I have had so many similar stories sent to me that I don't feel alone any more and truly believe something extraordinary occurred. Each story I have been sent shows how a divine voice brought protection, love, warmth, inspiration and joy during times of challenge, struggle, crisis and chaos, when all hope appeared lost.

By a wonderful coincidence one of these incredible stories hit the headlines as I was writing this chapter. I've summarised it for you below.

The voice of an angel?

At 10 p.m. one day in March 2015, Jennifer Groesbeck's red Dodge hatchback swerved off a road in Northern Utah, USA, flipped over and crashed into the ice-cold Spanish Fork River. The impact was so strong that the windscreen shattered and the roof crumpled. The car floated for fourteen hours until an angler spotted it and saw a hand coming out of the broken window.

Four police officers arrived and their panic was captured by the body camera one of them wore – the clip can be viewed online. They can be seen running into the ice-cold water (seven policemen and firemen were treated for hypothermia afterwards) to try and help get the person out of the crushed car. Approximately two minutes into the body-camera footage, the sound of an adult voice crying for help can be heard. It is not clearly audible and the sound is muffled on the footage, but Officer Warner can be heard replying, 'We're helping, we're coming.' As the footage continues you can see the rescuers turn the car around and remove the body of a woman driver, who is dead. Then there is a shocking revelation – her eighteen-month-old baby, Lily, is discovered in the back seat. She is upside down and strapped into a child seat that had protected her from the water. She is unconscious and hypothermic, but is taken to hospital and recovers.

The miracle of Lily's survival against insurmountable odds made headlines around the world, and it wasn't until a while later that the policemen discussed the rescue. All four remembered the female voice they had definitely heard coming from the car. Officer Beddoes, who went on to publish his story in book form, believes it was a heavenly guardian who had saved the baby's life, then called out for help when the officers arrived. They all agreed that if they hadn't heard the voice they would perhaps not have attempted to flip the car over so soon.

This mysterious story isn't the first one to hit the headlines, and many similar stories have been reported over the years. Perhaps the most famous story dates back to the World Trade Center attacks in New York on 9/11. Financial trader Ron DiFrancesco was on the eighty-fourth floor when the second hijacked plane smashed into the eighty-first floor. Others scrambled to escape down a staircase, but he lay down in panic until he heard an 'insistent' male voice urging him to get up and head for safety. He also sensed an invisible physical presence and felt his hand being grabbed. He was the last person to leave the tower before it collapsed and is convinced that an angel rescued him. Going further back to 1983, scientist James Sevigny fell 2000 feet down a Canadian Rockies mountain, breaking his back in the process. He curled up in the snow expecting to freeze to death, but then heard a female voice urging him to get up and giving him the advice he needed to make it back to the campsite. It took him two years to come forward and tell others about the experience, as it was so powerful and overwhelming.

Stories like this are picked up by the media, but similar ones have been sent to me over the years. They are equally amazing, though the people who witnessed or experienced them opted not to go to the press. I feel deeply honoured and humbled that they wrote to me instead, and that I can share their stories in my books. Lana's experience provides a wonderful example of such a story.

Shattered

Last summer I had the most incredible near escape. I was sitting in a friend's house and watching my five-year-old daughter play with her four-year-old friend in the conservatory. There was a glass window in the front and the sun was streaming through, but it wasn't burning hot, just pleasant. My daughter and her friend had their noses pressed against the window while they were watching a cat jumping around in the grass chasing a butterfly, and they were giggling. I remember thinking that I should give my mother a quick call as we hadn't spoken for ages, so I reached into my handbag. As I did so I got this high-pitched ringing in my ear. I only heard it for a few moments, then it stopped. After that I heard a voice – and the voice told me to get the children out of the conservatory, *now*.

When I heard the voice I knew I had to obey it as the tone was so serious and strong. I put down the phone, told the children it was time for milk and biscuits, and walked into the kitchen. As soon as we got to the kitchen I heard a violent shattering noise. I rushed outside and into the conservatory, and there was glass everywhere. It wasn't clear to me what had happened at first, but later I found out that a stone had been thrown at the window, shattering it completely. I can't imagine how terrible this would have been for the girls if they had been there with their noses up against the window.

If the voice had not sounded so urgent I might have questioned it or myself, as isn't 'hearing voices the first sign'? Theresa, the voice I heard was anything but mad. It was completely sane and may have saved us from serious injury. It was not shouted but quiet and calm, as if someone was standing beside me – but there was no one else in the house. I know this sounds nuts and that's why I am careful who I tell the story to. I'm not nuts, just incredibly grateful I heard that voice.

Lana's story is revealing. She mentions a gentle, high-pitched ringing in her ears, then a voice. I wrote back to her and asked her if she could identify the voice. She replied that she didn't want to say, as she could be wrong with everything happening so fast, but the voice sounded as though it belonged to her best friend Rachel, who had passed away six months before of lung cancer. The two of them had known each other from about the age of five and she felt her loss deeply, as they would talk to each other virtually every day and had gone through school, university and so much together. Lana said it made her quite emotional to think that it might have been her best friend warning her in spirit. Then she told me something even more revealing. The friend her daughter was playing with was Rachel's daughter. I wrote back to say that in my heart I felt that it was her friend in spirit who had warned her, and that this was not something to cry about. Rather, it was something to celebrate, as it showed that death had not cut the bonds of love between them.

Michelle's story, below, also features a voice of warning sent to a mother to protect her child.

Falling

I heard the voice of an angel and it saved the life of my precious son. I will never forget it. My son was only a few months old and I had to hang some washing on the roof as I did every day. To do that I needed to go up some steps that didn't have a banister. I would take my son up first to the washroom in his bouncer, then take up the washing. On this day a voice told me not to take my son up in his bouncer. I actually argued back, but the voice said it so strongly a second time that I had to obey it. I went upstairs without my son. I got to the top where there is a door leading to the washroom and went to grab the handle, but it came loose and pushed me back, so that I fell a storey down into the garden. I landed on a plastic table that got crushed, but happened to break my fall.

I think I was knocked out for a few seconds, but as soon as I woke I realised what had happened and ran to my son. I was so relieved, and shaky at the thought of what might have happened if I had been carrying him up the stairs in the bouncer. I thank heaven for those words from above every day.

I have received a number of stories from mothers who said that they felt a strange, irrational urge to check on or call their child, or heard a voice urging them to do so, and that this saved the child from danger. This is often called a mother's intuition. I can vouch for it myself. When my son was five a clear, loud voice in my head told me quite firmly to phone his school. When I called they told me he was absolutely fine, but about five minutes later they called back to say he had just been hit on the head by a stone thrown by another child. They said he was all right, but they were going to take him to the hospital just to make sure and I should meet them there. Mercifully, everything was fine and it was just a minor cut.

It is not just mothers who hear voices of warning and guidance. I have stories illustrating this phenomenon whenever the bonds of love are powerful and intense between two people. Martina's moving story is empowering because in her case the warning was not to protect a loved one, but to protect herself.

Time to stand up

I was with my boyfriend for two years. During that time he did everything in his power to control and manipulate me, to the point where I lost confidence in myself completely. The turning point came one night when my boyfriend repeatedly told me that I was worthless and was lucky to be with him. I curled into a ball of tears on the sofa as I had done many times before. This time, though, something incredible happened. Don't think I'm crazy because I'm not, but I heard this voice. It was gentle and firm and said, 'You need to get up now, Kathy.' I sat up expecting there to be somebody else in the room, but it was just my boyfriend. Again, I heard the voice, 'Kathy, you really need to get up now.'

Shakily I got to my feet. My boyfriend instantly got up to confront me, but there must have been something about me because for the first time he looked unsure of himself. I walked straight past him and left his flat and his life for good. I don't know how I found the courage, but the voice was the catalyst.

My world has changed completely since that night. I used to live in a world expecting bad things to happen, but now the world I live in is different. I expect better things now.

Kathy clearly went through a hard time in her relationship, and I don't know the circumstances so can't comment on them. However, as a spiritual writer I am often asked what happens to people who have caused others pain and suffering when they die. Do they go to heaven? My answer is yes and no. From what near-death experience stories reveal, there is an afterlife for people who have been cruel to others in this life – and in the next life they will experience the suffering they have caused others. It is not so much punishment, but the only way to help them understand and evolve as spiritual beings: on Earth they completely lacked empathy, but in heaven they have no choice but to feel the impact of their actions on others. This suggests to me that the heaven each one of us experiences after passing on is very much one we create with our thoughts, feelings and deeds on Earth. In this way, what you are thinking, feeling and doing right now is creating the kind of heaven you will experience. What an awesome and life-transforming thought!

The 'difficult time' theme continues in this next story, but in this case the power of touch triggered a powerful experience of clear hearing for Josephine, who had written to me previously about her afterlife experiences. Her story has some similarities to my own experience of clear hearing, in that what I heard in spirit when I was driving towards a junction reminded me of what my mother had often said to me while she was still alive.

In the next room

My nan always liked turquoise and frequently wore turquoise jewellery – and funnily enough, so do I. Consequently, I tend to feel closer to her when I touch and wear turquoises.

Well, having gone through a very difficult time recently, with extremely poor health, I was struggling to function and wasn't sure how I was going to cope with going out and doing what I needed to do. One Friday I suddenly found myself being strongly drawn to the pieces of turquoise in my jewellery box, and felt a sudden need to hold them. You may not be surprised to hear this, but as soon as I held a piece of turquoise in my hand, I immediately heard my nan's voice, saying, 'You can do this even if you think you can't. I'm only in the next room.' That's what she used to say to me years before she passed away, and it was those words that assured me I could cope that day, which I did. Even feeling as ill as I did, I still managed to do all that I needed to do and even started to feel a bit better for it later in the day.

Being the down-to-earth character my nan was, on the rare occasions when she gave advice, it was always very direct and to the point. There was no mistaking that voice or those words when I picked up the turquoise that day. Just hearing her voice when I needed to hear it the most helped me to carry on. Yes, it brought tears to my eyes hearing her again, but there was something about her no-nonsense, practical but reassuring approach that was exactly what I needed that day.

As you're aware, this is certainly not the first time I've felt and heard my nan's presence, as she does tend to pop up from time to time when I need her. Each time just reminds me that she hasn't really gone and is still there waiting for me in the next room.

Josephine instantly recognised the voice that spoke to her, but sometimes, as Martina's story shows, there is no recognition of the voice at all.

Lost in thought

A few months ago I was driving my car to a friend's home. It was a bad time for me personally and I was lost in thought. I was driving along a main road and the output of this road was a dangerous roundabout. To be safe, you don't slow down, but have to stop, because you can't see anything on the other side. That day I was totally absorbed in my thoughts, and didn't realise I was going to get to the round-about without braking. I was looking but not seeing, if you know what I mean, but I heard a voice – not mine or that of anyone I recognise – screaming. 'Brakes!! Stop!!' It wasn't a classic 'voice in my head'. I am sure of this, because I heard it with my ears and my mind. I got scared and immediately braked just in time to dodge a car. Did the voice of heaven save my life?

In my opinion, Martina did hear the voice of heaven. Demelza's story differs slightly from the previous one, in that the voice she heard didn't seem to come from outside but appeared to speak to her in her mind.

The voice that saves my life

The first experience happened in 2011 when I was about to be made redundant and was mother to a then two-year-old. I stood on the station waiting for my train to work and thought, 'Oh, what will I do?' Just then, a voice that seemed to speak in my mind but wasn't me said, 'You will be OK.' With that voice came a feeling of happiness and contentment in the knowledge that everything was fine, even though moments before I had been in despair. I simply knew I would be fine – and I was from then on.

The second occurrence a few years later happened when I was waiting for a bus in the morning. It was taking a long time and I thought I would be late, so I was going to start walking, but a voice much like the one before, only firmer, said, 'Take the bus.' I was a little shocked and turned to walk again, but the voice repeated the command, only with more urgency this time. I knew I had to listen. As the bus arrived I noticed an ambulance and police car rushing by, and while on the bus I saw an overturned car on the very pavement I would have been on minutes before. The voice had no doubt saved my life.

In the stories above the voice of heaven seems to come out of nowhere, and none of the people involved can explain how or why it happened. They are just incredibly grateful it did as it saved or transformed their lives.

Anna's life wasn't saved by a voice, but her heart will never be the same again because of what she heard. Here, in her own words, is her story.

You will know

My dad died at the age of seventy-eight of heart disease in his chair having his dinner while my mam was in the kitchen washing up. We were devastated. I was devastated. Dad was my hero. Dad and I often talked about the afterlife because he had experienced things throughout the years. He always said that when it was his turn he would do something to

show he was still around. I said, 'Dad, don't you show yourself to me. I would totally freak out.' He laughed, and said, 'I
would never frighten you, sweetheart, remember that. I will
do something when you are not alone and you will know. I
promise you will know and say, "That was my dad."'

So, here I was in Mam's kitchen with my older niece and
my husband, sitting at the table filling out a council tax form
for me mam. This was like four or five days after Dad passed
away and I had just come back from the funeral home. I had
actually put a letter in the coffin with my dad, and in it I asked
him for a sign. Mam was in the living room with a neighbour,
and the door was shut so they could talk.

All of a sudden there was a whisper. I say a whisper
because it was said like they were whispering, but it was
loud enough that all three of us heard it. It said … ANNA.
I stopped writing and thought that sounded just like me
dad … did I just hear that? And my husband said, 'Anna, did
you just hear your name?' My niece freaked out, saying, 'Oh,
God, I heard that, too.' It was like it took all three of us a few
seconds to actually realise what we had heard. I said, 'Where
did it come from?' My husband said he felt like it came from
over the bannister at the top of the stairs and he went up
to check. He said, 'Nope, there's just us here and your mam
in the living room but the door is shut tight.' To me and my
niece it sounded like it came from all around us. I sat there
for a few minutes and said, 'That was my dad.' He did what
he promised and it made me feel on top of the world.

Sarah also heard the voice of heaven but not externally;
the voice she heard spoke to her on a profound inner level.

The whispering angel

I wrote to you a few months ago when I was in a very dark place – a very dark place indeed – and your book opened my mind and reminded me of all that I already knew but had forgotten. I devoured the book within a few hours and during that time I had a very hard look at everything in my life.

At the time I was suffering from depression, anxiety and insomnia. I felt like a ghost walking around in my every-day life. I felt like a puppet, with my strings being pulled at constantly by those who were supposed to love me. I soon realised that I wasn't really living for myself – I was living for everything else. I was thirsty for something real. So, so thirsty …

And you gave that to me, quite literally. I believe that the afterlife is real. Without a doubt. You helped me remember that and I'll be forever grateful to you. The most amazing experience has happened to me since. There were no shafts of golden light or beating wings or even a halo, just a clear and profound voice that spoke clearly to my heart.

Each night for the last few nights I have fallen asleep and seen a silhouette walking towards me. Everything is dark and silent, and this silence always echoes through me. It is so, so peaceful. I hear my heart begin to beat slowly and then faster, like a very loud drum, and suddenly I feel a burning in my heart. It isn't painful, rather it sizzles and splutters into a flame. A red flame hovering just above my chest. I know this because I always wake up when I feel it and see it floating there – a small flame with so much hidden power and life. It fades after two minutes or so, and I close my eyes and wait.

A child's voice echoes through my mind, 'The whispering lady.'

That voice never seems to fade and ever since I have heard it, I can't help but see the divine in everything I see or touch. I have found what has been missing – I have found my passion and my drive. I am going to share it with the world. I will grow throughout this life, and love all that I see, touch, taste, smell and hear. When I have doubts, I will close my eyes and listen to the world's song, wrapped around the simple whisper of a child; reminding me that the whispering lady is the divine spark within and around me that will always give me inspiration and hope.

Sarah's story reminds us that we can all hear the voice of heaven, and frequently that voice speaks to the part of ourselves that is innocent, childlike and trusting, often called the inner child.

This next story from David about a voice in spirit was sent to me close to ten years ago, but it is one that I simply can't forget and want to include here.

Backseat driver

We'd only been married a year when my wife died. She was fine in the morning, but in the afternoon she kept complaining of headaches. I didn't think much of it because when you're a doctor (as we both were), headaches – along with bags under the eyes – are part of the job. She went to work as usual, then I got a phone call telling me she had died of a cerebral haemorrhage. As a doctor, I'd given people news like this on many occasions, but it's a whole different ball game when it happens to you. For the next few days I was literally numb. I couldn't cry. I couldn't think. I just busied myself with the funeral arrangements. I was told to take time off work, but that was the last thing I wanted. I needed to be distracted. So a few weeks after the death of my wife I was back at work.

One morning after a twenty-hour shift I was driving home listening to the car radio. I felt my eyelids grow heavy. I was so familiar with the feeling of barely being able to keep my eyes open that it didn't bother me. Besides, I had driven the journey to and from work so much that I drove on automatic. Then, as I turned a corner I heard a clatter. I looked in the mirror to see if there was any traffic behind me, and there in the passenger seat I saw my wife as plain as day. She smiled and blinked several times, then said in the voice I knew and loved, 'Open your eyes.' I screwed up my eyes in disbelief and when I opened them again she was gone.

Wide awake now, I put my foot on the brake to slow down, and as I did oncoming traffic rushed by. I realised that without my wife's warning to, 'Open your eyes,' I would most likely have run off the road or straight into the oncoming traffic. Sarah (that's my wife's name) had woken me up while I was asleep at the wheel and saved my life.

I've never told a soul about what happened to me that night on the motorway as they would just think that I was losing touch with reality, and my family worry enough about me already, but it was a lifesaver in so many ways. I still miss Sarah terribly, but there is no doubt in my mind that she is watching over and guiding me, and that on that night when

I drove home her words of warning saved my life. Clearly, Sarah thinks I have more to give and wants me to live my life to the full. For one thing, telling partners and relatives about the death of a loved one isn't as painful an experience as it used to be because I know that death is not the end. I have my proof and try to offer what empathy and comfort I can.

Several times in afterlife encounter stories you will notice the theme of spirits of departed loved ones or heaven watching over us on Earth. Don't get alarmed by this concept, as it is in an energy sense not the physical sense. My research of near-death experiences suggests that they don't see our physical bodies but our spiritual bodies, or the energy created by our thoughts and feelings.

The stories so far have been miracle reads, but every story that I am sent is unique and wonderful in its own way, even when, as in the case for Bethan below, the circumstances aren't necessarily dramatic or a matter of life and death.

Turn around

I was going through a hard time in my second year of university. I felt very alone and it was extremely difficult for me to live where I was at the time for a number of reasons I don't want to go into.

One morning as I was walking down the street to spend the day on campus, having made the decision that I could no longer live in the student house, I clearly heard whistling as I walked along. No one was around and the whistling was very clear and very loud, right near my ear. I walked into the

supermarket. Before I reached the main doors I heard someone very clearly call my name from behind me. My name isn't
a common one and it doesn't sound much like any other
name. I turned around but no one was looking in my direction, and I couldn't see anyone I knew, or anyone who could
have called and sounded so clear. As I turned back around
I heard it again. I looked back and again saw no one there.

   I can't explain the whistling or the name calling, but they
gave me a feeling of courage and contentment. I knew I was
going to be all right, and from that moment I was – and still
am – all right.

What the people in these stories share is something deep
and intense – they clearly don't care if what happened to
them was 'real', or coincidence or psychological. All they
care about is that something out of this world happened to
them, and gave their life spiritual hope, direction, meaning
and comfort after a period of difficulty or loss. For these
people the truth is not a matter of great concern because
their experience felt real and true to them. They heard
heaven calling out to them and in that moment their lives
were never the same again.

Perfectly natural

If you've had an out-of-this-world experience, or heard a
voice speak to you, the chances are that, like many people
who write to me, you haven't shared it with many people
for fear of judgement or ridicule. You may be worried that

others will think you are making it all up. I often wonder what compels other people to doubt and judge the experiences and honesty of others in this way. Is it fear of what they don't know?

It troubles me that in our day and age, when even respected scientists (*see page 184*, and appendices, *page 289*) are finally beginning to recognise the reality of afterlife encounters and engage in the first clinical trials to determine their validity, people still remain reluctant (and apprehensive) to share such profound moments in their lives. Why do they feel uncomfortable? Why can't we freely discuss the afterlife and messages or signs from above? I hope that through this book I will be able to help make talk of the afterlife more normal and acceptable.

The sound of heaven

In this next mini collection of stories the medium of sound is used again, but this time the voice of heaven is gently disguised. Don't be deceived by the subtlety, as the impact on the receiver is equally profound. Here is Tara's story.

Can't be dismissed

My mum passed away in 2008. We were extremely close and I still miss her a great deal. I have found it particularly sad that she never got to meet her two granddaughters. A few months ago I was driving home from Saturday morning surgery and a song came on the radio that reminded me strongly of the time just after Mum passed away. I had a very vivid feeling that she was sitting next to me in the car. It passed after a minute or so, but the feeling was so strong that I don't think it can be dismissed as nothing.

It certainly can't be dismissed as nothing because music is a heavenly calling card (a subject discussed in more detail in Chapter 8). Ann heard heaven sing in a different way.

Free as a bird

Although my mother had me quite late in life, I was fortunate enough to have her with me just months before her hundredth birthday. She lived alone and was very independent up to her last two years, when ill health took hold. I visited her regularly and we would sit and talk for England. We always had a giggle as she kept her sense of humour. One day I asked her what or who she would be if she could choose. Without any hesitation, she replied, 'I would be a bird.' I wasn't expecting that answer. 'Why a bird?' She laughed and replied, 'So I could fly hither and thither!' I never forgot that conversation, but didn't realise how important it was at the time.

A couple of years later my mum died. It was only three weeks before Christmas, and all the happy celebrations around me seemed to make the effects worse. I was feeling very low, then a friend invited my husband and I to a New Year party. I thought she was being insensitive to invite me so soon after Mum's death, but decided I should make the effort for my husband's sake. I reluctantly went to the party and put on a brave face. We arrived home at 2 a.m. It was a bitterly cold and frosty night. As we were getting out of the car we noticed a little bird sitting on top of the carport singing its heart out. It sounded so chirpy. What was a bird doing, I thought, singing in the middle of the night? It wasn't fazed by our appearance and just stayed where it was.

The next morning I awoke first. It was only about 5 a.m. I wasn't sleeping well anyway, and an early start had become the norm. I heard a bird singing again, though there were no other sounds. I slipped out of bed and opened the curtains, and there on the frost-covered fence sat the little bird. I stood and listened. Once again it made no attempt to fly off. I returned to bed and my sad mood seemed to have passed. I thought of my mother's words about being a bird. I felt the bird had brought me a message. My mum had suffered at the end of her life, but I knew now that she was calling out to me and telling me in the most beautiful way that she was as happy, free and singing like a bird.

In these next two stories, from Lynn, then Bea, no song or voice can be heard, but they are both convinced that they heard heaven call out to them all the same.

Tick, Tock

Not long after my father died, my mum told us all that she could hear a ticking noise and it meant that Dad was nearby. This happened quite frequently and we got used to it, but didn't really believe she could hear anything. We felt she needed to believe Dad was near because my father always wore a pocket watch and used it all the time – when he approached you could often hear the ticking announcing his arrival.

The following summer my friend and I took a holiday job, working at the Cairn Hotel in Harrogate, where I live. We worked each day and had to be there by around 5 a.m. for an early start. We had to clean 15–20 bathrooms and had a floor each. It was always quiet that early in the morning. I can remember vividly what happened one morning while I was kneeling in one of the bathrooms washing the floor. I distinctly heard a clear ticking that seemed to actually get louder.

I had not heard this before, and there was no clock or watch in the bathroom. I couldn't understand it and stood up, determined to find out where the ticking was coming from, sneaking in to the nearest bedrooms and bathrooms. There were no clocks, watches or anything else that could make a ticking noise such as the one I was hearing. I went back to my work in the bathroom and continued washing the floor – the ticking ever present and really loud. I can remember it vividly even today. It felt strange and there was simply no explanation for it.

At home a few days later I was with my mum when she said suddenly, 'Your dad is here – I can hear the ticking!' It was only then that I realised that I too had heard the same thing as my mum. I told her what had happened at the hotel, and what she told me gave me a real jolt. My father had been head waiter there many years ago, before he worked for the railways, and had been very happy there. I had never been told that before.

The impossible

I thought you would be interested to hear about my experience recently, following the death of my mother, who I had looked after for sixteen and a half years. Mum was ninety-two and beginning to need more assistance in getting out of chairs and the like, so a few months before she died I bought a doorbell so she could summon me if I was in the garden or at the other end of the house. She had the bell push on her walker, so I could respond when I heard the 'bing-bong'.

We were very close. My favourite time of day was when we were in her bathroom getting her ready for bed, and we would spend the time chatting about all sorts of stuff, singing silly songs and giggling helplessly about nothing in particular. About two weeks before she died, I jokingly said, 'If you come back to visit me, you'd better ring that doorbell so I know you're here.'

Sadly, Mum died soon afterwards, at the end of February last year, of a massive heart attack, but she was serene and accepting that she was going to a better place. At the beginning of October last year I moved into a smaller house in the village, which I had fallen in love with the moment I saw it, despite it needing a lot of TLC and renovation. One day I came across mum's doorbell. I decided to put it to its intended use, so stuck the bell push on the front door, a glass one that opens directly onto my large lounge.

Mum's ninety-third birthday would have been on 22 October, and that day was not as difficult as I anticipated it would be. The next day around lunchtime my middle sister, who lives close by, rang me, and we ended up 'having words'. I put down the phone, leaned against the back of the sofa near the front door, and said out loud, 'What am I going to do?' Almost immediately the doorbell rang, but not with its usual 'bing-bong' – it played the full Westminster chimes, something I didn't even know it was able to do. I could also see through the glass that there was no one at the door.

I was quite spooked initially, but after a few minutes I realised that it had to be Mum's doing, and that she had rung the bell as requested to let me know she was there, which I found very comforting.

Eight days later, in the late afternoon on Halloween, it happened again, so I said 'Hello, Mum, what are you doing here? You don't like Halloween!' I rang my sister to tell her it had happened again (the bell incident had reunited us), and while we were on the phone some kids came to the door trick-or-treating and rang the bell – which rang with the 'bing-bong' sound. The doorbell rang with the Westminster chimes seven times over the next few weeks, the last time being on 19 November, reverting to the 'bing-bong' sound when a real person rang the bell.

I recently found the instructions that came with the bell, and it turned out that in order to play the Westminster chimes you have to take the back off the bell, physically remove a link from two pins and put it on another two different pins, so there was no possibility that wires had crossed or anything like that. I asked a friend who is an electrician if he could think of any logical explanation for why this could happen and he said, 'No, it was impossible.'

It is hard to read stories like these and not think that the hand, or should I say voice, of heaven is at work. Arthur certainly feels that way.

Are you OK?

I believe my deceased mother somehow managed to activate her musical box, which was not working. I had taken it from her apartment two months earlier during the clear-out of her possessions. The box started to play its musical tune as I was lying reading in bed at around 1 p.m. in the morning. I looked over at the musical box (which was wall mounted), and it was playing its little tune. I waved to it and said, 'Hi, Mum. Are you OK? Is everything all right with you?' I felt a nice, calm feeling around me, which I am sure was my mother's way of letting me know that she was fine. It also felt very peaceful in the room.

This story from Sara is deeply moving and inspiring. I find it hard to read it without a tear coming to my eye.

Sweet laugh

I lost my little girl when she was just two years old. She was a true angel baby, and never a day goes by when I don't miss her. I read your book and wanted to tell you how I hear her sweet laugh. I hear her sometimes when the wind blows, if that doesn't sound too strange. I live very close to a park and sometimes when I go out at night to put out the rubbish, or to let the cat in or out, I stand and look at the stars and talk to her in my heart. Sometimes when I do that I can hear her laugh in the wind. It only happens for a split second, but when it does I am mesmerised. I am with my baby in heaven.

Even since I read Sara's story I have listened to the wind with angel ears. I truly believe heaven can speak to us in such ways.

Messages from the other side

One of the most unusual but increasingly well-documented types of afterlife encounter comes from the online world, and involves receiving a text, message or phone call from someone in spirit. Here's Ethan's story.

Text me

The last thing my best mate Steve said to me when he sped off in his old banger of a car – it was a real pile of junk – was 'I'll text you.' It was the end of our first term at college together and we wouldn't see each other until the following October. We'd got on well in our first year. We were on the same course and supported the same football team. I hadn't been very happy leaving home for the first time, but as soon as I got to know Steve I had a ball. The year had raced by.

I got a job in the summer and started to save up for a car of my own. After a few weeks I thought I should text my friend, but then I remembered that he had said he would text me. So I didn't get in touch, and before I knew it I was getting prepared for the new academic year. The day before I was due to leave home I finally got that text from Steve. It said, 'Sorry, mate, 4 not txting. C U around.'

When I arrived back at college I looked around for Steve but couldn't see him anywhere. Then I got the bombshell. He was dead. He had died two weeks after I had waved goodbye to him on a motorway pile-up. That was more than two months ago, so how come I got the text a day before the start of term? I got in touch with Steve's parents and they told me that his mobile had been crushed in the pile-up. It's a mystery and I'm hoping you can clear it up for me.

One person who has studied this phenomenon in scientific depth is an award-winning parapsychologist based at Northampton University, called Callum Cooper, who is author of *Telephone Calls from the Dead* (*see page 311*). According to Cooper, most of these calls happen within a day after the caller's death, but some have been reported weeks or several years later, others at the actual time of death. In most instances the call is a kind of farewell or warning, or the imparting of useful information. Of course, it is impossible to prove whether these are actual phone calls from the dead, but no satisfactory explanation has yet been found for phones acting up and sending random but deeply meaningful messages.

One well-documented case occurred on 12 September 2008 in the aftermath of a train crash in San Fernando Valley, USA. Twenty-five people were killed and among them was forty-nine-year-old Charles Peck. His death was instant, but in the eleven hours following the crash as the wreckage was being searched to discover his body, thirty-five phone calls were made to his loved one from his phone.

Another fairly recently recorded case that was featured in the *Daily Telegraph* involved the actress Maureen Lipman, whose husband, the playwright Jack Rosenthal, died in 2004. She believes her late husband admonished her by text on her mobile, after she criticised her son Adam's first draft of a novel about a character called Enk. On the same day she received a text message from Jack. It said: 'The lad's done well – Enk.' The actress could not believe it and does not know how it happened, as the message was from Jack. Sure, it could have been an old message that had somehow reappeared, but with the name, Enk? Maureen truly felt it was her husband's way of telling her to encourage their son more.

If you think about it, the phone is extremely mysterious in that it disembodies our human senses, and the person we talk to is both present and not present, as a departed loved one is. Fiona believes she received a phone call from the other side.

Sisters

Not sure you will believe me when I tell you this, Theresa, as I still struggle to believe it myself. I've only told my brother and he doesn't know what to think. Anyway, about a year ago I fell out with my twin sister. We both said some pretty terrible things to each other and I went away for a weekend to clear my head.

On the train back home I felt much clearer and calmer,

and decided to call my sister and see if we could work towards a solution as I do love her deeply. I called her and there was no answer, but then five minutes later she called me and we had the most beautiful chat. She told me she too didn't want to argue over petty things, that she had always loved and admired me, and that she was incredibly proud of me. I was so happy and felt tears in my eyes. I suggested we go out for a meal as soon as I got back home. She told me she would love to do that but not right now, as she had a few things to attend to, but she would see me again soon.

After the phone call I heard lovely music in my mind and drifted off to sleep, only to be woken up by my phone ringing again. It was my brother. I felt so peaceful and tired that I decided not to answer it and switched my phone to silent. I then fell into a deep sleep for the rest of the journey home.

When I got home I saw dozens of message. I answered them and to my horror heard that my sister had died a few hours previously. She had gone running, tripped and fallen head-first onto a stone slab. Her death had been instant. I sobbed my heart out and the only thing I had to cling on to was the phone call I had had with her. I searched my phone records for comfort to see her number, but it wasn't there.

Later, I was to learn that my sister had fallen and died just as my train was leaving the station. She had also not taken her mobile with her on her run. They say that twins have an incredible bond, but my sister and I were not identical twins and had never been that in tune with one another. In fact, we often found ourselves pulled in different directions. I truly did have that phone call and sometimes wish the train carriage had not been completely empty at the time, because I would have put an advert in the local paper to ask if anyone remembered me speaking on the phone. So, I can't prove anything. All I can do is write to you and tell you hand on heart I am not making this up. Something pulled our spirits together that day, and I believe it was sisterly love.

Certainly, from the stories sent to me I have noticed an increase in the number involving phone, electronic and online communication. Once you start to open your mind to heaven speaking to you in ordinary but extraordinary ways, you will begin to see that spirit is constantly sending you nudges, whispers and signs through the medium of sound, and as most of us are plugged into our phones and computers these days, heaven is going to adapt itself to that medium. You just need to shut out all the distraction going on around you and listen attentively.

Listening to heaven

Increasing your sensitivity to the world of sound can enrich your spiritual development. I have gathered the following tips over the many years I have been researching and writing about the afterlife. They will help you tune in more clearly to the divine vibrations within and all around you.

Listen This sounds fairly obvious, but one way to increase your psychic sensitivity to the world of sound – both physical and non-physical – is to take some time whenever you can to pay close attention to the sounds going on around you. In fact, you may want to try now. Put this book down and just sit and listen. First of all listen to the obvious sounds around you. Perhaps you can hear people talking, music playing, dogs barking or cars driving by. Now take a moment to listen to sounds that are more subtle and easily ignored, like your breathing, the beating of your heart and the click of your computer mouse. In time start to notice the difference between the sounds of things that are not alive, like an alarm going off, and the sounds of things that are alive, like people laughing. Pay more attention to the thoughts, feelings and inspirations that living sounds inspire in you, because these are the sounds of the psychic world. Let those living sounds fill you up inwardly.

Talk less Extend your enhanced listening skills to the people in your life, too. Instead of thinking of an answer all the time, try to listen more to what people are actually saying to you. Just let them talk and you will be amazed how grateful they will be for being truly heard. Of course, you have to take part in the conversation, but focus more on listening than on talking. The more you practise listening to others in this life, the more you develop empathy, which opens the lines of communication to the next life.

Self-talk Start to notice the way that you talk to yourself. If it is more negative than positive, make a change, as heaven tends to respond better to positivity, love and joy. Fear, guilt and self-depreciation pollute the communication channel between you and the other side, so from now on every time you hear yourself saying something hurtful or self-depreciating, counter it with something positive to balance things out. Hopefully, in time negative self-talk will become a thing of the past when you understand how it is blocking the pure voice of heaven.

Dawn chorus Birds and heaven have a powerful connection, and listening to birdsong – at dawn if you are an early riser or at dusk or anytime you can – is an inspiring way to invite spiritual sounds into your life. So, try to seek out the melody of birdsong when you can. Simply listen and drink it all in. Listening to music – great music that lifts your soul – is another way to hear heaven speak, so try to find time to listen to your favourite pieces more.

Water There is a deep, mysterious and powerful world beneath the surface of water, so seek out a stream, river, lake or the sea. Listen and wait to see if the water speaks to you, not through words but through sound, and note the feelings and thoughts that sound fills you with.

Protect your ears You may notice that when you start increasing your sensitivity to sound, you begin to feel the need to protect your hearing from loud noises or noisy groups of people that perhaps didn't bother you as much before. Even the sound of a mobile ringing loudly may start to grate, and you find yourself increasingly wanting to seek out peace and quiet, or to soften or quiet down your voice. This is positive as not only are you protecting your hearing, but you are also tuning yourself into the sounds of heaven from within and all around you, and 'hearing' the voice of spirit with your emotions and your thoughts rather than with your ears.

The greatest virtue

I want to end this chapter with these touching words from Sally.

> Thank you for reading and listening, Theresa, to my experiences. I've told you everything about my beloved John in spirit and how I believe he talks to me through little things, like meaningful songs or sending me comforting voices, thoughts and feelings when I need them the most. I want you to know that for me it is everything. It has changed my life.

In many ways Sally's words pretty much sum up this book, in that it is all about discovering the extraordinary in the ordinary, or heaven in a grain of sand. Yes, there is no definitive proof for the existence of heaven ... yet. Sceptics point to the lack of concrete proof as evidence that there is no life after death, but equally there is no evidence to suggest conclusively that heaven does not exist. One view is right and the other is wrong, and until science comes forward with something concrete to disprove the afterlife completely, it remains a question of individual experience and trust. I'm not trying to prove or disprove authenticity or probability with this book. I am simply hoping that what you read here speaks for itself. In my opinion, something from the unseen world is giving the people who submitted their stories to me incredible relief and a sense of meaning when they thought all love and meaning were lost. I believe that something is heaven talking to them.

Above all, I hope that what you read will at the very least open your mind and, more importantly, open your heart to the idea that there could be an afterlife. Sceptics have closed their minds. If the sky turned orange they would keep their heads down and insist it was still blue, and it is impossible to debate with people who always think they are right, regardless of evidence or opinions to the contrary. In my opinion, an open mind is the greatest virtue. An open mind can lead to new perspectives, and with new perspectives comes the possibility of transformation and growth. An open mind can lift the veil between this world and the world of spirit, where time does not exist and life does not end with death.

In the next chapter I invite you to open your eyes, mind and heart to the magical possibility that heaven can truly be seen on Earth.

To love is to receive a glimpse of heaven.

KAREN SUNDE

CHAPTER THREE

CLEAR SEEING

When you open your eyes heaven is yours to experience.

RON RATHBUN

Clairvoyance means 'clear seeing' and, although it is uncommon, seeing visions of departed people and angels can happen and, of course, these stunning visions are a defining feature of near-death experiences. Far more likely, however, are the following experiences – some of which may already have happened to you, but because they appeared so ordinary you didn't realise their profound significance at the time.

- Insights tend to come to you through internal visions, typically in the form of lights, symbols and colours. Sometimes it feels as though there's a film screen inside your head with images scrolling across it. Sometimes you see something happening inside your head and later that event occurs just as you visualised it.

- From time to time a certain picture, painting, photograph or visual image totally absorbs you.

- Sometimes you catch a glimpse of someone or something in the corner of your eye, only to discover there is nothing there.

- You can see pictures or shapes in clouds, and cloud watching is deeply relaxing for you.

- You are fascinated by your dreams, and more often than not have clear and vivid dreams that you recall on waking and that linger with you through the day. You are also prone to daydreaming.

- Feathers, birds, butterflies, flowers blooming for unusually long periods of time, coins, numbers or other signs that have personal meaning and significance offer you an unexplained feeling of reassurance and comfort, or closeness with a departed loved one. Objects lost and found, lights flickering, clocks stopping, bulbs blowing and other unusual visual experiences often give you pause for thought and make you wonder if there is more to this than what you see.

- Sometimes you pick up a book or magazine, and open it at random. The words you read offer invaluable insight into a problem you are having, or give you comfort and hope. In the same way you may notice a poster, sticker, number (typically the number 11), or other such sign, which is significant and feels as though it is speaking just to you.

- You notice a fair number of coincidences in your life and always feel deep gratitude for them when they occur.
- Some people notice orbs or strange spheres of light, coloured mist, sparks or sparkles hovering close to someone or in isolation. They describe the experience as similar to seeing a bolt of lightning in that the orb is there, then gone in a flash. More commonly reported are orbs that can be seen in photographs and can't be explained away technically or as dust specks. In some photos faces can even be seen in the orbs.
- You have had a near-death or out-of-body experience. These experiences are becoming increasingly common with the improvement of resuscitation techniques, and those who have had them report very clear visions of heaven. They also come back from the experience absolutely certain that they have seen heaven. For them, there is not a shred of doubt about this – they know it is so. Due to the importance of these exceptional experiences, I have devoted an entire chapter to them later (*see Chapter 6*).

Must be an angel

I begin here with true stories of angel sightings. Although in the strictest sense an angel is not the same as the spirit of a departed loved one (in that an angel is a pure celestial being that has never incarnated on Earth), I have come to believe that any experience which reminds us that we are eternal spiritual beings is a call from heaven. Therefore for me, sightings of angels and spirits of departed loved ones are all one – and proof of heaven on Earth.

Laura had a full-blown angelic sighting that certainly spoke to her.

Second chance

Back in 2006 I had a nervous breakdown and doctors recommended that I stay in hospital for a while. Despite the diagnosis they didn't give me any medication to help.

Stuck in the hospital it was one big black hole that I couldn't escape from. No matter how much I tried to fight the 'demons' they always seemed to win. It was a living nightmare until one night on 27 March 2006, at around 3 a.m., I was sitting on my bed in my dorm, wide awake and trying to block out dark voices and visions, when all of a sudden a rush of warmth and love swept over me. In the mirror opposite my bed appeared to me what I can only describe as a beautiful angel with no voice. The being's glow was warm, and a lovely aura of blue/neon/white – like no colour on Earth – bounced around her. Her hair flowed perfectly and it was so blonde that it was almost golden.

Then the most amazing thing happened. The being of light spoke to me not in a physical sense, but on an emotional level. She moved her lips (although there was no physical sound), and said, 'Everything's going to be all right!' She then faded away. I was a little sad to see her leave, but knew that from that moment on my life would be better forever. The whole experience must have lasted around thirty minutes.

At my assessment the next morning, I had improved so much that I was allowed to return home, and slowly but surely my life began to improve. The ironic thing is that earlier during the day on the night of my 'visit', for some reason I went to chapel and decided to ask heaven to send me a message. So I guess you could say that my prayers were well and truly answered. I really do believe in angels and can feel their presence each and every day. I feel truly blessed to have received such a visit, and believe this angel saved me and gave me a second chance.

Sometimes heaven chooses to speak to us through an angel sighting, perhaps even of an angel complete with wings and halo if that is our cultural or religious understanding of heaven – but as I hope you are starting to see, there are countless other ways for heaven to call out to us. Heaven finds a way that speaks to you personally, and uses religious or angelic imagery if that grabs your attention and tunes into your heart.

One angel sighting that grabbed the attention of the media occurred in 2008. The story can easily be found via Google but, in brief, it concerns fourteen-year-old Chelsea Banton, who was suffering from pneumonia. Doctors told her mother that the kindest thing to do was to switch off her daughter's life-support system. At that moment Mrs Banton glanced at the room's camera, and she is convinced that she saw there an angel with wings. This vision gave her the courage to defy the doctors and keep the machine switched on. Chelsea began to recover within an hour of her decision, and the doctors were at a loss to explain how that happened. Chelsea's mother believes it was through divine intervention. I have been sent many similar stories about angelic visions saving lives, so I'm inclined to agree with her. Here's what Tia told me.

Brought to tears

When my mother was a child there was a terrible fire in the flat she lived in. She was on the thirteenth floor with my uncle, and panic set in as all possible exits, apart from the windows, were blocked. In desperation, and knowing the fall might kill her, she was about to jump out of the window. However, she then saw a big white glow at the window. It was shaped like a human figure and was pure white. There were other angels, but the main angel up against the window pointed to the cupboard and told my mum and uncle to go inside it, which they did.

Afterwards, when the fire brigade came, they said it was a miracle that my mum and uncle had survived the fire. She says that the memory of the event still brings her to tears.

Many people who write to me believe in angels. I am happy for them because angels are a blissful spiritual concept. In my mind they represent the spiritual force of goodness, light, kindness and love in this life and the next. Anything that connects us to this force, from a hug or the kindness of strangers, to an afterlife encounter, is proof of angels.

Visions of spirit

Equally astonishing as angel sightings are visions of departed loved ones. Such visions bring a tremendous sense of relief. No one has ever written to me to say that a vision of a departed loved one caused them alarm. Sometimes there is shock, but it soon subsides into bliss. The next three stories – the first sent to me by Dalia, the second by Joseph and the third by Rachel – illustrate the soothing and healing effect of an afterlife vision.

True light

We are a very religious and spiritual family. Twenty-three years ago my darling brother passed away at the age of twenty-four. He was, as we say in Hebrew, a true *tzaddik* (righteous) person. At the young age of eight he had a benign brain tumour that crushed his optic nerve. He went totally blind in one eye and could only see a quarter with the other one, and it made him squint. It also left him with lots of complications, though he never complained and always kept his faith. It is still very painful to talk about his death when he had a big epileptic fit in our swimming pool and swallowed too much water. I heard afterwards that water provides one of the best ways to pass on.

Anyway, during what we call the Shivah (mourning period) week, my mum was in her room and she suddenly saw my brother next to her surrounded by a golden light. His eyes were straight, and he looked peaceful and happy. My mum called his name and said 'Ari, Ari, what are you doing here?' He answered her by saying, 'I've come to tell you I'm with

God and can see properly again, and I am so happy!' My mum, dad, sister, and other family and friends were so comforted by this amazing vision. We still miss him very much but we know that he is at peace. He is truly an angelic being, basking in the true light.

Seconds

For me Christy was a special brother. He died unexpectedly at his home on 6 February 2013. I wasn't at his side when he died, but I attended the wake at his house after the postmortem. He looked as though he was asleep.

Christy was buried with full military honours in fine sunshine on 9 February 2013. He was laid to rest in Reilig na Naomh Uile, a mile west of Kilrush, Ireland, overlooking the mouth of the River Shannon and Scattery Island.

The good news is that Christy appeared in a vision to me three days later beside the door to my bedroom. I now call this *doras na n-aingeal*, which means the door of the angels. The vision occurred on 12 February 2013. Christy was dressed casually in his blue jumper and jeans. Around each of his feet were lights about three inches in height. I reckon there were 7–12 lights around each of his feet, but I can't be sure of the exact number as the vision was brief. I believe the lights were those of the power of heaven. In the adjoining bedroom were celestial female voices. I think these could have belonged to a deceased friend of the family and our mother. The vision lasted seconds. I was lying in bed awake at the time and there was Christy. It was awesome!

To rewind for context: in 1984 Christy and I visited the

family grave. I remarked that most people die at the ages of 48–55 in Kilrush, and asked Christy to promise that if he died before me, he would make sure to came back to let me know he was all right – and I would do the same if I died first. He laughed and promised. Memories in the making. The light of heaven is shining on Christy now.

Seven weeks and one day

My amazing dad was taken away from me twelve weeks and a day ago. He was the funniest man I knew and I miss him. I never imagined how I would feel when someone I loved so very much died. Well, I felt nothing – as though he'd never existed. I never thought it would feel like that. I always thought I'd feel him around me and with me all the time. I just didn't, at that time.

Seven weeks and a day after he passed away I was in bed alone. My husband was downstairs and my son was in bed. I think I was in that stage where I was neither quite asleep nor awake. I suddenly heard a burst of choral, church-like music, and I opened my eyes. There, just outside my bedroom door, stood my dad. He was staring intently at me, not smiling. He was wearing his favourite navy blue fleece. I stared back at him. He looked solid but had a golden glow around him. I blinked and he was gone. I suddenly felt anxious, but then the feeling changed to utter peace and tranquillity, and I went straight to sleep.

I replied to Rachel to say that feeling numb with shock after the death of a loved one is common. The stages of grief are discussed further in Chapter 7. I also told her that the only reason why her dad wasn't smiling was that he was concentrating so much. In Appendix 1 you can read an enlightening interview I recently did with world-renowned medium James van Praagh, in which, among other things, he talks about the energy vibrations he detects in spirit. According to Praagh, to appear on Earth spirits need to lower their energy vibration or levels dramatically. This is because in spirit the vibration is so much higher than on Earth, and it is very hard – sometimes impossible, as spirits need to grow spiritually in heaven and this increases their vibration even more – to lower the vibration enough for us see spirits with our physical eyes. That's why it is easier for spirits to appear to us in gentler ways that don't require massive energy shifts, such as dreams, signs and coincidences.

This next story from Tina is touching because it has such a normal, matter-of-fact feel about it. It shows that in death loved ones simply need to know we are all right, and that a hug can be one of the most priceless gifts in both this life and the next.

We'll meet again

My father died in January this year. My mum was very ill in the same hospital and luckily we were able to get her to my father's ward in a wheelchair, so she was there when he died (of pneumonia). He was ninety-two and they had been married and in love for sixty-seven years. My mum's health improved and she was able to attend his funeral and burial.

She has since been hospitalised several times and had a serious operation. She is back at the family home now, living alone but with frequent visits from family and friends.

Yesterday I saw my mother (eleven months after my father died). We were talking about the wording we should put on my father's headstone. I suggested 'We'll meet again', as it was a favourite song of theirs and it was played at the funeral. I also mentioned that I genuinely believed that they would meet again. She hesitated, then said she had already met him again and told me the following story.

In October this year my mum told me she got up one night to use the bathroom. She returned to bed and my father was lying on it, dressed in the suit he had been buried in and without shoes on. My mum lay on the bed and asked him what he was doing there. He said he needed to see that she was all right. She said she was. He said that they hadn't given him any shoes and his feet ached (he hadn't been able to walk properly for several years before he died). He lay with my mum and hugged her for a while, then vanished. She absolutely insists this was not a dream and I believe her.

My mum said that this visit gave her great comfort as my father looked well and not like his corpse, which was not a good memory for her. She hopes he will visit again, but even if he doesn't she now believes that there is something after death. It was so typical of my father to check to see that she was all right, as they were best friends for so long.

Tina mentioned in her story that seeing the corpse of a loved one was not a good memory for her mother. I have also had letters from people who say that seeing a loved one's corpse is helpful because they look so peaceful. When I worked as a weekend care assistant in an old people's home for a year before I went to university, I saw several corpses, and yes, there was a peace and grace about them, but their bodies reminded me of discarded clothes – the spark and the essence had gone. It wasn't them lying there any more. So for me personally, I would always prefer my last memory of someone to be of them alive, but I realise that this may not be the case for everyone.

It is not uncommon for me to get stories, like the one below from Hilary, about parting or deathbed visions.

Reaching out

A couple of months ago we had to put my mother in a home. She was suffering from Alzheimer's and needed twenty-four-hour care. Luckily we found a good one that treated all its patients with dignity.

My mother was happy until the day she died. She was taken to hospital in May this year with septicaemia and never came out. She passed away peacefully with my sister and me by her bedside. Although she struggled a bit at the end, we kept telling her to stop fighting and that it was all right to go. When she was more lucid in the beginning, she kept talking about a woman at the end of her bed who she some-times stretched out her arms to. She also mentioned other people she hadn't talked about for years, so I am convinced they were all gathering ready to help her cross over.

Since then, although it was sad to lose her, I have never

felt she really left me. I chat to her now all the time, knowing she hears and understands everything.

This tender story from Samuel suggests that at the moment of death heaven is closer to us than ever. It is intimate and deeply moving.

A smile

My grandson died last spring and the bottom fell out of our world. He was a sick baby from the start. He lived for eight short weeks. Nothing would have made me happier than to be a grandfather again for the third time, but it wasn't meant to be.

My son and his wife were in great distress and I'd have given anything to ease their pain, but the manner of his death brought some comfort and healing. We had been told by the hospital that he didn't have long to go. As we gathered around his cot he opened his eyes for the first time since he was born. He looked at his mother and father first for several seconds, then he looked at me. It was a look of such mature understanding and connection that I will never ever forget it. Then he moved his little head and looked at the ceiling. As he did so he raised his arms and started to smile; that smile stayed on his face as he closed his eyes and gently died.

I know there may be medical explanations for his fleeting moment of lucidity at the point of death, but they don't interest me. What mattered to us all that day was that we believed there was an angel in the room waiting to carry him to heaven and comforting him with a smile.

Clear vision

The first thing that probably comes to your mind when you read stories like this is that perhaps these people were seeing things or hallucinating? That was my first thought, too, but the more I have investigated heavenly visions over the years, the more I have become convinced that this could not possibly be the case, because hallucinations tend to be accompanied by drugs, medication, poor health or loss of awareness of current surroundings. With the exception of deathbed visions, the stories sent to me were from people who were not suffering from poor health, and who did not lose awareness of their current surroundings. Also, hallucinations tend to be random images with no coherent meaning, involving visions of the living. However, these stories were coherent and only involved spiritual beings such as angels, or visions of people who had died. In short, the people who sent me their stories were perfectly sane and lucid, and in no doubt that what they saw was not a hallucination but a vision from the other side.

For decades I longed to have visions like these people did. I wanted to see spirit with my eyes open, but I had not properly understood the nature of clairvoyance. I tried in every way I could to 'see' heaven, and it was incredibly frustrating for me that I had no results. I didn't 'see' anything. As you've probably gathered, I may have been extremely passionate and knowledgeable about the psychic world, but I was also a slow developer spiritually and it took me years to understand two very important things. First of all, heaven wanted to connect with me visually as much as I wanted to see heaven, but I was creating blocks that made that connection impossible (later in this chapter I discuss these common blocks). Secondly, I needed to learn that for the great majority of us heaven reveals itself to us when our eyes are closed rather than open.

It took me a while to figure out that for most of us clairvoyance is an internal rather than an external experience. I did not realise that it is extremely rare to see spirit with our physical eyes, though most of us have the potential to see it with our inner eyes. I didn't think of vivid dreams as a form of clairvoyance, or that heaven could talk to me through images in my mind. If you have ever seen something happen inside your head almost like on a film screen, with images passing across it, you are already receiving messages from heaven through clear seeing. Perhaps you have 'met' a departed loved one in a dream. You may have seen yourself in a dream, or in a daydream, passing an exam, or relaxing on holiday before you did these things – then, when you experienced them, you found that your internal image was accurate.

If you are a visual person and tend to think in pictures, or notice what things look like rather than how they sound, feel, taste or smell, you may be particularly sensitive to developing clairvoyance. Seeing from the inside out is a stunning way to connect to the invisible world, but don't think it is the only way. Quite the contrary. Heaven is constantly finding new ways to reveal itself to us, as all the stories in this book prove.

Coincidences

One of the most common but frequently discounted ways to see heaven at work in our lives is through the magic of coincidence, or synchronicity to use its spiritual name. How many times has this happened to you? You are thinking of someone, then your mobile phone rings or beeps and there is a call or text from them. Or you pick up a book, open it up at random, and find that the words you read offer invaluable insight into a problem you are having. Is this coincidence, or heaven answering your prayers?

The dictionary defines coincidences as 'striking chance occurrences'. However, when these remarkable coincidences happen to us we need to ask, 'Is that all there is to it?' It feels as though it's something so much more, and few of us can dismiss what Carl Jung called the 'synchronistic phenomenon' so easily. In my opinion, coincidences that have a major impact on your life – saving it or turning it around – give witness to power from a higher source. Because our human minds are limited, a coincidence can seem like mere chance – for example, hearing a song that seems to speak directly to you, or finding yourself in just the right place at the right time. But if we stop trying to examine and question, and simply acknowledge that something magnificent is in tune with us, then when coincidences occur our lives can be transformed.

I am firmly convinced that there is a spiritual power behind coincidences, and focusing on their deeper meaning is a way to see heaven on Earth and discover what you are meant to do. Coincidences have played a huge part in shaping my life and I hope they will continue to do so, because for me they are heaven's way of remaining anonymous. Indeed, as finishing touches were made to this book – a book about the different ways heaven speaks to us – news of the long-awaited sainthood for my namesake, Mother Teresa, a woman with a potent sense of spiritual calling who inspired me deeply (see Appendix 7), was announced close to twenty years after her death. This book was published around the time of her canonisation in September 2016 and has the title *Heaven Called My Name*. Coincidence or the language that heaven speaks? You decide.

One of the greatest joys of getting older is looking back with hindsight and seeing how neatly things have stacked into place in your life. Even though I wasn't aware of it at the time, every experience I have had has brought me to the place I am in now. Think about the people who are touching your life right now. What amazing coincidences have brought you all together? Think about all the situations in your life when things just seemed to fall together perfectly? What other coincidences are out there waiting for you to find them?

Over the years I've learned that the more I become aware of coincidences and the more I express appreciation for them, the more likely I am to encounter and be guided by them in my life. Feelings of gratitude have a truly awesome power in the world of spirit and invite magic into your life.

After considering all that I have experienced, read and been told about coincidences over the years, it is my firm belief that heaven is calling out to us through them. Like countless other people who have been inspired, saved or comforted by the miracle of coincidences, Lucy is in no doubt that a higher power was making decisions for her.

All for a reason

In the year before I was due to start my third year at university, I learned to drive and passed my test. I saved up enough to buy my own car and got a wonderful secondhand Mini. It run beautifully as the previous owner had barely used it.

After spending summer with my parents I was looking forward to driving my very own car to university. I packed my bags and said my goodbyes, but the car simply would not start. I could not explain it. My parents tried to start it. My brother, who is great with cars, tried and failed to start it. We called the AA but it was a very busy day and they couldn't promise to arrive soon as I was a non-emergency, being at home, and not in danger. It was upsetting, but my parents took pity on me and let me drive their old Range Rover instead. They said they would get the car fixed, drive it to the university, then drive home in the Rover.

Fortunately, I was insured to drive my parent's car and jumped at the chance. It was raining very heavily on the way and I could barely see through the windscreen. I think a deer or something ran in front of me. I swerved and skidded, and the Rover crashed rapidly down a hill and into a ditch. I was wearing my seatbelt, but I'm convinced that being in my parent's Rover saved my life – I ended up with only a broken wrist.

I called for help and was taken to hospital. The weirdest thing is that when I called my parents, they tried my car again to see if they could get to me as quickly as possible – and it worked the first time. I think something from above saved my life. It has to be more than a coincidence, because if I had

been in the little Mini I don't think it would have been sturdy
enough to protect me. I'm very lucky and blessed.

Lucy is right that events such as this are more than coincidence – they are heaven playing a guiding hand in your
life. In Chapter 9 we return to the subject of coincidences, as
they are the driving force behind the subject of that chapter,
which is about afterlife signs, or calling cards, but for now
start noticing the coincidences in your life as they are one
of the first ways heaven will try to talk to you, guide you
and inspire you. Another way in which heaven will try to
initiate contact is through your dreams.

While we are sleeping

Along with coincidence, another common but frequently
ignored way for us to see heaven (because it is so gentle and
least likely to cause us anxiety) is in our dreams. While we
are sleeping messages from heaven can enter our unconscious minds – the place where all true magic begins and
where there is no time and space, just infinite possibility.

When we dream we suspend disbelief and enter a world
of unlimited potential where the extraordinary is the norm,
and in this way dreams can be important spiritual experiences. Indeed, dreams were the medium through which
I first made contact with the world of spirit. With all my
heart, I desperately longed for a sign when my mother passed
away. I got increasingly frustrated and disillusioned when
nothing seemed to come, but then I had the most soothing

dream. Nothing dramatic happened in it. My mother simply appeared in my bedroom and tidied up some clothes that were on the floor. However, the experience felt so real that I knew when I woke up that this had been so much more than a dream. My mother had visited me in my sleep.

Over the years I've lost count of the number of stories I have read from people who have absolutely no doubt at all that they saw, heard and spoke to departed loved ones in their sleep. I call these kinds of dreams *night visions*, and defining features of them are their vividness and realistic feel. They are also impossible to forget for days, months and years after they occur, unlike other dreams that have more of a symbolic function and are easily forgotten.

Dreams may feel confusing at times, but psychologists regard them as important for mood regulation and in helping people to work through problems in their daily lives. Many people think they don't dream, but everyone dreams every night. The reason why people think they don't dream is that they can't remember their dreams. This is because dreams tend to fade from our memories as soon as we wake. So before you go to sleep, tell yourself you will remember your dreams when you wake up, and keep a pen and paper beside your bed so that you can record your dream immediately when you wake up. Don't wait until you have brushed your teeth as the memory might fade – write it down straightaway. The more attention you give to your dreams, the more likely you are to recall them. Even reading this here may trigger a dream memory the next time you wake.

Do bear in mind that most of your dreams will be symbolic and should not be taken literally. In most dreams your thoughts and feelings about yourself and others, or about your life, are turned into a series of images or pictures to trigger associations, so you can become more empowered and insightful in your waking life as a result. In this way your unconscious mind acts like an inner therapist. Sometimes the symbols can be quite confusing, and confusing and symbolic dreams are easy to forget. However, no translation is required at all when you have what I call a night vision.

Night visions

A night vision is a message direct from heaven. It is typically brilliantly vivid, with a sense of reality you can feel, touch and sense. It is also impossible to forget. Night visions can feel as real as waking life and you remember them for a long time – typically for decades. You also have a sense that they are something more than a dream – your inner sense is right because heaven is talking to you through night visions. Examples speak louder than words. I begin with this truly heart-wrenching account from Nicola.

It's time

It was the year 1994. I was twenty-five years old with two small girls, and twenty-eight weeks pregnant with a third child. It was August, warm and humid. Up until this point I was having a good pregnancy with no problems. Without going into too much detail, I had an abruption on 8 August. If you don't know what that is, it's when the placenta suddenly falls away from the side of the womb and your life's blood pours into your womb. Yes, it's extremely serious and life-threatening. I was told that the child had no heartbeat and that I had to deliver it naturally because the doctors didn't think I would survive a caesarean section. My kidneys and liver were failing, and I was given 8 pints of blood and 14½ pints of salt water. After seven hours of labour and doctors preparing my family for the worst, I gave birth to my son Thomas. He was born asleep. I didn't know how poorly I was. All that mattered to me was my little boy. My little Thomas. Oh, Theresa, he was gorgeous. He weighed 3 pounds 4 ounces.

Once I was out of hospital and the funeral was over, you can imagine how I felt. Empty. Numb. I was told by my doctor that he was amazed I'd got through it and that it was nothing short of a miracle. I often thanked heaven for that, as I still had two small girls to care for. But all I wanted was Thomas, to smell him and touch him. So one day while at his grave I said, 'Please let me hold him one more time. Please let me smell him and kiss him.' Theresa – I kid you not. That night I had the most amazing experience.

I went to bed as normal and fell asleep. Suddenly I was in a dark room. I wasn't scared at all. There was a table in the corner with a glass of wine on it. Two ladies stood in the doorway. I never saw them, but knew they were there and that they were my nana and grandmother. I had known my nana when she was alive, but my grandmother died before I was born. I was shown a chair. I sat down in it in the centre of the room. My grandmother was standing in front of me. I couldn't see her face. I was just aware of her body. She put

Thomas in my arms, Theresa. He was right there in my arms. I can't tell you the joy I felt. My grandmother didn't speak, but in my head I heard her say, 'This is just for a little while.'

I kissed Thomas. I stroked his little face and kissed his hands. I told him that I loved him and that Mummy would always love him. I could smell him. I cherished every second. Then my grandmother with my nana at her side bent down to take him and I said, 'Oh, no, just one more minute,' which she let me have. After that precious minute I said goodbye to him and kissed him. Gently, she took him from my arms and said to me without speaking, 'It's time.'

And then I woke up. I felt I had just been there – that I had just that minute held my baby in my arms. I could still smell him. I ran downstairs to my then husband and said, 'Oh, my God, smell me – I can smell Thomas all over me.' I've since told friends and family, and they say, 'That's nice you had that dream.' Theresa – I know that was no dream.

Alex had a night vision that didn't just reassure her that her father was alive in spirit. It also gave her a new-found sense of direction and meaning to her life.

Endless

My dad and I were so very close, and when he died five years ago from cancer that started in his bowel and spread to his liver, I felt as though I didn't belong in the world any more. I had no idea how I was going to move forwards with my life – I just felt an endless sense of loss and emptiness.

Six months after Dad's death my wife booked a holiday

in Canada for me and herself. I think she was trying to help me move on, but even though I appreciated her concern and love for me I missed Dad terribly. I felt lost. The night before we were going on holiday I helped my wife pack our bags, but went to bed early with a splitting headache. I remember crying a little before I went to sleep. When I woke up the next morning I felt completely different. My headache had gone. I had energy, and best of all I had a memory of the most stunningly vivid dream I have ever had. That dream has convinced me that death is not the end.

In my dream I floated through a tunnel of intensely bright light. It was very bright but it was not blindingly bright, just energy bright. As I floated I heard whispers. I think they were female whispers, but can't be sure. They told me that Dad was waiting for me, but that once I had seen him it was time to get back to the business of living. That was the exact words they used, 'the business of living'. I didn't actually see Dad in the tunnel, but I knew he was there because I felt his love. On top of that I felt something even greater – a love for everyone and everything. It was the kind of love that can only be experienced in a dream, I think, because it was so intense, strong and energising.

When I woke up I didn't feel empty and sad any more. I felt calm and knew that Dad wanted me to move forwards with my life. From then onwards I haven't looked back. I also know that even though I can't see, hear or touch Dad any more, he is with me every moment of every day and night. The dream I had of my father was different from any other dream I have ever had. I remember every detail vividly and know I will never forget it. I know I am going to see my father again one day and that life is endless energy, potential and, most important of all, endless love.

Rachael's story below speaks to the heart rather than the mind, but it shows yet again the remarkable power of a night vision to provide relief, healing and absolute conviction that this life is not all that there is.

Priceless

I lost my mum four weeks ago to cancer. Although we'd known she was poorly, we hadn't realised how bad she was and we lost her quite quickly. I am comforted by the fact that I was there when she passed away, but it was not in the nicest way and I am haunted by the last few minutes of her life. I searched for answers after her death, but finally resigned myself to the fact that I would never find them, since the only person that could do so was Mum and she was no longer here.

My experience was a dream, but it was so much more than a dream. It was so real and intense and something I will never, ever forget. In the dream I took a seat in the park. I was aware of someone or something behind my right shoulder. I saw a shadow face and knew immediately that this was Mum. I could hear her voice as clearly as if we were having a conversation. She touched my cheek and I felt it. She told me she had not been in any pain when she passed away and that I was not to worry. She told me she loved me, we held hands and I can still feel that today. She had a bright light behind her and she asked me if she could 'go'. I told her I wasn't ready for her to go and begged her to stay. She kissed my cheek and told me she would stay for now.

At this point I woke up sobbing my heart out. I knew I had just seen and spoken to my mum. I knew she hadn't crossed and that I'd asked her to stay. I do feel a little guilty about this as now I feel she hasn't been able to cross over and is staying here for me, but at the same time I have found such comfort in the dream. I now have to find a way to let Mum go and be completely at peace, and I think writing to you is the best starting point.

As I write this I feel a weight has been lifted, that I am able to share this experience and not be laughed at. I read my words and every one of them brings me back to that one moment when Mum and I shared something so priceless.

I wrote to Rachael and told her that she should not worry as her beloved mother has crossed over already, but that she remains close by her always in spirit – and it was this closeness that she experienced in her dream.

As previously mentioned, a sense of brilliant vividness and reality are hallmarks of night visions or visitation dreams, and this can be seen clearly in Sara's story.

Left with his smile

I lost my uncle in 2012 and that was a very difficult time for me as we were very close. The couple of dreams I have had involved my uncle and grandparents.

The dreams were so vivid that I didn't feel as though I was asleep. The day after I had them I was filled with happiness inside, and felt so thankful that I'd had them. I am always talking to my uncle and grandparents as I have pictures of them in my room, so they are the last people I see before I go to sleep at night.

The last dream I had was very close to the anniversary of my uncle's death in July this year. I was suffering with shingles and felt quite unwell. I asked my uncle if he would come and visit me in my dreams and told him how much I missed him. The dream was very clear. He gave me the biggest hug, which seemed to last forever, and when he let go I was left with his smile. It's as though he knew I needed to see him. I have read about visitation dreams and believe this definitely was one.

The power of love to triumph over death also shines through in Angela's night vision.

The perfect time

My sister passed away in 2005 at the age of forty from a very aggressive form of cancer. When she was in her last couple of months she kept telling me to go to the doctor if I noticed anything different about my habits, or any pain I couldn't explain. I was busy at the time and kept putting it off. After she passed away I was not paying attention to myself as I was in a very depressed, self-blaming mood. I had not spent enough time with her. My life was very busy, as was her's, and I would always make excuses and say that we would have time together when our children had grown up and we'd retired. We never got to that perfect time.

One night I had a dream that was very lucid. My sister came to the side of my bed and sat down as if she was going to talk to me. She smiled and said hello. The room was lit by a gorgeous glow. I felt very warm and could feel love swelling in my heart when I looked at her face. She was smiling but calm and peaceful. I did not move and did not want to move. She then took her right hand and reached right into my stomach, clasped my left ovary, and telepathically said, 'Get this checked.' I was shocked at her words and woke up immediately with them still ringing through my head. Anyway, that day I made an appointment and got a referral to a gynaecologist.

To cut a long story short, I ended up having a full hysterectomy, which was necessary due to cysts on my left ovary and endometriosis.

Angela's night vision is fascinating because if she had ignored what she saw in her sleep she could have got seriously ill or worse. In spirit Angela's sister clearly wants her to live her life on Earth to the full, and to not let poor health get in the way.

While we are sleeping our unconscious minds (the place where heaven speaks to us) tend to be more receptive to messages from heaven because our conscious minds (the home of our ego and the voice of fear) are off duty. A night vision is one of the most calming, gently reassuring ways for departed loved ones to let us know that they are still with us. It may well be the first sign and the wisest, especially for those who are deep in the grieving process. When my mother died I was so deeply traumatised and filled with tears that my heart and mind couldn't see anything else. I just wasn't ready for more direct communication.

If you aren't sure if your dream was a night vision, there are some hallmarks you can look out for. In a night vision a loved one enters a realistic or familiar setting – more often than not the bedroom of the dreamer – and either talks to them, or stands or sits beside them. There is typically no story or narrative in this type of dream, and there are no other images and symbols – which is extraordinary as most symbolic dreams are littered with symbols competing for attention – and when the dreamer wakes there is absolutely no doubt in their mind that the experience was real. The personality of the departed loved one is so recognisable and familiar that it feels like a visitation – which again isn't the case for symbolic dreams.

Grief therapists often suggest that dreams like this are a part of the grieving process, a kind of natural pain relief, and to a certain extent I agree, but I also believe them to be powerful messages of love and hope from beyond the grave.

Night shift

For me it is perfectly logical that through dreams we can glimpse heaven. If you think about it, every dream you have, whether symbolic or a night vision, is pretty remarkable. Your body is asleep but your consciousness continues to work, explore and experience. I have even had stories sent to me over the years from people who believe that their spirits left their bodies while they slept. They describe visiting places they have never visited before, or flying through space or even crossing over to heaven to meet loved ones. Some rare stories, like this one sent to me by Tara, describe how they believe they offered comfort or healing to those who are in crisis or crossing over to the other side.

Left behind

I had been the on-call general practitioner at work that day and was all packed up ready to go home at 6.30 p.m. when my phone rang. One of our terminally ill patients needed a prescription written out for some pain-relief injections. It was one of the community nurses calling – apparently the job should have been done earlier in the day, but for some reason it had been missed. I stayed behind to sort it out, then went home.

That night I dreamed that this patient was in my room at work and I knew she was about to die. I put my arms around her and held her hand and she passed away. At the moment she died an incredible energy and light filled the room. Again, this feeling was very powerful and real. I woke in the middle of the night and could not get back to sleep straightaway, as it was such a dramatic feeling.

In the morning I found out that the patient had required two doses of pain relief overnight before passing away. My interpretation of the dream is that after she had had the morphine, she was able to be at peace and was 'transition-ing' to the next life. She came to thank me for sorting out her medication. I had been feeling rather negative about work recently, as a huge amount of my day-to-day work was dealing with trivial issues and administrative paperwork. This was a sign to me that I do still have an impact on people's lives – and that I still have a purpose.

Have you ever gone to bed and woken up the next morning feeling drained for no reason? You can't understand why you feel tired because you have not been doing anything strenuous, have eaten and drunk healthily, and are not on medication. If you can't think of any rational explanation for this, perhaps you could hold this incredible idea in your mind: when we sleep our bodies may be at rest, but our spirits are very busy and perhaps even helping others in their times of need, or when they transition to the other side. We just can't remember this when we wake up.

Light years ahead

Here's another incredible idea to get your head around: dreams that catch a glimpse of the future. Just as night visions bridge the gap between this life and the next, I believe that they can bridge the gap between past, present and future, and time and space. These night visions are called flash forwards, or precognitive dreams, like the two sent to me by Pat and Leanne.

Travelling light

My brother passed away recently, and had been very poorly. Two days before he died he came to me in a dream. I knew he was going to pass away as he had his suitcase with him, and I felt he was telling me that his time here was over. I have many dreams that tell me things – is this possible?

Too soon

One morning as I came downstairs for breakfast, my mum was just pulling the toast from the toaster and buttering it with a knife. I was about eleven years old at the time. I told my mum about my dream from the night before. I had dreamed that my aunt, who had sadly recently miscarried a child, was pregnant again. 'No,' said Mum, 'It's too soon – they were going to wait a while before they tried for another baby.' As she finished her sentence and was buttering the toast, the phone rang. It was my aunt to say she was pregnant. Mum dropped the knife and stared at me in astonishment!

Again, there are ways to tell the difference between flash forwards and precognitive dreams. Symbolic dreams are like a series of unconnected images – rather like watching a music video. A flash forward, on the other hand, is vivid, feels realistic and includes events that make sense or have a distinct and logical story line. Jenny, whose story is next, had a flash forward in a dream.

I saw her

I can't explain this at all. It has never happened before or since. I woke up at 4.40 a.m. to the sound of a baby crying, although there are no babies in my house. It was very dark and it took me a few minutes to realise that there wasn't a baby in the house. I even grabbed my dressing gown and rushed to my daughter's old room from when she was a child. It was only when I got there that I realised I must have been dreaming, because my daughter is in her early forties now.

Then memories of a vivid dream came back. In my dream my daughter was holding a baby girl in her arms, and the baby had lots of dark hair and blue eyes. Even though it was early in the morning something told me to call my daughter to ask if she was pregnant. My daughter laughed and she said that wasn't possible because she was too old now, and taking care of her boys was more than enough. A week later she phoned me to tell me the news – she was pregnant and the pregnancy was unplanned. Eight months later a little girl was born. Just as in my dream, she had dark hair and blue, button-like eyes. Incredible.

Precognitive stories like these are tantalising, but flash forwards that offer glimpses of *potential* futures are far more common. They are not as sensational in that they may not play out in real life, but what they do is offer the dreamer a chance to experience, or 'live through', potential futures if a certain course of action is followed. I think heaven sends us glimpses of potential futures to motivate us to make changes if the future that is glimpsed in our dreams is not to our liking. In short, precognitive dreams show us what *could* happen, and that we all have the power to take control and change our lives for the better.

Hold on to these ideas as I hope they will encourage you

to think about dreams as significant spiritual experiences, proving that our consciousness is most certainly not limited to our physical bodies, and that while we are asleep we can all communicate across time and space. When we dream, barriers of time, space, fear and disbelief melt away, and this gives us easier access to the world of spirit and the infinite possibilities waiting for us there. That's why as a way to catch a very real glimpse of the other side, I would urge anyone to pay far greater attention to their dreams.

How to see heaven

As mentioned previously, most of us won't experience full-blown clairvoyance with our eyes open. We are far more likely to see heaven in our dreams or in our minds, or in daydreams. You could call all this your imagination, but your imagination is used as a way for heaven to initiate a conversation with you. The secret to releasing this ability is to start thinking in pictures, not words. The following suggestions will help you do just that.

Get curious From now on start looking – really looking – at the world around you. Notice what you haven't noticed before. Many of us don't take in the details of our lives. It is as if we walk around with blinkers on, only focusing on our target or what we know. Take a look at the leaves on the pavement as you walk, notice the structure of buildings you walk into, watch the people around you. It is amazing what things you can see when you truly open your eyes.

Cloud and star watching Clouds can create magical pictures, and the world of spirit can express its love to you through images up there that inspire and guide you. Don't stare intently at the clouds. Be sure to avoid direct sunlight, and just gently gaze at the clouds and see what shapes they create for you. Trust your imagination and allow heaven to speak to you in this way. You can do the same with star gazing. Spending a few moments star or cloud gazing is a simple but extremely powerful way to develop your clairvoyant ability and something you can do at any time – as long as there are stars and clouds.

Magical pictures Another simple method to help you think in pictures (the language of clairvoyance) rather than words involves buying a heavily illustrated children's book, preferably one about fairy stories. Think back to when you were a child and remember your favourite books. The chances are that they were the ones with the most beautiful and magical illustrations. The story was secondary to the pictures. Find books like that. As you look at them again with adult eyes, notice feelings inside you that feel familiar and unfamiliar. This is a positive sign as it shows that you are starting to kick-start your imagination, which is your direct path to clairvoyance.

Keep a dream journal It goes without saying that paying more attention to your dreams helps you to think in images and stimulates your clairvoyant ability. Before you go to bed each night, tell yourself you are going to remember your dreams the next morning. The moment you wake up, write down all that you can remember – or better still, try to draw what you saw. It doesn't matter if you are a terrible artist. Just try to capture what you saw in the best way you can – this is for your eyes and spirit only.

Take charge of your dreams Once you get into the habit of remembering your dreams you may even try to take a giant leap of faith and start controlling them. This really is possible, and the technique is called lucid dreaming. Basically, it means awakening your sense of self and becoming aware that you are dreaming within your dream, so you can take control of the action. Just think of the magical possibilities that lie ahead for you if you can master that technique. Not everyone can do it, but if you are intrigued, do some research online about lucid dreaming techniques, and enter a world of limitless potential.

All these exercises gently trigger clairvoyant ability and help you see heaven all around you, when you are both awake and asleep.

Breaking down barriers

You may well find that you try these exercises, but won't make as much progress as you would like. Perhaps the images you see are unclear or confusing, or maybe you can't see anything at all. If this is the case it is entirely possible that fears are making it harder for you to see heaven than it should be.

First and foremost, to receive images from heaven you need to have as positive and relaxed an attitude as possible, and trust that something wonderful is going to inspire you. It is very hard for heaven to break through doubt and negativity. Don't worry that you might see things that are frightening, as everything that comes from heaven is loving and positive. If anything does frighten you, that will be your ego doing the talking. If you approach your clairvoyance with an attitude of love for the purposes of healing yourself and others, you can't go wrong.

Also don't fall into the two traps I have often fallen into: lack of self-belief and trying too hard. If you have never seen clairvoyantly you may doubt your ability to ever do so, but this is your fear trying to distract you from remembering who you really are and reconnecting with your spirit. If you take anything away from this book, I hope it will be the realisation that you don't actually need to see angels or talk to dead people to hear or see heaven – heaven is within and around each one of us. Heaven is for everyone. Equally detrimental to clairvoyant progress is trying too hard, as when you try to force this you are operating from a position of competitiveness and fear, which blocks any spiritual progress. Also let go of any expectations you might have about what heavenly visions will look like – sometimes you may just get the simplest of images or something totally unexpected.

Bear in mind that your spiritual blocks may have something to do with people in your life who have strong negative views about you or your belief in the world of spirit. If that is the case, remember that no one makes you feel or believe something without your consent. You are in charge of your thoughts and feelings.

If any of the above resonates with you, don't think you are a lost cause. Even the most spiritually evolved people have fears and blocks. The difference is that they are aware of their limitations and try to find ways to work around them. A good place to start would be to completely avoid people and situations that drain your energy. Protect yourself from those who manipulate you or make you feel unhappy. Keep boundaries. Helping others selflessly is admirable, but not if it harms you. Remember, you can't give to others if you don't give to yourself first.

Mixing with like-minded people who share your passion for spiritual development – whether at meetings, workshops or online – can be extremely encouraging and will motivate you to stay true to your beliefs. Also never underestimate the importance of taking good care of your physical health by avoiding toxins, eating and sleeping well, and exercising regularly, preferably in the fresh air, as this will make you a clearer channel for heavenly communication.

Taking care of yourself also means taking care of your thoughts. You are probably beginning to see from the stories in this book that everything in this life and the next is spiritual energy, even your thoughts. If you constantly think negative thoughts you will only attract negative energies back to you, so be the positive change you want to see in your life and the world. Create your world with your loving thoughts.

Don't forget to change the way you think about your spiritual development. Get into the habit of telling yourself over and over again that you can receive images and messages from heaven. Keep doing this and sooner or later it will become a self-fulfilling prophecy. Whatever you focus on expands – that is a universal spiritual law of attraction. The more you think about heaven and about attracting only what is beautiful, magical and loving into your life, the more likely you are to draw it to you.

So, from now on focus your energy on reprogramming your thoughts – your prayers – heavenwards. As you'll see in the next chapter, wherever your thoughts go your heart will follow.

Your vision will become clear only when you look inside your heart. Who looks inside awakens.

CARL JUNG

CHAPTER FOUR

CLEAR FEELING

*I can no longer see you with my eyes,
touch you with my hands but I can feel
you in my heart forever.*

ANON

Sensing divine guidance or the presence of a departed loved one through your feelings, or sometimes through touch and smell, is called clairsentience. This is perhaps the most neglected and ignored channel for divine communication, because many of us suppress or deny our emotions instead of noticing, understanding and working through them. It is highly likely that you have already felt heaven call your name through your heart, but that you simply haven't recognised it as such a calling at the time. Do any of the following sound familiar to you?

- Sometimes you get the distinct feeling someone is standing or sitting behind you, but when you turn around there is no one there.
- You may feel a strong sense of familiarity and the presence of a departed loved one around you for no apparent reason.
- On occasion you could have sworn someone or something invisible touched your cheek, stroked your hair, held your hand, hugged you or gently pressed your forehead.
- You sometimes feel a cool breeze for no reason.
- Perhaps you smell certain scents that have no recognisable origin, for example perfume, flowers, lavender or vanilla.
- At times you experience a tickling sensation on your body, like shivers down your spine. You may also get a tense feeling in your stomach or a bad taste in your mouth when things don't feel right.
- Sometimes when you meet someone you feel elated or drained for no reason. The moods of other people, especially those closest to you, influence you greatly. You have an uncanny ability to feel the atmosphere of a room you walk into. You also sometimes appear to know how another person feels without them having to tell you.
- You may feel unexpected surges of joy and comfort for no reason – and it feels like drinking a warm cup of hot chocolate on a winter's day.
- Spending time with animals or communing with nature makes you feel calm and inspired.

- If you have ever felt abandoned and in crisis, but then a feeling of warmth engulfed you and gave you the strength to move forwards, or hopeless and directionless, but then you were suddenly filled with a clear sense of purpose and meaning, this was spirit talking to your heart to let you know you are never alone.

The uniting theme in all the above is that divine guidance always feels soothing and warm, so if you aren't sure if this is heaven talking to you, use that guideline as your criteria.

Through the eyes of a child

There are two categories of afterlife stories that belong in a chapter all about heaven speaking through the language of our feelings. The first involves children and the second pets. Let's begin with Liz's story, which shows how a child can touch hearts and lives in a divine way.

The little boy who is the best friend of the world

I love being inspired by other people. Yesterday, my husband and I were waiting in the car at some traffic lights with our windows open, when a woman carrying a little boy aged about two or three walked past with her friend. I assumed his mum and her friend were chatting about people, because suddenly the little boy said to his mum, 'The whole world is my best friend.' As he said this he had the most angelic smile and his face was beaming with light. He expressed it with such love and happiness in his voice. It was very moving. I just hope he doesn't lose that magical innocence, but I suspect he will as he gets older. If only we could all view the world as our best friend, it would surely be a better place.

To me this little boy's statement, his angelic/cherubic way of saying it, and the look of bliss in his face was heaven's way of communicating with me. I felt very blessed to have been there to hear and experience it.

I love hearing children talk about heaven as they have the innocence and ability to suspend disbelief and see the world with angel eyes. Sadly, as we get older fear and doubt tend to rob us of our natural ability to see magic in everyone, including ourselves. I love how readily children accept and don't question what they see and hear. They talk in such a matter-of-fact way, without any doubt that what they are experiencing is real. We could learn a lot from their open hearts and minds about connecting to heaven. Could anything be more simple and obvious than these next two stories sent to me by Tara, then by Nick?

Seen her, heard her

My husband had been at home looking after the girls. When I got home I asked Sofia, my five-year-old daughter, what she had been up to with Daddy. She said they had been in the garden picking strawberries. She said there was a loud noise outside and she didn't like it. She then said that her nanny (who has passed away) had told her that there were too many people cutting their lawns. I queried if she really meant her nanny and she said, 'Yes, my nanny, your mummy.' I asked Sofia if she had seen or heard her – she said both. She told me her nanny had held her hand. She said she was wearing blue trousers and a blue top.

After talking to my husband he says he did recall Sofia going off quietly to a corner of the garden for a short while. I have not wanted to press Sofia on the issue at the risk of putting words in her mouth, but I do think she is too young to be able to make up such a detailed story out of nothing. My feeling is that as I was reading your book I was having doubts as to how seriously to take the stories in it, and Mum came in spirit to tell me it was real. It fills me with a lovely feeling to know that she popped in to see her grandkids.

Big brother

I'm surprising myself by writing to you because I truly don't believe in this kind of thing, but my wife has been reading your book about angel babies. Something has happened to give me pause for thought and I would love to know what you think.

About seven years ago, before the birth of our two children, now aged four and six, we had a stillborn baby boy called Michael. It was the saddest and hardest experience of my life. Fortunately we went on to have two healthy children after that, but it remains a scar on my heart. Something happened recently, though, to ease my pain considerably.

We have never told our children about their sibling in spirit. Last week our six-year-old son, Jake, came home from school one day with a gold star for his family file. It was just pictures and colours, and we laughed at the drawings of Mummy and Daddy on his parent page (we looked enormous) and the page for his little sister (she looked like a hedgehog), but then we turned the page and he had created a page for his big brother. I told him that he didn't have a big brother — we have never spoken to him about Michael and no one else has either, on our request — but he shook his head and said he did. I told him again that he didn't, and again he insisted he did. The drawing was the best of the bunch as it clearly showed a boy of around Jake's age kicking a ball. I said to Jake that he had drawn himself here, and Jake again shook his head.

I decided not to press things and looked through the rest of the 'Jake's Life' file. On the back page I saw a drawing that sent shivers down my spine. It was the letter M in very large writing. I asked Jake why he'd drawn it, and he said M was the best letter in the alphabet. I asked him why and he gave me one of those 'are you a complete idiot?' looks only young children can give adults, and said, 'Because it just is, that's why.'

The story of little Jake reminds me strongly of a poem by the romantic poet William Wordsworth that made a great impression when I first encountered it in my school days. It's called 'We are Seven' and describes a conversation between a man and an eight-year-old cottage girl. The man asks the girl how many siblings she has and she insists on there being seven children in her family, even though two are in the graveyard. The man says that if two are in the graveyard then there must only be five children, but the girl insists on the number seven. Here's a stanza from the poem that expresses the child's total disbelief in the deaths: her departed siblings are alive to her even though they have been buried in the churchyard.

> 'But they are dead; those two are dead!
> Their spirits are in heaven!'
> 'Twas throwing words away; for still
> The little Maid would have her will,
> And said, 'Nay, we are seven!'

Many parents write to me asking if I think their child is making it all up, and I tell them that the best way to determine if it is a true experience is the child's response. Is the child unsettled in any way? If there is fear, panic or uncertainty the experience is not typically heaven sent, and may have more to do with attention seeking or too much exposure to frightening images on television, for example. But if the child is matter of fact and feels safe and comforted by the experience, then I believe it to be genuine. Of course, the child could be imagining it or even making it up, but imagination is the beginning of creativity and a window into another reality.

Sadly, many adults react with fear, disbelief and suspicion whenever a child opens up and talks about what they can see, hear and sense from the world of spirit, and this distrust can cause anxiety and confusion for the child. They start to doubt themselves, and the more they doubt themselves, and their ability to see magic all around them, the less they are able to communicate with spirit.

The more we encourage our children to stay young at heart, and the more we get in touch with the child within each one of us whatever age we are, the more we can move away from the blocking fears and self-doubts that adulthood brings and start noticing heaven all around us – for the child within our hearts is where heaven is likely to speak to us first. All the suggestions here about the different ways to see heaven are designed to reawaken your inner child, because the child inside us is the place where all eternal magic, wonder, spontaneity, innocence and openness live.

While I am discussing the beauty of an open and trusting heart, this book would not feel complete without mention of afterlife encounters involving beloved animals.

Pets from heaven

In much the same way that children can open our hearts and teach us profound spiritual lessons, I believe animals can teach us a great deal about compassion, empathy, healing and the power of unconditional love. Stories like this one, sent to me by Moya, exemplify this.

Richie

After my husband Richard died, I was as you might expect a mess. We had been married for a happy thirty-three years and he was my soulmate. I miss him every moment but am coping better than expected because of Richard's Labrador, Richie – yes, Richard couldn't resist giving him a similar sounding name to his own. He hasn't left my side since Richard died, and on the first night, when I thought sleep would be impossible, he did the most simple but comforting thing. He crammed as many of his toys in his mouth as he could and brought them to me – offered them to me one by one. It was so lovingly done that I could not help but smile through my tears. He sleeps beside the bed and sometimes on it at night. As soon as I start crying he wags his tail and is right beside me. It feels as though Richard wants him to be there for me.

I've had equally remarkable stories sent to me about the spirits of animals that continue to visit their owners from the other side. I don't doubt this one jot because I believe my beloved cat, Crystal, visited me in spirit soon after she died. I had just started university and missed her terribly. She died just before I left home as if her role as companion during my childhood was over. Anyway, one night in my first term I woke up and heard her familiar purring, then felt her padding my legs gently as she used to. It really felt as though she was there with me, although of course she wasn't. John had a similar experience.

Billy cat

I went to bed last night really missing my departed cat Billy. I wanted him to visit me and even said that out loud. I woke at about 3.30 a.m. I was just thinking about getting up to make a cup of tea when out of the blue I felt him on my feet, then on my leg. It wasn't a heavy feeling, just gentle pressure. I knew it was him. It was a beautiful feeling although my heart was pounding. I've been wondering this morning how he got that message asking him to come. How had me uttering a few words before bed resulted in him coming? It blows my mind. I can't comprehend the magnitude of it at all. Have you any theories, Theresa?

Of course, I have my theory. I believe pets have eternal souls that travel over to the other side and they don't stop loving us in heaven.

Trevor's beloved dog Molly may well have come back for one last goodbye.

One last time

For fifteen years I walked my little dog, Molly. We took several different walks, but her absolute favourite was through the park and into the woods where we lived – especially in autumn time as she loved scampering around in the leaves and trying to get as many conkers in her mouth as possible. Molly was my best friend and when my wife died eight years ago I can honestly say she helped me get through that pain.

Molly has been gone for four weeks and sometimes I wonder if she is still around me. Yesterday I was walking to the local shops and I suddenly decided to course correct and go on Molly's favourite walk. I don't know why, but I just felt I had to. I walked through the park and there at the edge of the woods I swear I saw Molly. She was wearing her bright red collar and when I called out to her she ran into the woods. I followed and saw her jumping around in the leaves, just like in the old times. It made me so happy to see her. I felt tears in my eyes. I longed for her to run to me and she seemed to sense that, because she stopped playing and stood very still.

For about a minute we looked at each other, then she gave me her familiar two barks, followed by sitting down on her haunches – always a secret sign between us that she wanted me to pick her up. I was about to go and pick her up, but then I heard children calling out to each other in the park behind me. I looked back, turned around again and she was gone. I didn't try and find her because I knew she had gone to a better place. I'm convinced she was just saying one last goodbye.

Was the dog I saw a stray or did I imagine it? If it was a stray the likeness was uncanny, given the exactly same red collar and the same mannerisms. The dog clearly knew me. There was that strong connection. If I imagined it I must be going mad, and I assure you, Theresa, I am not.

Don't think it is only dogs and cats that bring heaven into our lives. I get stories about all types of pet – horses, rabbits and even goldfish. I also get stories about wild animals and even insects, especially butterflies and ladybirds, and they all in their own unique way bring a message of love and hope from the other side. Love is the most important and powerful energy or force in the universe, and it doesn't matter what form it takes. Human or animal love, it is eternal and speaks to us directly from heaven.

I've often been told that animals don't have souls, but I believe that all living things do, and that it is possible to maintain communication with beloved pets and other animals after death in the same way that communication can be maintained with departed human loved ones. I think this very special poem by an unknown author says it all.

The Rainbow Bridge

Just this side of heaven is a place called Rainbow Bridge.

When an animal dies that has been especially close to someone here, that pet goes to Rainbow Bridge.

There are meadows and hills for all of our special friends so they can run and play together.

There is plenty of food, water and sunshine, and our friends are warm and comfortable.

All the animals who had been ill and old are restored to health and vigour.

Those who were hurt or maimed are made whole and strong again, just as we remember them in our dreams of days and times gone by.

The animals are happy and content, except for one small thing; they each miss someone very special to them, who had to be left behind.

They all run and play together, but the day comes when one suddenly stops and looks into the distance.

Suddenly he begins to run from the group, flying over the green grass, his legs carrying him faster and faster.

His bright eyes are intent.

His eager body quivers.

You have been spotted, and when you and your
special friend finally meet, you cling together
in joyous reunion, never to be parted again.

The happy kisses rain upon your face; your hands
again caress the beloved head, and you look
once more into the trusting eyes of your pet,
so long gone from your life but never absent
from your heart.

Then you cross the Rainbow Bridge together.

Surprised by joy

Heaven can often try to speak to us through our emotions. I know that, not just because of my own experiences and the stories I receive from others, but because of the absolute joy that fills my heart as I write this chapter. I have no doubt that the stories you read below, starting with Diana's, will fill your heart with joy, too.

Wish you were here

On this day as my uncle and cousins were entering our new house, we were walking down the stairs towards our kitchen when I said to myself in the most genuine way, 'I miss my aunty and wish she was here.' In that very second I was stopped in my tracks by a force that went right through me, which I believe in all heartfelt certainty was my aunty. I feel very fortunate to have had this experience and am so grateful that she could give me proof without a doubt that we truly are spirits having a human experience.

As Mary explains in her brief story below, she just experiences feelings, but they are feelings that makes complete sense.

Saved by heaven

I have lived on my own since my husband passed away almost five years ago now. My house is empty. It feels empty most of the time. Sometimes, though, as soon as I open the door I feel as if someone is in the house. It just has that feel. One time after an evening at my craft club it felt so inhabited that I went into every room just to make sure there was no one there who shouldn't be. I know it's my late husband. I feel it, Theresa. After he died I had a dream where he came into the house, and it was so real. I asked him what he was doing here, and he said he had simply come home.

Enid didn't feel the presence of spirit with such force as Diana or Mary did, but is equally convinced that what she felt was heaven sent.

Picking up

When I was in my early twenties I was dating a man who I was really keen on. We saw each other whenever he was not working, and as time went by I thought he was the one for me, and that we would eventually get married. I lived for the weekends when he came to see me, and we would go out together. We seemed to be getting close, and we enjoyed our time together.

One weekend about six months into the relationship, he abruptly told me he was going away to work in another country. It was like a bolt out of the blue. He said he wouldn't arrange to see me again because he would be working in a very dangerous area. To say I was upset would be a huge understatement. I can barely recall what happened, but at some point he left me to my tears, and that was that.

The first time we met was at a mutual friend's house, and for some reason I decided to go back there. I skipped work, put some clothes into my car and drove down to her. I stayed for 2–3 days, but it didn't help. Going back to the place where we had met was a big mistake, and it just made me even more upset. I felt as though my life had ended. I got back into my car and set off home again.

The road home was normally a lovely drive, out in the countryside, fields and trees all around, but this drive just felt terrible. Everything was going round and round in my head, and suddenly it occurred to me that I could crash the car and all the unhappiness would come to an end.

The moment that thought crossed my mind everything changed. A warm yellow, cloudy light enveloped me in the car, and I suddenly felt loved and happy. I had the absolutely wonderful knowledge that everything would be all right. I do believe I smiled and laughed. I had very little knowledge in those days of spirit or angels and, as is often the case when profound things like that happen, it was only years later that I knew I had been saved by heaven. How powerful that event was. I had some way to go before I felt right again, and had some bad times in the following weeks – sometimes I thought I could see my ex-boyfriend in a crowd, and I lost my way for a while – but I didn't go back to how bad I had felt before, and gradually picked up my life again.

Looking back that feeling was heaven sent. It saved my life and inspired it.

Ann's story, below, is a conflicted one because it involves an important relationship on Earth that still needs healing, but it also shows that in spirit there is only love and healing shining down.

Apart but together

It was the day of my mother's funeral. She had been ill for a long time and was now at peace. This day was doubly upsetting for me because my daughter was there, too. She had fallen out with me years beforehand, and had refused time and time again to rebuild our relationship. I hadn't even seen her for ten years or met the man she had married.

As we followed the coffin down the aisle before the service began, I felt protected from the soul-destroying situation. I could see everything, yet I felt in some kind of protected bubble. This was not the way I expected to feel at all. My daughter pulled her husband away from me to the opposite side of the church just as we were about sit in the pews. I felt that my head was being gently turned away from having to even look at her and feel the overwhelming hurt of cruel rejection. I stopped even wanting to look her way. I was comforted and protected in the strangest but sweetest of ways. I was able to keep hold of all the swirling emotions for both my mother and daughter.

After the service my daughter and her husband avoided joining the mourners who shook the vicar's hand on the way out. Instead, they went straight to the waiting funeral car, which drove off leaving my husband and myself to follow the hearse in our own car. It was unbelievably cruel, yet the feeling of love and protection was supporting me. She couldn't hurt me any more. I just sent her my love. I had been carried away somewhere safe by protecting angels – not just one but a few of them – and when it was all over they even sent me a message from my mother via her will. She had written her will by hand when she was very old. It read, 'My hand is sore and so is my heart. Ann, don't grieve for me because I love you very much.' Heaven was telling me that even from the other side my mother knew how I had been treated at her funeral. Yes, I am sure of that.

I will never forget that day and how heaven comforted and protected me in a way no human could have. I may never experience that divine presence again, but once was beautiful enough to treasure for the rest of my life – of that I am certain and am so very grateful for it.

I'm often asked what happens when there are unresolved issues and a loved one passes away before there is a chance to heal and forgive. Every near-death experience account I have read shows that if there were any disagreements, departed loved ones rise above all that and have absolute understanding. They see the bigger picture and no longer judge or feel resentment – as judgment is a very human thing. Instead, they view us with compassion. Spirits in heaven are blissfully happy even if the circumstances of their passing on were violent. They don't take that shock with them. It is harder to resolve feelings of despair in spirit than it is on earth (because despair is a human experience not a spiritual one) but heaven works with them to heal the spiritual wound they inflicted on themselves and others.

To return to the theme of feeling heaven on Earth, here's Keiry's experience.

Gentle feeling

When I was in my early twenties I used to feel my nana sitting on my bed. It was a very gentle feeling. I also sometimes felt as though she was standing at the side of my bed. This was accompanied by a slight prickling at the back of my neck, which went away once I turned and looked. I then had a very strong sensation that she was standing at the side of my bed, almost as though she had opened the door and walked in.

Keiry's story is intriguing because it mentions the 'behind you' phenomenon. Has this ever happened to you? For no reason, you feel as if someone is behind you, but when you turn around there is no one there. This has happened to me many times, most especially when I am at my desk and writing my books. I typically get a prickling sensation, then sense someone standing right behind me even though I know I am alone in my office. It used to alarm me a bit, but now I feel deeply reassured by it. If it happens to you stay calm and take a deep breath. If you are outside it is, of course, important for your safety to make sure you aren't actually being followed, but if you are certain you can't possibly be in danger, relax and enjoy the bliss of being watched over from above.

Clara, whose story is below, felt heaven's touch in a different way, but the impact on her heart and her life was just as transformative.

Hand of heaven

In 1979 I decided to leave my job as a social worker with an agency in the city of New York. I was very close to my boss, and although I enjoyed my job I could not turn down the opportunity to work as a school social worker. My boss was upset with my decision but understood. He'd wanted me to stay and be a supervisor. Unfortunately, he had just been diagnosed with lymphoma cancer but was still working.

An important factor here is that I am blind and travel with a Seeing Eye dog. My dog had recently died, and I had to go and get a replacement. When I came home my intention was to meet my boss with the dog. He loved dogs, and also missed the dog that had died. I knew he would have loved to see my new dog.

I never got that opportunity. My boss was taken to the hospital as they wanted to do an experimental treatment on him. The treatment did not work, and he died immediately. For many reasons, when I heard this news I was devastated. I clearly remember what had happened while I was at home crying hysterically, and calling out his name. I was all alone in my house at the time. As I was changing my clothes I felt his hand on my shoulder, and he briefly spoke to me. He said, 'I'm all right, it's all right.'

When I put my right hand on my left shoulder there was nothing there. Initially I was very frightened and thought I was losing my mind. Soon after I felt tremendous peace in my heart and spirit, and I never mourned his loss again because I know in my heart he hasn't died.

This kind of soothing experience that speaks directly to a person's heart is something I have had stacks of mail and messages about over the years, and which I had personal experience of a few years after my mother died. It was on the day of my daughter's first birthday. I missed my mother terribly and wished she could have seen her granddaughter. Suddenly, a feeling of joy and peace filled me. She was there celebrating my daughter's first birthday with us.

Typically, a feeling of love, peace and calm will descend for no particular reason, or you will feel your hand being held or a gentle kiss on your cheek. During that moment of bliss you just know that a departed loved one is close by. It is such a tragedy that there isn't more talk about these kinds of uplifting and surprising experiences following the death of a loved one, and the extraordinary relief they bring. My dream is that one day such experiences, and learning how to encourage them and tune into them, will be considered an essential part of grief recovery and healing.

Spirit doesn't only reach out to us during times of grief following the loss of a loved one. As Leanne's story shows, the hand of heaven can reach out and reassure us at any time.

Unstuck

I was sixteen and taking my GCSEs. I had revised well and was ready for my exams, but was dreading my maths exam and becoming increasingly nervous about it. When the day for it arrived, after little sleep and feeling sick to my stomach, I arrived in the exam hall and began the test. At question eleven, I was well and truly stuck, sweating and wondering how I would ever get through it.

Suddenly, I felt the room spin, had tunnel vision and was in total panic. As this happened, I felt a strong hand grasp my shoulder and squeeze, as if reassuring me that it would be all right. Assuming this was a teacher comforting me after noticing my fear, I turned to smile at them for their kindness. There was no one anywhere near me – the staff were all either at the far front or the rear of the hall and, as during all exams, the desks were spaced so far apart that no one could have touched me. I understood immediately what had happened, my panic subsided, my heart was filled with joy and I continued the exam full of energy and purpose, knowing that whatever would be would be.

Martina believes the touch of heaven actually saved her life.

Into the woods

When I was about eight or nine years old, I went with my family for a walk in a hilly place. Walking and walking, we found some lovely woods to stroll in. I was with my mum and sister in the highest part of the forest, and saw my father further down and decided I wanted to run down and join him. Attempting to go down the cliff I put one foot on the ground to go down slowly, but it was too steep, so I slipped. I tried to cling to trees to stop myself, but could not. I rolled down many, many yards until something or someone stopped me. I was rolling fast and clearly felt a touch behind my back. It was as if the strength of two hands had stopped me and placed me gently on the ground.

I was young, confused and frightened, I didn't believe in certain things, but I was sure someone had saved me. Lying on the ground, I saw a huge, sharp rock a few inches from my head. If I had fallen only a little later I would have hit my head on the rock, and certainly would have done much harm, not to think the worst. That day my mother said to me that she thought it was my departed grandfather who had saved me. I don't know about that − all I know is that something or someone from the other side protected me from harm. It's an incredible thing and fills my heart with joy because it makes me feel that I was saved for a reason.

For Lorraine there was a strong feeling that spirit was present. Her inspiring story follows.

Frozen

Over the years I have had various signs and feelings, but have usually paid little attention to them and simply lived my life. A very prominent memory was of something that happened not long after my favourite and closest aunt passed away. At that time I was feeling quite despondent about life. I had been married for about eight years. My husband was in the army and away on duty. We had been trying for a baby for some time, without success. In fact, I suffered a miscarriage shortly before my aunt died.

One evening I was stressed due to work pressures, and was feeling particularly down when I went to bed. As I pulled the duvet over my head, I distinctly felt my aunt's presence in the room. I knew immediately in my heart that it was her, but was not able to move to see for myself. It was as if I was frozen. My eyes were open, but I could see only the duvet across my face. I heard her voice clearly and loudly. I had not heard it for some time, as she had lost her speech due to a long illness before her death. She told me to stop worrying. She said, 'It is only a job and it doesn't matter. You are going to travel the world and have a wonderful time. You will have that baby of yours! Now stop worrying and stop being so silly.'

The next thing I knew it was morning and I was awake. However, I remembered what happened very clearly and I know that it was not a dream. Incidentally, my aunt was quite right. Little did I know it at the time, but I did go on to travel around the world for a while. My husband was posted to Canada shortly after that and we lived there, before moving to Germany and later to other parts of the UK. In between all the moving, we applied for adoption. Then, soon after, I became pregnant and gave birth to a healthy baby boy. Three years later, we had another son.

Although I have never forgotten the two main incidents above and have been aware of occasional spiritual moments, it was not until I read your book that something changed within my heart. It has made me stop and think today, about the here and now. About how I have been caught up in the humdrum everyday of life, running here and there, working full time, letting the small things get to me, giving so much to my job and possibly too little to my family. I have been feeling quite stressed and ill lately and now realise that I need to look within myself.

I feel revitalised now, filled with love and ready for change and life.

The situation Moira describes below is, of course, different, but the euphoria, the life-transforming feeling of elation, when there is a realisation that heaven is real and loved ones do not die, is familiar.

Miracles happen

Growing up I was very close to my uncle. Sadly, he suffered from problems in the stomach and as a result was diagnosed with colon cancer, which unfortunately spread. He only lived nine months after his diagnosis.

I'm nervous around ill people, especially when they are close to death. I visited my uncle a number of times, but when he was reaching the end I stopped going to see him, although I prayed deeply for him. I am a very spiritual person by nature. On the last day of his life I simply could not be by his side. I dropped off my parents at the hospital and waited in the car so that they could spend their last precious moments with him.

As expected my uncle passed away peacefully that day

under the spiritual guidance of my aunt, who helped release him from his pain through prayer. I come from a religious background, and my aunt believes strongly in miracles.

A day after my uncle's death I experienced a sense of euphoric peace that I cannot explain. My heart burst with joy. Well, this is what happened. I was sunbathing on the beach when I felt the presence of my uncle close to me. He gave me the message that I should have visited him when he was nearing death, and that it would have been important for him. He wasn't angry with me, though, for not being there. I could tell that he understood. I think he wanted to make sure the message he gave me was one I would remember and not forget, because it was so personal to me. I do remember it clearly. Especially, I remember the intense peace I felt in my heart.

The stories so far have tended to have grief, stress, depression or extreme crisis as the setting for heaven or departed loved ones to flood hearts with comfort but, as you'll see when we discuss peak experiences next, such moments can happen at any time, even when you feel content and happy. The only requirement is an open heart.

Reaching the peak

If you ever feel a rush of joy, peace or euphoria for absolutely no reason, take a deep breath and enjoy it, as heaven is calling your name out loud and clear through the power of your heart. Pat, then Laura describe their experience of this in the two stories below.

Overpowering

I think I may have had a little touch of heaven a couple of years ago, which I have not told anyone about. I was driving home and twenty minutes or so into my journey, something very strange but wonderful happened to me. All of a sudden a feeling came over me that was really strong – it was as though I was being covered in an energy. I felt an overpowering feeling of love and happiness. It was so overwhelming that in those few minutes of emotion, I would have given my last shilling to someone in need. I've never had the feeling since, but remember that it was truly heaven.

No reason

I sank so very low after my divorce. I hated my ex, my life, myself. I was bitter. My husband had an affair with my best friend. For three weeks I couldn't leave my house. I hid from the world. I barely ate and slept loads. I cried for several lifetimes. Then one morning I woke up feeling amazing. I wish I could say that a great dream (or an afterlife encounter with my mother) had been the catalyst, but it was nothing as dramatic as that. I just woke up feeling as though I could fly. I drew my curtains for the first time in weeks and looked at the sky. There was a hint of a rainbow and I gazed at it in awe. For absolutely no reason I felt inexplicably happy and grateful to be alive. It was a gift from heaven, and although it faded pretty soon – about ten minutes to be precise, when I looked around my house and realised I needed to clean it up – I will never, ever forget it because I think that is what it must be like in heaven: sheer bliss for no reason. Thank you for letting me share this with you.

For Charles, life became colourful again after his peak experience.

Turning a corner

About a month ago I was taking part in a cycling marathon. It was a beautiful day and I was keen to improve on my time. I had done this marathon every year for the past nine years, and a lot of my year was devoted to preparing for it. About a third of the way through the marathon it started to rain gently. I thought nothing of it, but then after the rain had eased and I was turning a corner, I saw the most lovely rainbow. Even though I knew it would mess up my timing and put me behind I had to stop and gaze at it in awe. I think I stood there for a good ten minutes.

As I stood there it felt as though my heart was getting bigger and bigger inside my chest. The rainbow started to glitter, and the grass and trees by the side of the road were in glorious Technicolor. I knew in that instant that everything was alive and interconnected by an eternal spiritual energy. I felt as if I had stepped into a different world. I noticed all the other cyclists swish by, and one of my friends called out to me asking if I was all right. When I said yes they shouted at me to get back on my bike so I didn't lose too much time. I just let them ride by. I didn't understand why they couldn't marvel at the beauty I saw in the same way as I did. I felt sad for them. I imagined their lives and sensed all their feelings. It was as if I knew them all from the inside out.

I never finished the marathon that day. I wanted to fly on my bike to the end of the rainbow. Any desire I had to beat my previous time vanished and I owe it all to a rainbow. It was quite incredible because ever since my mind has been on fire with new ideas for my business. I feel happier and healthier, and wherever I go or whatever I do I look for the magic, the colour and the infinite. I see infinite possibility and connection. I see myself in everyone and everything.

Studies have shown that these kinds of peak experience are often triggered by extreme turmoil, but they can also occur for no reason at all when you are among natural surroundings or in a gentle meditative state, sometimes called the 'flow', or just feeling content and peaceful. When these higher states of being occur, it is tempting to think of them as different or outside our normal state of being or everyday reality, but perhaps what we are glimpsing in these moments is not an illusion, but our eternal and true spiritual reality. Near-death experience accounts confirm this, as all those who have seen heaven for real describe their afterlife experience as euphoric and blissful.

Into bliss

During our lives on Earth I believe there are various stages of spiritual development culminating in the peak or bliss experience. The first stage is one of *being* where your life and relationships tend to be self-serving and chaotic, as your heart hasn't discovered its true power and potential yet. It's vitally important during this stage that you are involved with people who are more spiritually evolved, as they will help you find your true meaning and purpose.

The second stage is one of *belonging* and occurs at times in our lives when we get our identity from others – be that a religion, group, job, vocation, or even family and friends. During this stage we imitate or copy the beliefs and rules of other people, and it is a stage that typically attracts young or impressionable people looking outside themselves for a sense of identity, as it did me in early adulthood. It can also appeal to the elderly and vulnerable in need of support and companionship.

For some people the belonging stage is their true spiritual calling and the stage they choose to remain in all their lives. This is only negative if you start to think that your spiritual way is the only way, and belittle or try to cause harm to others who do not share your beliefs. However, if you respect the opinions and beliefs of others and find joy, companionship, fulfilment and a sense of community in your chosen belief, then right now you have found your spiritual path. There may come a time when you want to rethink your options, or that time may never come. Either way, heaven is revealing itself to you through belonging to a community of like-minded people who are your spiritual family. You take care of each other, and in a world where loneliness is a growing problem and compassion is in short supply, this is a truly miraculous and wonderful thing. However, if you start to feel unfulfilled and that your life lacks meaning, as I have done countless times in my life while seeking the truth through religion or spiritual groups, you are being called by heaven to another stage: *becoming*.

My gut instinct tells me that a lot of you reading this book are in this third stage of becoming. It is the stage I often find myself in and often am in right now. You are someone who has perhaps experimented with religion or a belief system but have not found fulfilment, or someone who has never been religious but who has always thought there must be something more to this life than the everyday. You could experience moments of great clarity and insight, but these glimpses are fleeting.

The highest stage that can be reached on Earth is one of *bliss*, and for most of us it can only be experienced in dreams, flashes of intuition, peak experiences or during meditation. Those who have near-death experiences typically describe this stage of your eternal life as heaven. If you are lucky enough to experience it on Earth, you sense the unity and unconditional love between all people and things both in this life and the next. You see only beauty, wonder and magic within yourself and in everyone around you. During this stage you completely accept that spiritual growth is an unending process and that your life is eternal. Your only guide and teacher is love, and you become a true original, a free spirit whose inner light glows brightly and brings glimpses of true and pure beauty to Earth.

In my life I have certainly experienced moments of transcendent beauty and bliss in mystical and material ways. Vivid dreams, flashes of intuition, stunning coincidences, and hearing and sensing my departed mother's presence have given my spirit wings, but so have human experiences such as falling in love, having children and, more recently, the euphoria I feel whenever I get a letter or message from someone who says that my books have inspired or helped them in some way. If you don't feel that you have experienced anything like this, dig deep into your heart and mind. It is possible that you have but you just haven't associated it with heaven at the time. Have there been moments in your life when you have felt overwhelmed with feelings of love and gratitude, or when your soul has been lifted by something inspiring, such as a rainbow or glorious sunset?

The peak experience is the highest state of spiritual awareness you can achieve on Earth. So, from now on if you experience a surge of unexpected joy or peace, don't think of it as abnormal – instead, see it as a temporary glimpse of the reality of your eternal life awaiting you in heaven. Each time you remind yourself of the existence of spirit within and all around you (by reading a book like this, by focusing less on the material and more on what really matters, or by living intensely and gratefully in the now, spending time with people you love or doing what you love), you are taking a step closer to living as you will when you cross over to the other side.

How to sense heaven

Developing your clairsentient potential is perhaps the most rewarding way to kickstart your spiritual development, because it makes life feel more fulfilling, deep and colourful. You start to develop compassion for yourself and others, and see the spiritual connections behind everyone and everything. Here are some practical suggestions to help you tune in to your heart.

Develop empathy The ability to understand the feelings of others is essential for opening divine channels of communication. A simple way to fine-tune the skill of empathy is to go somewhere busy and observe someone you don't know – without them noticing you are doing so. Take a good look at them and imagine what they are like and what they do for a living. Put yourself in their shoes.

Listen to your gut You may be surprised to learn that your stomach is a kind of primitive brain with its own intelligence – so the term gut instinct does make sense. If you ever feel sick when you are worried, or get butterflies in your stomach when you are excited, you will know that the area below your ribcage is very sensitive to emotion. Start to think of this area as having a mind and will of its own. Start to notice what your gut is telling you. Do you feel happy, sad, angry, nervous or calm when you meet someone new, walk into a room or imagine doing something in the future? Your feelings know what your spirit desires, so listen to them.

Be healthy If you eat unhealthily, and don't get enough exercise or sleep, this will impact your mood, energy levels and health in a negative way, and negativity of any kind can block you from connecting to heaven. It really is very simple. The healthier and fitter you are in body, the easier it is for you to tune in to your emotions.

Trust your body Listen to your body in general more, too. Notice your physical sensations when you need to make an important decision or meet someone new. Does a part of your body tingle or tighten in any way? Heaven is talking to you, but are you listening?

Trust your heart The mediums I have spoken to often tell me that they make contact with the other side solely by sensing the emotional energy of those who have departed. When they pass on information to their clients they typically have no idea what it means. They simply have to have absolute faith in the feelings they sense. In other words, the more you have confidence in your feelings, however irrational they may seem at the time, the more your clairsentient potential will develop.

Smell the flowers Flowers and plants in general can help open up your heart. If you can, surround yourself with them. The colours green, as well as yellow, blue and pink, are often associated with emotion in colour therapy, so find ways to surround yourself with these colours.

You choose

Spiritual or peak feelings of love, goodness, compassion, peace and bliss are gifts from above that reveal a glimpse of your eternal spiritual reality, but all other feelings belong to this life and are therefore within your control. This may come as a surprise to you if you are a very feeling, focused person, but just because you feel angry or sad does not mean that you *are* angry or sad. You, the eternal you, which this book is dedicated to, are merely experiencing feelings of anger and sadness, and it is up to you to choose what you do with them. Negative feelings simply don't exist in heaven. Love is the only reality, and many near-death accounts suggest that our souls are sent to Earth to learn and grow from human emotions. Seen in this light, life on Earth is very much like 'school' for your spirit.

Every emotion is either an opportunity to grow, or an obstacle to keep you from growing. You get to choose. So, the next time you feel angry, guilty, frightened or sad, remind yourself that you are making the choice to feel this way. No one can make you feel anything but yourself. You are the one who chooses how you feel. Why not wake up one morning and simply decide that you don't want to feel frightened, guilty or angry any more, ever? When you become aware that your emotions do not define you, it truly is possible to rise above negative emotions.

Managing your feelings requires you to step outside yourself and observe feelings passing through you. Remember, every time you do this you are developing spiritually and reminding yourself that you are a spiritual being independent of the physical.

Protect yourself

With practice you will find that it becomes easier and easier for you to tune into and trust your feelings. As you do you may well find that you start noticing things you haven't noticed before, and can't zone out of things that you used to. As enlightening as it is to become more sensitive to the world around you, there are risks. You may, for example, start to confuse the negative emotions and feelings of others with your own. This can lead to depression without you understanding or knowing why, especially if you work in the caring professions. So be sure to protect yourself and take regular time out. I don't like recommending techniques, but some people find it helpful to imagine themselves surrounded by a protective bubble whenever they feel overwhelmed. Don't feel this is you being uncaring or cold, because you are not the source of another person's happiness – they are – and you are not arming yourself against love, just the bonds of codependency and fear.

Heaven wants you to be empathetic, kind and compassionate towards others, but not if you damage or harm yourself in the process. Indeed, the more drained and damaged you feel, the less energetic and uplifting you can be to others, so in this way protecting yourself when you feel fragile is a way to help others.

It is also important that you try to spend some quiet time alone, even if it is for only a few minutes. It doesn't matter where you do this, even if your only option for peace and quiet is a bathroom. When you feel overwhelmed by social interaction, take some time out for yourself to recharge and find your calm centre.

Go within

The fastest way to discover heaven is to go within and open up your heart to divine guidance. Sure, there are some things that can encourage this inward-looking process, but at the end of the day it is you who must discover divinity – or feelings of love, empathy and compassion – within yourself. This is because what you are actually rediscovering when you reconnect with these divine feelings in your heart is who you already are – a spiritual being.

Everything begins and ends with your heart, and it is through your heart that heaven and departed loved ones are most likely to talk to you first. Your heart opens the door to heaven, but to let divine guidance in you need an open and intuitive mind – which is the subject of the next chapter.

The kingdom of heaven is not a place
but a state of mind.

JOHN BURROUGHS

CHAPTER FIVE

CLEAR KNOWING

Knowing heaven
is what heals us on Earth.

MITCH ALBOM

When you know a departed loved one is close by or communicating with you, or you simply know exactly what to do, without knowing how you know, this is clear knowing, or claircognisance. It is a sudden – often unexpected – certainty or knowledge that takes you to a place beyond doubt. Some people call this kind of thing an intuition, a sixth sense or a hunch – but I think of it as heaven talking to you and guiding you.

Claircognizance is more common than you might realise, but because people tend to focus on visions and hearing voices, it is often overlooked. However, like clairsentience, heaven is far more likely to reach out to you through your thoughts and feelings than through the rarer forms of heavenly communication – visions and voices.

Too many of us dismiss claircognizance when it happens not only because we expect voices and visions, but also because we think that what inspiration we have is obvious and nothing special, or not to be taken seriously. We don't trust our thoughts. The moral here is to accept your intuition as something relevant, possible and helpful in the here and now. It is a voice from heaven requiring you to change your mind or a situation in some way, or simply reminding you that a departed loved one is close by.

How clear knowing works

Here are some examples of ways in which heaven may speak to you through your thoughts.

- For no reason at all you know that a departed loved one is close by, guiding or protecting you, or talking to you in some way. On rare occasions you know when someone has passed over before anyone even tells you about it.
- You know what someone is going to say next or what is going to happen next, and your thinking is proved to be correct. For example, you have a sudden knowing about something current happening without reading or hearing about it – like the death of a famous person. This sudden knowing

can also occur when you visit a new place or meet someone new. You know things about them, but have no idea how you know them.

- You meet someone and have an inner knowledge that they are lying or can't be trusted, and later you are proved right. In much the same way, you can have a deep knowledge that someone is good news and are proved right.

- Something inside you tells you that acting in a certain way is a good or bad idea, despite evidence to the contrary, and you are proved correct.

- Like a bolt out of the blue, you have an 'aha' moment of sudden realisation, or knowledge, clarity or understanding of what you need to do.

- You have a problem that is causing you anxiety, but wake up one morning knowing the solution or the best way forward.

Can you recall those wonderful moments in your life when you know something with absolute certainty? Feels divine, doesn't it? I've had a handful of such moments of golden illumination, and each time they have affected me profoundly and sometimes changed the course of my life. I'm one of those people who is a bit of a worrier, and have lived much of my life in a state of doubt or hesitation, so you can imagine what a blessed relief it is to just 'know' something for sure. Here's a story about a sudden knowing I had while at university that changed my life.

The book of revelation

When I started my academic life at Cambridge I was committed to my Christian faith, but there was always a quiet voice inside me that didn't feel entirely satisfied or settled. I could not tell, however, whether that voice was to be trusted or not. Then, to resolve my doubts, I had what can only be described as an 'aha' moment.

The memory of it remains vivid and powerful to this day. I was in the university library trying to gather notes to write an essay about the Old Testament Book of Job, and to compare that with notions of suffering in other world religions. If you are not familiar with the Book of Job it tells the story of a humble and devout man who — for reasons only his loving God understands — has unimaginable pain and suffering inflicted on him to test his faith. Job passes the test, but the book has always left a bitter taste in my mouth, and I was wondering how I was going to manage to remain objective in my essay. I was also pondering the Hindu law of Karma, and again trying to reconcile the 'you reap what you sow, if not in this life then the next' philosophy with the suffering of innocents. It felt as if a headache or migraine was about to come on, so I sat down in a quiet corner to take some deep breaths and find my calm centre. All the new knowledge I was trying to get my head around was making my head hurt.

I remember feeling overwhelmed and confused. It was winter and the library was dark and musty, as the lighting wasn't efficient. Then a sudden shaft of light came in through the window and hit me right in the eyes. I was blinded briefly and couldn't see anything. I shut my eyes and saw flashing, colourful lights.

After a few moments I opened my eyes. The light had completely gone. There was no trace of it, and the library was all quiet and dark as before. I looked outside the window and couldn't figure out where the light had come from. It was grey and dusky, the setting sun was hidden behind dark clouds and the streets were quiet. The whole episode was surreal, but even more astonishing was the dramatic shift in my energy levels. I wasn't tired any more. I was bursting with energy and my headache was completely gone. I felt as though I could fly, as if I had tasted heaven.

I can't explain the incident, but from that moment onwards I instinctively knew that there was great power and profundity in every religion, not just Christianity. The idea of committing myself to one religion now felt limiting, as I could see with a clarity I hadn't had before that there were glimpses of heaven in each one, and that hearing the voice of heaven was not exclusive to Christianity – as all religions place emphasis on a need to find truth through an inner reflection and realisation. Each takes a different path or route in its quest for awakening, but they are all seeking the same profound truths.

My mother had often told me when I was growing up that we are all spiritual beings having a human experience, regardless of our religion, background and culture, but being young and out of place in a family of spiritualists (because try as I might I couldn't actually see spirit), I had tried to seek my identity in religion. I knew now that she had been right – you do not need to be religious to be spiritual.

Perhaps more significantly, I knew with an absolute certainty that I can't explain that I had been searching for heaven in all the wrong places, and that spirit could never be found in books, ancient dogma, ritual or creed. Heaven wasn't out there and something I would know about only after death. Heaven was within me and all around me right now. It was not a destination but a state of mind and heart – an interconnection of dynamic, loving energy that sustains and guides us both in this life and in the next. To be born again was not about following or imitating others, or joining a religion or group, but about becoming myself – finding heaven within me.

This moment of divine insight only lasted for a few moments, but it changed my life forever. From then on I was an obsessive seeker of spiritual truth.

My experience of clear knowing was a spiritual wake-up call, but for Wendy, whose story is next, it was more a case of divine intervention.

Crossing over

About six years ago my son, aged eight at the time, and I were about to cross a very busy road. The lights were green for us to cross and my son started to move forwards on his bike. I knew I had to stop him from crossing. Something made me pull him back and as I did so a car on the opposite side of the road jumped the lights at speed. It doesn't bear thinking about but if I hadn't stopped him the car would have hit him for sure. The strangest thing about it was that I was calm afterwards. I definitely think we had some heavenly intervention.

In times past, people who were intuitive would have been highly valued by a tribe because they could alert it to potential danger before it happened. Wendy's story shows that intuitive people are still saving lives today. In the next story Karen explains how clear knowing, or as she prefers to describe it, 'her angels', has saved her own life on several occasions.

Motorway

I'm a taxi driver. I had just dropped off some passengers at the airport. I had a rule that I never answered my telephone while driving, even if I was alone in the car – this was because the areas I would have to stop at to take a call were far from savoury. I was on the motorway and my phone rang with a private number. Normally I would have ignored it, but this time something made me answer it. I don't really know why – I only knew I should answer it. I pulled over quickly in an unsavoury area, which was a notorious hotspot for crime and hijackings, and told my client on the phone that I would call them back when I got back to the office.

I drove back on the motorway feeling angry with myself for stopping when I should not have, even though I couldn't have stopped for more than two minutes. As I drove around the corner I saw a man running towards me from his 2-ton truck. Strewn all over the road for about 100 metres was corrugated iron sheeting with huge, thick, long metal chains that had broken loose from the back of his truck. I now know the angels orchestrated the phone call that forced me to pull over in an area I would never have dreamed of stopping at before.

There's more to tell. For about a month I kept getting strong intuitive messages regarding tyres. I'd just collected four corporate directors from the airport and was driving them to a business meeting, when I simply knew I had to pull back from the sixteen-wheeler truck in front of me, even though there was a safe distance between us. As I dropped back to widen the gap, one of the biggest tyres I've ever seen broke off from the truck and started bouncing towards us, getting higher and higher each time it hit the road surface. It was heading directly towards us. Being on the motorway, I couldn't move to the left or right. Just as I thought the tyre was going to come crashing through the window and squash the car, it fell over and landed next to it with a thud.

The truck driver, however, was still moving and unaware of what had just happened. I picked up speed to try and warn him, when another tyre alongside the one that had come off popped off, and the whole process started all over again. It was like watching a rerun, so I gritted my teeth, mumbled a few choice words and thought that this couldn't be happening again. The tyre bounced higher and higher. Then, all a sudden, it shot forwards and raced along the highway at an enormous speed, shooting between cars. Then it bounced over the barrier, where it came to a halt.

By now the truck had stopped and was leaning over to

the side. I pulled over and phoned the traffic police. All the men in the car were cheering my good driving. I took a few deep breaths, thanked my angels that no one was injured and couldn't believe that not one car had been touched. After that day the messages I had been receiving about tyres totally stopped.

Trusting her clear knowing or intuition was a life-saving matter for Sonia, too.

How did I know that?

I wish to share a story that happened to me about fifteen years ago. At the time I was working in a temporary job. I took my lunch at roughly the same time every day. I was a creature of habit and went for a walk each lunchtime, always using the same route, which goes around a sharp bend.

One lunchtime I headed towards the doors of the office with the intention of going for my usual walk. However, on this occasion, as I went to walk out of the doors I suddenly felt as though something had grabbed me from behind in order to stop me. I instinctively knew that I shouldn't go on my lunchtime walk. Instead, I turned around and had my lunch in the work canteen. I wasn't very keen on the canteen, so for me to have my lunch there was most unusual.

I heard that afternoon that a tanker with toxic load had overturned on the sharp bend at around the time I would normally have taken my lunchtime walk. Wow! How did I know that?

John, whose experience is described below, told me that he 'just knows' what his wife (who had died) would be saying sometimes, and how he 'just knows' that she is with him in spirit all the time.

Just knows

We were married for twenty-seven years – Lynn and I. As happens in most marriages we had our ups and downs, but we always managed to meet each other halfway. She was my wife and my best friend and I miss her beyond words but, Theresa, the strangest thing is that when she died last year I just knew she would not leave me.

I was right. I don't feel alone in our house because it feels as though she is still there. I feel her presence, her spirit. She feels so real that sometimes I talk to her and hear her talking back to me in my mind, and I dream about her all the time. I was in the toy shop the other day buying some toys for our grandchildren. I am a terrible gift buyer and very indecisive, but my wife took over. She chose the presents and guided me to them. I did not have to think. I simply knew the right thing to get because she was guiding me. When everyone opened their presents at Christmas they were very happy with my choices. I never did the food shopping in our marriage, either, and didn't think I would have a clue. Again, my wife is looking after me and help-ing me to make the right choices. I cook myself the finest meals, even though I was always a poor cook. I listen to my wife guiding me. She is with me in the kitchen. I know she is.

Please don't think I'm in denial. I'm not at all. I do cry a lot because I realise I can't hug my wife any more in this life, and that is hard to bear. But feeling her around me so closely in spirit, and knowing she is still here in spirit, makes her loss so much easier to bear. Lynn has gone but in some ways I feel closer to her now than I ever did, if that makes sense, because I know we can never be parted again. Her spirit is within me, a part of me now. Where I go, she goes.

John's story is a wonderfully moving testimonial to establishing a living connection with a departed loved one. I know what he means when he says that in some ways he feels closer to his wife now than he ever did, because in spirit there is never any physical separation again as there was on Earth. You can take your loved one with you everywhere.

For Pauline there was simply a moment of profound real-isation. Her story spoke to me on a very deep level. I tend to worry about things too much sometimes, and she showed me the way forwards by stating something very obvious that I had overlooked in the past: that worry achieves absolutely nothing.

Deep knowing

Before I had Julia there had been four miscarriages. I worried constantly. The emotional high of finding out that I was pregnant was followed by the excruciating low of miscarriage, with both the physical and emotional pain to deal with. My body ached to become a mother. It was all

I thought about, so when I became pregnant for the fifth time I was, of course, overjoyed, but at the same time the familiar worry and fear began. I'd always miscarried before twenty-one weeks, so a month into my pregnancy I decided to go on bed rest. I lay there day after day absolutely terrified to move, then, at twelve weeks, the unthinkable happened and I started to bleed. Waves of panic came over me as this was all too horribly familiar, but then – and I don't know how or why – I had this deep knowing that panic, worry and fear weren't going to make any difference. If I was going to miscarry I would do so, and panic was futile.

As soon as I made the decision to not waste my energy worrying any more, I had a moment of serene awareness. I knew everything was going to be all right. I was taken to hospital and my deep knowing was proved correct as the baby was fine. I went to full term and delivered Julia.

I didn't have an out-of-body or near-death experience, just a deep knowing that worry was pointless and Julia was going to be fine. I truly believe that deep knowing saved Julia's life because she needed me to be calm. I was connecting to a very deep part of myself – the part of me that belongs to heaven.

Pauline's wise words at the end of her story are spot on. Whenever there is that sense of absolute certainty and a feeling of natural rightness, this is heaven doing the talking. The question is: how can you tell the difference between just knowing and anxiety or fear?

Overcoming road blocks

I know from personal experience how confusing thoughts and feelings can be, because they can often be very subtle, and our fear-based ego can be extremely persuasive, but there are ways to know when heaven is doing the talking.

Feels right When you think something and it just feels right, go with it in a quiet and calm way. Fear may initially make you think it is right, but then there will be lots of long, drawn-out explanations, confusing changes of direction and self-talk running around in your head. This won't be the case with your intuition. There won't be confusing twists and turns – although the details may build, the key idea will remain the same.

Enriching Divine communication will always be about enriching your life and/or the lives of others spiritually, or helping yourself or others in some way, because when that is your motivation the universe will respond with opportunities to help you succeed. The chances are that it will require hard work and not be a quick fix. Sure, there may be financial rewards or recognition from others but these will be side effects and not the prime motivation. Messages from heaven usually involve the words 'you' or 'we', and don't begin with the word 'I'. If you feel as though you are talking to yourself, this is your ego and not heaven talking.

Energising Messages from heaven raise your energy and never pull you down. If you feel as though you want to fly, this is heaven talking to you.

Empowering The voice of heaven is commanding but in an empowering way that fills you with confidence and a sense of purpose, not fear. If the thoughts in your head are filled with guilt and self-doubt, this is fear talking, not heaven. Spirit is never judgemental and harsh, so if your thoughts tell you that you aren't good enough or that you are a loser, this is your fear and not heaven speaking. Guidance from above may tell you that something doesn't feel right or that you should rethink your approach, or there may be no words – just a thought or feeling that you need to make a change. In short, heavenly guidance is warm, uplifting, positive and empowering. It will build your confidence, not tear it down, and will make you feel comforted, safe and warm – as if you are being given an invisible hug or kiss.

Natural Things will feel familiar and natural for you, and there will be a sense that you are not alone. Fear, on the other hand, will make you feel anxious, out of step with things and alone. It will also push you into extreme thinking.

Live dangerously Guidance from above can sometimes require you to try a radically new approach, put your interests aside for the sake of others or fly in the face of conventional opinion. You may have to go against the advice of strongly opinionated people, and that isn't always easy to do. It won't be the safe option. Thoughts and feelings inspired by fear won't be like this, as their primary goal will be ego and security based, and designed to protect you from embarrassment, failure or taking a leap into the unknown.

Out of nowhere When heaven speaks it will usually do so suddenly and unexpectedly, will require no explanation because you understand it immediately, and will typically have nothing to do with what you are currently working on or thinking about. By contrast, fear-based thinking builds up over time, slowly and gradually, and always requires endless explanation for you to interpret and understand. Having said this, another hallmark of divine guidance is that once the message has been given it will gently repeat itself. You won't feel pressured by that persistence, merely quietly certain that you are doing the right thing.

Make sense Divine guidance will not confuse you in any way. It will be pure and to the point, and will make sense. The opposite is true of fear-based thinking and feeling. There will also be a sense of strong familiarity when divine guidance strikes – as if this was meant to be and you are 'coming home'.

Feel real If there is any loss of awareness of your surroundings when you receive guidance, then it probably isn't coming from above. There is typically total awareness of current surroundings during such occurrences.

As I write this chapter heaven speaks to me again through my inspirational readers. I got a message from Susie, one of my readers, saying that she was walking along the beach yesterday, and wondered if thoughts that inspire or offer solutions come from ourselves or from spirit. I replied saying that I believe they are from both ourselves and our spirits, because both are connected, as this story from Alexander illustrates.

When the soul awakens

Ten years ago I was stuck. I never really got over the loss of my son James, aged eight, in a hit-and-run accident. I experienced seething anger and resentment because the person who killed him got away so lightly, with only a minimal fine and a six-month jail sentence that he didn't even serve. The thought of him walking around free made my blood boil. My marriage didn't survive the death of James, and I struggled through life and several other relationships. Nothing brought me real happiness, but then I had an experience that transformed everything.

As you often say in your books, it happened in the most ordinary of ways. I was watching the news online and there were the usual sickening war images, but one in particular jumped out at me. It was the picture of a boy cradled in the arms of a soldier who was protecting him from an explosion. The picture was no more harrowing than others I have seen from war-torn countries but it brought a tear to my eye because the boy looked so fragile and scared.

As I was pondering the picture a thought came into my head from nowhere. It told me that that boy was James. I looked in more detail at the picture, and apart from the fact that the boy looked as though he could have been aged around eight, the age James had been when he died, there was no other similarity in appearance. I didn't immediately understand what my thoughts were trying to tell me, but the idea of this boy and James being one and the same stayed with me all day. The next morning I woke up after dreaming of James and I had complete understanding.

I believe that heaven was telling me that we are all one. James is alive today in every child. We are all interconnected in this life and the next and my pain was everyone's pain, as was my joy and happiness. There was no separation and I could see James again in every child I encountered. He had not died. He was alive everywhere and within everyone, especially within me.

From that moment of awareness onwards, I've felt as though I have taken a huge leap forwards spiritually. I still miss James but I don't let his death block my heart from loving and opening myself to others. I have even found a way within my heart to forgive the driver who killed him. Ever since I did that I have had many vivid dreams of James and feel his presence everywhere – whereas before I just felt his loss. It is very hard to write such things, as what I'm trying to describe is out of this world. It feels as though my soul or spirit has awakened to something greater than myself. Having read your books I think you will understand.

Many spiritual traditions teach the interdependence of all things. Near-death experience stories also nurture this concept of oneness and interconnection through the power of love and empathy. In my opinion, Alexander's moment of knowing was sent from heaven. I also like to think that it was his son James who longed to connect spiritually with his father but he simply couldn't do so until his father opened his heart and mind to spirit and empathy with others.

Alexander's anger and grief were blocking contact with the other side. The photograph and the empathy it inspired in Alex's heart were the trigger. It is often the case that empathy and concern for our fellow human beings can lead to profound bursts of intuition and spiritual awakening.

Boosting your intuition

As is the case with all the suggestions in this book, to establish a connection to the other side you need to find what works best for you. Here are some ways that I have found effective over the years.

Go for a walk Walking regularly can calm your mind, order your thoughts and sharpen your awareness so you can be more receptive to messages sent from above via your thoughts.

Keep an open mind It is positive to have opinions about things, because those opinions define our personality and nobody wants to be bland, but always keep your mind open to the possibility that you could be wrong or that there is new information which could impact your opinion. An open mind provides a clear channel for heaven to speak to you. A closed mind puts up barriers. Bear in mind, however, that there is a difference between an open mind and being suggestible and gullible. If you have heard other opinions, ideas or arguments and taken time to consider them but they just don't feel right, trust your intuition as the chances are that they aren't right for you.

Feed your mind Think of every person you meet and every situation you are in as an opportunity to learn something new. Look at the world as an open book, a treasure trove of secrets. There are so many amazing things to discover, so many insights to feed your unconscious mind, the storage facility for your intuition.

Listen to your thoughts Simply recognising that your thoughts are a way for heaven to speak to you, and committing to listening to them (and not automatically ignoring or dismissing them as foolish, unoriginal or irrelevant), will help you develop clear thinking. One way to give your thoughts more respect and a chance to express themselves, instead of being dismissed, is to get into the habit of recording them on your mobile or computer, or writing them down in a notebook. This is also a great way of finding out how often your thoughts or impressions of people and situations are accurate.

Just be There are lots of meditation techniques that promise to quiet your mind and connect with your inner vision/intuition, but the meditative state can't be created, learned or possessed; it just has to be noticed. It is about the lack of thought and simply finding a quiet moment to find your calm centre. That's why meditation techniques aren't always effective – because they merely put more thoughts into your head. What you need to do is stop thinking and trying altogether. Do, think and feel nothing. Just be.

Live backwards I have found this is a powerful way to kickstart your intuition. Every night before you go to sleep try to remember your day backwards, starting from when you went to bed and working back to when you got up in the morning. It sounds simple but is actually a lot harder than you think. The reason I am asking you to do this is that in near-death experiences there is often mention of a life review, where a person's life flashes before their eyes. This review starts backwards because in heaven past, present and future do not exist. They become one. So thinking backwards encourages your mind to connect to the world of spirit, the way things might be in heaven.

Step outside yourself Try to spend five minutes or so every day paying conscious attention to your actions, words, feelings and thoughts from within. If you can do that, something sensational will happen. You will notice that you can step outside yourself, and that you are not the same as your thoughts, feelings and actions. You are separate and this separate you is your spirit, the part of you that survives death.

Tune into the silence of you It can feel very odd at first watching yourself from the inside out, but distancing yourself from your thoughts, feelings and actions gives you remarkable inner clarity. You tune into the silence of you – the spiritual part of you that glows. When that happens someone else, typically someone who is also sensitive, notices your inner glow and is inspired by it. There won't be any words or physical interaction, but they will feel connected to you in ways they don't understand. They will sense a spiritual connection that will light them up from the inside. Then, in turn, they will inspire and light up someone else, and so on. What is happening here is a mystical connection between all people that near-death accounts express so beautifully; a sense of oneness with everyone and everything, which is basically another word for heaven.

Let me count the subtle ways

Remember, thoughts from heaven tend to be subtle and you may often receive divine guidance without even being aware that you are receiving it from above.

If at any point you have felt as though you are a part of something greater, or that there has to be something more to this life, you are connecting to a deep truth within. This could be when you gaze in awe at the stars or at the beauty of a sunset or sunrise, or find peace and stillness in nature or in anything that fills you with wonder and inspiration. It could be whenever you try to stay positive or think or send others happy thoughts because, although you may not realise it, what you are actually doing is praying; creating a message that is sent out to the universe. It is the same when you follow your intuition: you are talking to the divine part of yourself. Likewise if you value truth and respect your life and the lives of all living creatures, you are engaging in a spiritual dialogue.

If your heart longs to travel and experience the unknown, heaven is calling you to dialogue with and experience different expressions of divinity. If you naturally avoid negative people and situations that drain your energy, and are looking for people and situations that leave you feeling revitalised, you are again naturally inviting spirit into your life. In the same way, if you understand that you are in control of your mind and can choose to change your perception, you will know that there are no limits to your potential and again you are entering into a divine dialogue. Finally, whenever you laugh or seek out humour, heaven is talking to you. In all these ways heaven can call your name. You may not notice it with your eyes and mind, but your spirit and heart will hear it loud and clear.

Hopefully, this chapter has encouraged you to start trusting your inner knowing more. You will just know when heaven is speaking to you. Try not to rush or force things, and be patient when you make mistakes – because you *will* make mistakes and there is nothing wrong with that if you learn from your errors. Think of all experiences in your life, even negative ones, as opportunities to learn and grow in spirit.

We are all equal in the eyes of heaven – drops in the same ocean. Some people appear more intuitive and connected to the divine within and around them than others, and this is only because they are willing to trust, listen and believe messages when they come to them. The more open minded, trusting and relaxed you are, the easier it is for heaven to call out to you.

The call of doubt

Finally, if doubtful thoughts about the existence of an afterlife emerge – and they will – don't see this as a sign of

weakness or failure. Over the decades I have come to understand the awesome power of doubt, because whenever there
is doubt there is progress or a leap forwards – for example,
without the power of doubt we would still think that the
world was flat and that the sun revolved around the Earth.
Someone had to doubt accepted opinion for humanity
to take a leap forwards. It is the same with your spiritual
development. Doubts about the afterlife can be a catalyst for
serious awakening.

Typically for me, whenever I seriously doubt the existence of heaven it often finds a way to inspire me. After the
horror of 9/11 those doubts were stronger than ever. Stories
of unbearable suffering filtered out into the media, each
more heartbreaking than the last, but then the final phone
and text messages from people in the doomed planes were
revealed. You would have expected the final messages to be
filled with hatred and panic, but in many cases the last words
those people spoke were ones of love. They only wanted to
send messages of love. There was no time for, or interest in,
doubt. There was only heaven. Doubt had no relevance. So
if those people could find heaven within themselves in the
midst of hell, there was no excuse for me.

On another occasion I was filled with doubt when a
friend of mine went through the torture of losing a young
child, aged four, to cancer. Her life and heart were torn
apart, and everyone who knew and loved her shed tears
alongside her. Seeing a child suffer and die makes it very
hard to believe in heaven.

After her child died my friend asked me if he would
always be a little boy in heaven. When he crossed over

to the other side would he still be four? I was at a loss to know how to answer at first, as until then I had not thought about the concept of age in heaven, but then I dug deep into my heart and a sudden knowing came over me, perhaps inspired by the many near-death experience stories I have read and the way they describe eternal life in spirit as pure consciousness. As I spoke I could see my friend's face relax and soften, and it was a moment of peace after all the harrowing pain she had endured. I told her that her beloved child would be four years old in heaven, but every other age it was possible to be as well. I told her that he was now free to be a part of everyone and everything, and to live in her heart for all eternity.

To put things another way, when we die our consciousness, our energy, survives. Have you ever wondered which 'you' will go to heaven when you die? The 'you' as a child, or the 'you' as a teenager? The 'you' that existed yesterday? The 'you' that exists today? The yesterday 'you' and the child 'you' have gone, died, but you – your consciousness – go on, and it is your consciousness that lives on in spirit when you die. It is your consciousness, the eternal you, that never dies.

Doubt crushes your current idea about heaven, the idea that makes you think you know the answers, but we will never know all the answers in this life. Whenever you doubt it is heaven calling you to search even deeper within yourself for meaning, to grow taller spiritually and open your mind to a world of infinite possibilities.

The next chapter explores that world of infinite possibilities with some breathtaking stories from people who have actually visited the other side in near-death experiences. I have no doubt you will be amazed and inspired, as I never fail to be, by their compelling testimonies to the existence of an afterlife.

Death is no more than passing from one room into another. But there is a difference for me, you know. Because in that other room I shall be able to see.

HELEN KELLER – FIRST DEAF-BLIND PERSON
TO EARN A BACHELOR OF ARTS DEGREE

CHAPTER SIX

DYING TO LIVE

*It certainly seems like a good idea to talk about heaven,
meditate about heaven and read about heaven, because,
after all, that's where we are going to spend all eternity.*

DAVID BRANDT BERG

Perhaps the most powerful way spirit can speak to any one
of us on Earth is through a near-death experience (NDE).
All those who have had an NDE have absolutely no doubt in
their minds that heaven spoke to them with vivid clarity. They
know they went to heaven. Out-of-body experiences (OBEs),
when a person's spirit or consciousness somehow separates from
their physical body and can look down on it, are also often
associated with NDEs. Take a few moments to prepare yourself
before reading these next few stories. They are truly awesome
and the closest thing we have right now to actual proof of
heaven. Let's begin with this NDE sent to me by Rachel.

Lighting the way

At the age of eighteen I lost four babies via miscarriage. I lost my first baby in March 2005, and lost triplets in May the same year. I was devastated. I sank into a deep depression, the first of many to come, and stopped working, which I was also sad about as I loved my job (working with children with special needs). I cried most days, took rose petals to the sea for my babies, and begged heaven every day for the blessing of motherhood (I'd not been religious before losing my babies, but now consider myself spiritual). I married the father of my babies before Christmas and was thrilled to find out we were expecting again. I was terrified I would miscarry again and the whole pregnancy felt like a miracle to me. We found out we were expecting a girl, and I threw myself into preparing for her arrival. I was the happiest I'd ever been.

Four weeks before our due date, we found out that there was a complication with our daughter, and that there was a possibility she would need surgery at birth. Again, I felt too scared to hope, and merely prayed. My husband and sister were with me when my contractions started (via drip induction), and for fourteen long hours I cried and begged heaven to help me. By the time my daughter was ready to be born I was exhausted. I felt completely drained. I had an epidural and forceps were eventually used to assist with the delivery. During the labour I remember being violently sick, and while barely conscious, being asked to sign a form in case of the need for a blood transfusion. I didn't understand and tried to protest, but eventually managed to sign.

By some miracle my daughter was healthy and, despite

being born with an abnormality, she did not need surgery at all. They placed her on me and I just cried and cried with gratitude, happiness and relief. For two days we lay beside one another, both of us drifting between the ward and our dreams. I was told I needed a blood transfusion due to losing such a massive amount of blood during the labour, and was hooked up to a drip for about two hours before I noticed anything was wrong. I watched other women leave with their babies and kept questioning why I didn't feel right, why everything felt as though it was taking so long.

I asked heaven in my mind what was happening and continued to cry. I needed the toilet and somehow found the strength to stand. I left my daughter in her cot and dragged my drip to the toilet. I felt sick, hot and scared. My heart was racing and I was all alone. I went to the toilet and when I stood up I nearly collapsed. I suddenly felt frozen to my core. I stumbled back to the ward and tried to get warm under the sheets. My teeth started chattering and a woman opposite me asked if I was all right. I kept thinking, I don't know, but smiled at her and explained that I was just cold. I turned away and pressed my buzzer. Within moments there were four women around me. The drip was yanked from my arm, an oxygen mask was put on my face and the world slowed down. It was then, at that exact moment, that I knew I was dying. My curtain was closed, and I looked up at the ceiling and closed my tired eyes.

I then experienced what I now know was tunnel vision. Everything went black, but then I saw a little circular light ahead of me. I seemed to float down this tunnel and the light grew and grew until it was all I could see. Then, just like in an old film, my life quite literally flashed before my eyes back to front. I was watching my memories, but as an observer. I saw things I'd experienced as a child. I saw my family, our pets, the ocean, my wedding day and my daughter being born. It was all perfectly sequenced. The whole experience occurred in silence. I couldn't hear the nurses or the ward. I had left them completely. The last image flickered away and I was left with the purest light I've ever seen. It filled my entire being with love. I have never experienced love like that, before or after. I felt immediately that I was in the presence of an angel. I felt incredible. I felt unconditionally loved, beyond any measure. I felt understood, safe and at home.

The light held me in its presence for some time. I later learned that it was at this time that my husband was called and my family had to make the long journey to see me. I actually remember thinking about that while they put the mask on – that I'd never see them again. But all that fear disappeared when the light came. During my time with the light, I felt that I was being fed information which was incredibly important to my life path. There was no depression, no pain, and everything felt natural. I remember asking if I could stay and never wanting to come back to my body. That moment of wonder seemed to go on forever, but then I was told, by the light, that I needed to go back. An image of my new-born daughter flashed in front of me and my heart throbbed to be with her. I wanted to scoop her up and bring her with me, truth be told. The light told me I was special, I was needed, I mattered. It taught me the importance of each and every one of us, and I knew right then that only love really mattered. As soon as every realisation had hit me hard, I flew backwards, the light was gone and I was back in my body.

For a further three days I lay in and out of consciousness. My family came, but I would drift away and rest with the light. I was sweating constantly and wanted nothing more than sleep. I woke on the third day to the midwife feeding my baby and it triggered something in me to fight.

Rachel then went on to tell me that her sensational experience encouraged her to write about her trip to heaven and find her true meaning in life. She set up a support group online for people suffering from depression. It has helped thousands of people feel better about themselves. She tells me that people often call her an angel who saves people, but the truth is that heaven saved her and she is forever grateful.

Rachel's story is breathtaking but every time I read an NDE account I find it impossible not to be moved and inspired. Joanne's NDE below may be brief but it is no exception.

Millions of diamonds

Having had an operation under partial sedation with some complications, I was taken back to the hospital ward to rest. I wasn't feeling too bad, but was informed that I had suffered a small haemorrhage. I must have fallen asleep, and the next thing I remember was travelling at a fast speed down the brightest tunnel of light. It was unlike anything I had seen before, but I felt so comfortable. The nearest thing I could describe it would be as millions of diamonds catching the light at the same time. I travelled for a short distance before I arrived at a beautiful area of 'greenery', a bit like a woodland, but it was all surrounded in mist and I couldn't see clearly, though I wanted to. I wanted to walk forwards but something was stopping me. Then everything was black and all I could hear was a clearly spoken voice, saying, 'Go back, Joanne, it is not your time yet.'

The next thing I remember was a nurse standing by my hospital bed trying to lift me up as the alarm on my blood-pressure monitor was beeping. The nurse said that it was showing that my blood pressure had dropped off the scale. I sat up by myself and she looked at the machine and said it must have malfunctioned, so I should just have a glass of water. I lay there and wondered what on earth had just happened.

Death creates fear in our minds and hearts because it is the great unknown, but every NDE story I have read reassures me that fear should be replaced with peace, joy and courage. Swiss psychologist Carl Jung (1875–1961) famously described death as a 'the great adventure', because from his own NDE when he had a heart attack at the age of sixty-nine, he believed that he had witnessed something 'unspeakably glorious'. Here's a sparkling extract from his famous autobiography, *Memories, Dreams and Reflections*:

It seemed to me that I was high up in space. Far below I saw the globe of the Earth, bathed in a gloriously blue light. I saw the deep blue sea and the continents ... In many places the globe seemed coloured, or spotted dark green like oxidized silver ... Later I discovered how high in space one would have to be to have so extensive a view – approximately a thousand miles! The sight of the Earth from this height was the most glorious thing I had ever seen.

Bear in mind that Jung wrote this before humans had travelled into space, but it remains a fairly convincing depiction of what Earth is like viewed from space. Jung goes on to say that returning to Earth was 'profoundly disappointing' as his vision had been so incredible: 'In reality,' he wrote, 'a good three weeks were still to pass before I could truly make up my mind to live again.'

It seems that Jung's reluctance to return to life is not uncommon. Many people report conflicted feelings when they come back to Earth after they have tasted the unconditional love and joy of heaven. Lily's NDE story speaks for itself about the bliss of life on the other side.

I have tasted paradise

I didn't want to go back. The angel told me I must go back because there was more for me to do. But I didn't want to go back. That sounds horrible, doesn't it? I love my husband and children and my life so much on Earth, but when I was in heaven I knew that I was home. I was enveloped in love and feelings of bliss. I wanted to stay so I could send some of that love and bliss to my family on Earth, but the angel told me I needed to do that in my human form. Instinctively I knew that I would not feel the same euphoria in my human form, but the angel assured me that when I returned my life would never be the same again. The angel was right – my life has never been the same. How can it be? I have tasted paradise. I see the world in a totally different light. I know that death is not the end and that infinite love, joy, beauty and bliss await us.

Here is Olivia's account. Her story reads like a parable. There is so much to learn here about leading a life of spiritual fulfilment both on Earth and in heaven.

The grass is greener

In 1987 I tried to end my life. It was for a lot of reasons that I don't want to go into here. Mercifully I was found just in time by my college friend of one week and rushed to hospital. My stomach was pumped and I was in intensive care for several weeks, and nearly didn't make it. That first night when I was brought in, I had a vivid experience. I saw myself on the operating table. I was outside my body. There were three doctors in the room and two nurses. They were working silently, but I could see how worried they all were. Outside the door there were no hand-wringing relatives, just my new friend – she wasn't truly a friend since we'd only known each other a week – looking confused and shocked.

I didn't feel anything when I looked down on my body. It was like looking at a suit or dress you didn't want to put on. I was aware of feeling totally free. I'd been in emotional torment for so long, and the relief to feel free was intense. I watched the doctors and nurses work on my body with a sense of detachment.

Then I was outside the hospital, floating around the grounds and in the car park. I had an amazing sense of peace. There was no way that I was ever going back to the pain I had known on Earth. At last I was free. I could feel a light coming towards me, but just as I was reaching up my arms to be embraced by its warmth and comfort, I was back in the operating room. Once more I was looking down at my body and my stomach was being pumped.

Then I noticed two people standing on either side of me. They were watching my body on the table, and unlike me they looked very sad. I had never seen either of them before but knew they were both dead. I also knew they were sisters, and that they had died in a car accident some time ago. They were dressed in clothing in the style of the 1960s. I knew that the elder sister felt responsible because she had been driving the car. Her guilt was so strong that it made it impossible for her to leave her life on Earth behind. The younger sister loved her sister so much that she didn't want to go anywhere without her.

I felt concern for the sisters and asked them telepathically why they were hanging around in a hospital watching people die. I told them that they were no longer alive, and that they should leave this place and go to where they were meant to be. When I spoke to them I had an amazing feeling of peace, as if I was doing the right thing for the first time in years. They both looked at me with confusion and asked me — again telepathically — what I was doing there then, because I was alive and yet wanted to be dead. In their world I wasn't where I was meant to be either.

In an instant I knew that it was not my time to go yet, and

that I needed to go back. As soon as I realised this the sisters vanished. We all returned to where we were meant to be. The next thing I remember is waking up with a very dry throat in a hospital ward. Holding my hand was my friend. She was fast asleep with her head resting on a magazine.

I can't describe or explain it, but the warmth and love I felt for my friend and for everyone around me was incredible at that moment. I was intensely, deeply grateful to be alive, and all these years later that feeling has remained unchanged. I try to live each moment to the full because I know that everything we do in this life is being noticed, and that whenever the living don't appreciate what they have on Earth this causes confusion in the afterlife. I haven't seen the afterlife again, but I know that when my time comes to pass over – and I hope this doesn't sound too strange – I will also feel intensely grateful to be dead.

Jordan's NDE story below reminds us that signs from above are being sent to us all the time. We just need to open our eyes, hearts and minds to them. It also reminds us powerfully and poignantly that love never dies.

To the stars and back

I lost my dad when I was thirteen, and it left a gaping hole in my life. I missed him every day and also felt extreme guilt, as the last memory I had was of me telling him how much I hated him. He wouldn't let me go to a party because I had exams that week and I lashed out. I didn't hate him. I loved him to the stars and back and it has crushed my spirit knowing that the last words he heard from me were spoken in anger. Ever since, I have longed for a sign that he has forgiven me. My life has not felt complete these last twenty years.

During my NDE, Dad was the one to greet me in the tunnel, although for me it felt more like a corridor than a tunnel. It was dazzlingly bright and I felt unimaginable lightness and joy. When I met my dad the joy was indescribable. He told me in spirit that he had never ever stopped sending me his love and had always been by my side. He had been with me on my university graduation day (after Dad died my grades soared, as I stop partying) and on my wedding day; he had been in every moment of joy and pride and laughter in my life and in everything astonishing I saw, felt, heard and touched. He had been in the bright stars and in the white clouds. I just hadn't noticed him there watching over me because my guilt had blocked out the light and the truth.

There is much to savour from a spiritual perspective in Jordan's story – in particular the familiar life-review concept when a person crossing over 'sees' their life again in a flash. This suggests that everything we say, do, think and feel on Earth is being gently observed, and that our connections with loved ones are eternal. With that stunning idea in mind, are you living in a way now that would make heaven proud? If you aren't then perhaps reading about NDEs here is heaven's way of motivating you to make changes.

Jordan's story, like every story in this book, also illustrates the eternal power of love in this life and the next. If you have known injustice, cruelty or hardship, or are grieving the loss of a loved one, it can be especially hard to believe that love is the answer to everything, but it really is the only way out of the darkness. I'm not talking about romantic love here, or the unconditional love a parent has for a child, or the platonic love families and friends have for each other. NDE accounts show that although these kinds of love are certainly aspects of love, they are not the whole story in heaven.

People who have 'died' and gone to heaven talk about love as the most all-consuming force in the universe. It is so spiritually expansive that it is impossible to fully understand or express it in human words, but the father of a young child visiting the scene of the horrific shootings and bombings in Paris in late 2015 to lay some flowers came pretty close. The little boy asked his father how they could fight back, and the father replied, 'We fight them with flowers.' If ever words expressed the power of heavenly love to defeat darkness, those did.

Near-death stories suggest that it is only when we are in heaven that we fully recognise love as the spiritual force that lies at the very heart of the universe and moves through us. On Earth we understand love in a more limiting way. Those who have been to the other side, however, have glimpsed the earth-shattering force of love, and they also know that on Earth what or who we love is a reflection of who we are or need to become in order to grow spiritually. We give and seek love in our lives because we are seeking to connect with the divine, to become spiritually whole. Seen in this light, there is nothing more powerful and important than love in this life and the next. It is the reason for our being.

There is, of course, no guarantee that others will love you as you would want to be loved, because love is a choice you cannot force others to make. However, I promise you that the love you give unconditionally will always return to live in your heart, and you will grow stronger and more empowered in spirit as a result. Love is the force that overcomes death and connects you to the true meaning of your eternal life – and that true meaning is heaven.

Shift in perspective

Commonly accepted scientific opinion is that death is the ultimate end, but NDEs like the ones you have just read appear to directly contradict that. In the past any scientist who investigated the possibility of an afterlife or heaven would typically have had to face criticism from the scientific community, and lack of funding and support. In recent years, however, due to a number of highly significant developments, and the work of some pioneering and courageous researchers, that perspective has gradually begun to shift. There is still a long way to go, but what has been uncovered so far has the potential to make even the most sceptical of us wonder if perhaps death is really the ending we have always been taught to believe it is.

I'm aware that the evidence I present for the afterlife typically rests on personal or anecdotal experiences. I am not a parapsychologist, doctor or scientist. Having said that, in recent years I have started to reach out and interview leading scientists, doctors and researchers, and I want to take this opportunity to give you a brief overview of where the scientific search for evidence or proof of an afterlife is currently at. You'll see that we are a lot closer than you might think to proving that heaven is real, and the gap between science and spirituality is closing fast. I hope what you read below will give you goosebumps in the same way it does me.

Proof of heaven

Leading the way has to be the work of resuscitation expert Dr Sam Parnia, currently an assistant professor at the State University of New York, and a former research fellow at the University of Southampton. As well as being a pioneer in medical procedures that help revive patients after cardiac arrest, Parnia is fascinated by the idea of life after death. According to hundreds of interviews he has conducted with people who have had near-death or out-of-body experiences, Parnia believes his research proves that consciousness can exist outside the body and survive brain death – the moment when there is no electrical activity in the brain – for at least three minutes.

Out-of-body experiences certainly seem to suggest the survival of consciousness independent of the body. In his groundbreaking 2014 NDE study, which got all the major newspapers talking, Dr Parnia made special mention of a 57-year-old social worker who described everything that had happened during his resuscitation, despite being clinically dead for at least three minutes at the time. Among the things he remembered were two bleeps from a machine that makes a noise at three-minute intervals.

Parnia's research is so convincing that the scientific community has had no choice but to sit up and take notice, and Parnia and his team have been given the go-ahead and funding for another round of research into the survival of consciousness after brain death. This in itself is a massive leap forwards, and potentially very exciting for all those who seek scientific proof of heaven.

One of the reasons why Parnia is able to conduct his research is that in recent years the number of first-hand accounts of people claiming to have had NDEs has increased dramatically. This is in large part due to advances in resuscitation techniques pioneered by doctors like Parnia himself. Fifty or so years ago these people would not have lived to tell their stories, but now they are returning from the brink and their stories are utterly compelling. Some cases have truly captured the imagination of the world. Nowhere is this more so than in Dr Eben Alexander's case, as described in *Proof of Heaven*, a book perhaps treated with more reverence and respect than others because he is a neurosurgeon, and before his NDE he doubted the existence of life after death.

According to Dr Eben his brain was in a vegetable-like state for seven days, and was incapable of any higher thought or activity because it was offline. During this time – when he was due to die at any moment – he had the most sensational NDE and 'met' a biological sister who had died several years previously, but at the time of his NDE he had no idea he had a sister.

There have been plenty of attempts to discredit Dr Eben

and his story, which he has refuted, but his case is not an isolated one. Other bestselling authors, such as *Dying to be Me* author Anita Moorjani, have come forward with equally convincing accounts. If they are all telling the truth then their eyewitness testimonies cannot be ignored.

Indeed, if you study NDE accounts as closely as I have over the years, one of the most compelling things about them is how similar they all are. If they were just hallucinations or random workings of a dying brain, then surely they would all be different? Another fact that science has thrown up recently about NDEs, which is hard to explain away, is their hyperreality. Leading this research is Dr Stephen Laurey – a scientist who does not actually believe in life after death. When he started to research NDEs he expected them to operate in the same way that dreams or hallucinations did, and that memory of them would fade. Instead he found the opposite to be the case – that the memory became more clear, fresh and vivid over time. Years after their NDEs, people still had perfect recall, and in my own research I have found this vividness and clarity years after the event to be the case not just for NDEs, but for all afterlife experiences.

In addition, research has shown that people who had an NDE experienced positive changes in their approach to life afterwards. Almost all lost their fear of death, and became more positive, loving and outgoing, regardless of what their personality was like before. These kinds of psychological changes are not reported after hallucinations, and the most obvious explanation for them is that these people have been to heaven and come back to tell the tale.

Even more incredible are those who meet a dead relative in heaven, having no idea that they have died. Others have accurately described dead people they have never seen or met, and NDEs have been reported by children who met people in heaven they had no awareness or knowledge of before.

NDE research is leading the way when it comes to offering actual proof that heaven is real, but alongside that a growing number of respected doctors and scientists are currently devoted to the study of spiritual experiences and afterlife communication. At the forefront of this research are the Institute of Noetic Sciences (IONS) and the Windbridge Institute, both in the United States. It's not just in the States, however, that this cutting edge research is taking place. There are amazing academics, scientists and institutions all over the world engaged in it.

All the research currently taking place, and the fact that science is opening its mind to the idea that there may just be life after death, owes a great deal to modern quantum research and theory, which assign as much importance to the observer (our perception), as to what is observed in the creation of matter. An early person to link quantum science with the paranormal was Fritjof Capra in his seminal 1975 text, *The Tao of Physics*. In this book Capra explores parallels between eastern mystical traditions and quantum physics. In the decades that followed, influential supporters from the medical and scientific community, most notably the likes of Deepak Chopra, Dean Radin and Robert Lanza, went on to present an idea that the universe is in itself a product of our consciousness, and not the other way around as scientists would have us believe. To take this argument further, time, space, matter, life, death and everything else only exist because of our perception of them.

Don't worry if you find all this quantum science, or bio-centrism as Lanza has called it, mind-blowing, because it is. I'm simply trying to give you a brief overview of current research into afterlife science, so you can see for yourself that the dividing line between science and spirit isn't as great as you might think.

For me life after death is perfectly logical. I am no scientist but I believe modern physics tells us that everything is made up of vibrating strings of energy, and the way this energy vibrates determines how it manifests in the world. Our thoughts and feelings are energy in the same way that our bodies are, so it is entirely possible that this energy can survive in another dimension of reality. Nothing has been proved conclusively yet, but I believe that it is only a matter of time before all the experiences I have had, and all the amazing afterlife-encounter and near-death stories I have been sent over the years, are proved to be real. Right now if there is anything we can take from all this exciting research, it is probably that we shouldn't fear dying as much as we do. It isn't the last frontier we have been made to believe it is. Talk to anyone who has had an NDE and they may well tell you that it was the best thing that could have happened to them.

The truth is out there and it is the calling of all the pioneering scientists to try to find it for us. If you would like to know more, take a look at Appendices 1–3. In particular read my interview with visionary scientist Dr Julia Mossbridge of the Institute of Noetic Sciences. For now, though, it is time to leave the search for scientific evidence and step back into the world of the personal and profound, the discovery of the extraordinary in the ordinary and everyday.

The first person you meet in heaven

This chapter closes with a story that is deeply personal to me, as it concerns my mother and her NDE following a suicide attempt. There was whole variety of reasons why my mum attempted to take her life. Her Dutch Indonesian family had been torn apart by the horror of the Second World War, and the brutality of the Japanese towards the Dutch in Indonesia, where she was born. Her father and older teenage siblings were placed in concentration camps, but because she was only eight or nine at the time she was sent with her mother to live in Holland. She didn't have a penny to her name, felt utterly and completely alone, and suffered from taunts, sexism and bullying in both Holland and the UK. In short, as happened to millions of others, her life was torn apart by war and she lost all sense of meaning and hope.

To cut a long and complex story short, my mother, aged twenty-five, somehow ended up in a young woman's hostel close to Victoria Station in London, and overdosed on sleeping pills. Fortunately, on the night she chose to take her own life, one of her roommates was sent home early from work due to a vomiting bug, and discovered my mother in time. As her stomach was being pumped in hospital my mother had an NDE. She told me later that during her time in heaven she floated through a dark tunnel and walked into a garden of light, where the first person she met was not a relative or friend, but a woman she had absolutely no recollection of.

This woman spoke to her (my mother never speci-fied how and I wish I had asked for more details at the time), and told that her that she had been behind her in a cinema queue. The film was sold out and my mother got the very last ticket. However, my mother, sensing how disappointed the woman was not to get a ticket, gave away her ticket to her. As a result of my mother's act of spontaneous kindness, the woman ended up sitting next to the man she would later fall in love with, marry and have children with. After five years of love and laughter the woman died in a car crash. She wanted to be the first person to greet my mother in heaven because she wanted to thank her for enabling her to meet her soulmate. She also wanted to ask her why she had done it. Why had she handed over her ticket when she clearly wanted to see the film as well? My mother replied that she didn't really know why, but she must have felt that it meant more to the woman to see the film. Her heart told her to give her the ticket. This answer seemed to delight the woman, and she told my mother that she was now going to do some-thing wonderful for her in return. She told my mother that it was not her time to die as there was much left for her to do, give and learn on Earth.

My mother did, of course, return to Earth, but she also

made a serious point of telling me that as spectacular as her NDE was, it wasn't until a week later, when she felt sunshine on her face before stepping into a perfumed bath, that she truly felt the desire to live. She told me this to remind me that you don't have to nearly die, or go through extreme trauma, to see heaven – sometimes heaven can reveal itself in the simplest of ways.

As you can expect, it has taken me a lifetime to come to terms with the fact that my mother, the woman who inspired me to seek a spiritual life, actually tried to take her life. She waited until I was in my early twenties to tell me, and she told me during a time when I thought my life wasn't worth living, as I had just broken up with my first serious boyfriend and felt broken. She said she was always going to tell me it was just a matter of the right time.

At first I felt deeply betrayed and wounded by my mother's revelation, because she has always told me that life is sacred. However, in the decades that followed I gradually came to an understanding and acceptance. I often find myself returning in my mind to that pivotal moment when my mother told me about the NDE, and each time I feel that my mother is standing right beside me. Her experience taught me that nothing we say or do in this life is ever trivial. If my mother's roommate had not had a stomach bug, I would not be writing this book today, so even unpleasant things may have a higher purpose either for ourselves or for others who we may not become aware of until we cross over. In the same way, my mother simply handing over a ticket, because her heart told her to, had profound and unforeseen consequences that changed the life of the woman who received the ticket – and brought two new spirits into the world when she had her children. Incredible!

I'm sure you have heard of the butterfly-effect theory, which derives from the metaphorical example of the formation and path of a hurricane being influenced by the slightest thing, such as the flapping of a butterfly's wings weeks earlier. In other words a single happening, however insignificant or tiny, has the potential to alter the course of our lives forever. From a spiritual point of view the butterfly effect indicates the interconnectedness of our thoughts, words and deeds. Whether we know it or not, we are all connected in highly complex ways. While a single act, such as giving up your seat or ticket for someone else, arriving five minutes late and so on, may appear inconsequential at the time, it is impossible to predict all the potential outcomes that may be triggered by a single act, or the powerful spiritual connections that are created as a result.

Think about this the next time you hold a door open for someone or feel inspired to strike up a conversation with a stranger. It could all be happening for a reason, and what you say or do could change lives forever. If you think about everything in this way, how much easier it will be to listen to the guidance of your heart whenever life doesn't go as you have planned. How much easier, then, will it be to regard every moment of your life as potentially life changing or sacred.

Above all, my mother taught me that it is possible to glimpse the extraordinary in the ordinary. Many times in my life I have seen heaven in a shaft of sunlight or a blade of grass. I thank my mother every day for the gift of life on Earth she gave me, and the desire to understand and connect with spirit that she inspired in me. Indeed, I have devoted all of my adult life to this search for spiritual understanding and connection with departed loved ones.

In the next chapter I share more of what I have learned, most especially how to have a conversation with heaven during times of loss, suffering and the intense pain of grief.

There is a connection between heaven and earth.
Finding that connection gives meaning to
everything, including death.

JOHN H. GROBERG

CHAPTER SEVEN

GRIEVING WITH SPIRIT

Sincerity is the way to heaven.

MENCIUS

It is especially hard to believe in heaven during times of suffering and grief. I hope this chapter will teach you that painful life experiences, like the loss of a loved one or a relationship breaking down, can offer incredible opportunities for spiritual growth and connection to the afterlife. In brief, any time in your life when you feel vulnerable, confused and alone, when you feel you don't have all the answers, or when your world view shifts dramatically, is an indication that the spirit within you is awakening.

Sometimes spiritual awakening feels painful and wrong, as all your familiar beliefs, routines, ideas about yourself and your life crumble around you, but you have reached a crisis point when the demands of your spirit can't be ignored any more. It is spiritual evolution or nothing. Heaven isn't calling but yelling, because it longs for you to search deep within and find that life-saving connection to the eternal divine spark within and all around you. This famous quote describes the darkness before the dawn – the labour-pains-before-birth message I am hoping to convey here perfectly.

> *A pearl is a beautiful thing that is produced by an injured life. It is the tear that results from the injury of the oyster. The treasure of our being in this world is also produced by an injured life. If we had not been wounded, if we had not been injured, then we will not produce the pearl.*
>
> STEPHEN HOELLER

There have been many times when life has overwhelmed me, but two occasions stand out from the rest because of the intensity of the pain I experienced and the life-changing spiritual growth that followed. The first was the pain of heartbreak and the second was the pain of grief.

Heartbreak

In my early twenties, when my first serious relationship ended, my heart was smashed into pieces. I couldn't handle the pain. I had poured so much of myself into the relationship, it felt as though a piece of me was missing. I lunged into full-blown depression. It took the words of a wise

Earth angel on a Tube train, intuitively asking me why I was wasting my energy crying for someone who probably wasn't crying over me, to help me understand that heaven was closer to me in my heartbreak than ever. Clearly my partner didn't love and value me, so heaven (wanting only what was best for me) gifted me his departure.

Whenever people write to me these days about the pain of heartbreak when a relationship breaks down and how it challenges their belief in heaven, I feel glad I experienced that intense pain and can empathise with them. I try to encourage them to shift their thinking and find the spiritual meaning behind it all. When someone leaves or a relationship ends, don't think of it as rejection or failure. Think of it as a gift or sign from above that heaven only wants people in your life who truly love and value you but, above all, heaven wants you to search deep within and discover true love and a sense of completeness there.

Don't ever think it is self-centred to fall in love with yourself. There is a school of religious thought that equates self-sacrifice with piety, but I challenge that notion. You can't give to others what you don't have within yourself. Start thinking of your life as a love affair with yourself, and when you do genuinely love yourself you will find that giving to others comes naturally because it makes you feel even happier. You will also find that true love seeks you out, rather than the other way round, because your self-belief only attracts people into your life who truly value you. It might help to think of the relationships in your life as your spiritual mirror. If you don't love what you see in the reflection, the change needs to come from within you.

Grief is the last act of love we can give to those we loved.
When there is deep grief, there was great love.

ANON

The call of grief

In much the same way that heartbreak forced me to evolve spiritually, and to find love within myself rather than seeking it in others, I can see now that my utter despair following the death of my mother was a further spiritual catalyst.

After my mother died and I didn't immediately get a sign from her, I doubted heaven as I had never doubted it before. I longed for a sign but got absolutely nothing. Sometimes I would simply want to see a picture of her. I was terrified I would forget her face. I lunged into full-blown depression, and for a terrible eighteen months gave up all belief and hope in the idea of heaven. Then, gradually, through significant dreams, meaningful coincidences and bubbles of profound intuition, I met my mother in spirit again. It is clear to me now that her death and the darkness that followed forced me to search deeply for heaven and grow up spiritually.

Grief shakes us to the very core of our being, and all our beliefs about the meaning of life are thrown overboard with the shock, anger and pain. Most of the letters I receive are from people in the stages of grief when they long for a sign or some kind of reassurance from above, but feel utterly and completely alone. The phrase 'dark night of the soul' comes to mind but, just as in the plant kingdom, it is during the darkness of the night that the miracle of growth occurs.

As I worked on this chapter by heaven-sent synchronicity, I read a letter sent to me by a woman who has recently lost her young son to cancer. She tells me how her life has been smashed to pieces. The smallest of things set her off. The ringing of someone's mobile phone reminds her of a sound she heard on her son's life-support equipment, or she will see a boy wearing a blue scarf and remember her son wearing his favourite blue T-shirt. She doesn't know how to carry on with her life. Sometimes she goes for a drive and just pulls over, and cries and screams for hours. She tells me that she longs to see her son in spirit, but so far has seen nothing. 'The hardest thing,' she writes, 'Is that nobody wants to be around me any more. I have lost all my friends. I have been told I should just get on with my life but I don't want to. My life stopped when he died. I don't know how to start it again.'

My eyes fill with tears as I read her letter, but I am also filled with great conviction – because this mother's pain is the reason why I write spiritual books. I pray they will help people who are lost in grief understand that heaven is calling out to them in their grief and longing to show them a way forwards, where they can reunite with their loved ones in spirit. I also hope they will encourage other people to not avoid or stay away from grieving people for fear of saying something that might upset them further. As this lady told me, 'Even people saying the wrong thing to me would be better than saying nothing at all. Sometimes I feel invisible.' When a person is grieving they need the love and support of friends and family more than ever, and they do want to talk about the person they have lost. They want to keep the memory alive.

Beyond grief

The pain of someone you love dying is unbearable and isolating, but I hope this book will reassure you that although you can't touch or laugh with your loved one physically any more, you can enter into an amazing relationship with them in spirit. They can live forever in your heart and mind, and be with you more deeply and intimately than ever before.

It sounds so very easy to say this on paper, but anyone who has ever lost a loved one knows it is far from that. Many grieving people tell me how intensely they long for a sign to ease their pain, but it never comes. I reply by saying that their loved ones are reaching out all the time with gentle signs, but they can't get through the wall of grief and any signs they do send won't be noticed. That's why before spirits can offer us spiritual reassurance, there needs to be a period of acceptance of the passing first. We need to accept that the spirit of a departed loved one is never going to come back physically. Only when there is acceptance of the loss and we feel stronger emotionally can spirit break through. On occasion it can penetrate intense grief, but more often than not a departed loved one will not appear in such a dramatic way out of concern for you. They don't want to make your transition to life without them even harder to bear because, however comforting the vision or encounter, they can't ever come back into their physical body.

So a priority is to tend to the wound of your grief first. It is essential that you cry and mourn, and fully accept the physical loss. Grief is unavoidable because whenever there was great love there will be great grief. When my mother died the pain was so raw that I went into denial. I paid the price for this later, in that the wound grew larger and stopped me moving forwards emotionally and spiritually. I had to understand that grieving does not mean saying goodbye forever. It just means that I am human and missing human contact. I had to understand that my grief was a gift to my mother in spirit, an act of love, and only when I could release my grief could she find a way to speak to me. To risk repeating myself, grief truly is the darkness before the dawn. I needed to go through the dark tunnel of grief before encountering light or making contact with the other side.

I'm not a grief counsellor but there are counselling services (see Appendix 4) out there that can explain the complex feelings you will go through as you grieve over the loss of a loved one, and give you coping strategies. I know from my own experience that your emotions will include anger, guilt, fear and confusion. As intense as these feelings can be, it is important to remember that they are not good or bad – they are just feelings. It is only when you act on your feelings that they become good or bad, and you are the one in control here. I also know that if these emotions aren't accepted and acknowledged, this can result in depression somewhere down the line – that is what happened to me. Denial is never the answer and it is all right to cry and scream. You are not crazy. You are a human being reacting naturally to loss.

Everyone will travel a different journey through the pain of loss – some people will move fast while others will have a very slow pace. There are no rights or wrongs as you need to take things at your own pace. Grief cannot be hurried and there are no quick fixes to escape the pain. It will take time. The support of friends and family can often be invaluable, but if the help isn't there (which is sadly often the case because people just don't know what to do or say around a grieving person), talk to your doctor and ask for support. If someone offers to help, let them take care of you for a while. Think of it this way: if you had a heart attack you would allow yourself to be taken care of – it is no different for emotional wounds.

It goes without saying that taking care of yourself by eating well, exercising and trying to sleep properly is important, and after the initial first few weeks keeping in touch with the world around you is essential, too. At times you may feel guilty because you are alive and your loved one isn't, but never forget that you are a unique miracle. There is no one else here on this Earth like you, and heaven wants your spirit to remain on Earth as you have a purpose and a destiny yet to fulfil. Indeed, that purpose and destiny may even include one day helping someone else to journey through their grief, because you have travelled that road.

Time goes by

Everyone knows the old proverb, 'Time is the great healer', and like many proverbs it states the truth. I have lost loved ones and although the sharp pain of their loss is out of this world, trust me, the intensity of it does eventually fade and there is light at the end of the tunnel. This doesn't mean that you won't feel sad any more or will forget, it just means that stinging sadness no longer incapacitates you. Don't think of your life returning to normal again because it simply can't. Your life has changed dramatically and the old you doesn't exist any more, but key for you now is whether this change and the new you is going to be positive or negative.

Think about what your loved one in spirit would want for you. If you choose to live a sad and lonely, purposeless life then this isn't really a celebration of the time you shared with your loved one on Earth. What better tribute could you pay to someone you have loved and lost than to live your life to the full, and to remember the time you shared together with joy?

Again, I want to stress that this process takes time. Grief is like the wind – sometimes it howls, sometimes it is like a gentle breeze and at other times you barely notice it at all. In time you will come to a place when you can remember your departed loved one with a smile. This is the place where you can reclaim the part of yourself that you gave away to them. When you love or feel for someone deeply, you give a part of yourself away. This is truly wonderful as long as all your self-esteem and happiness aren't dependent on them, which wouldn't be healthy for them or you. There is a difference between need and love. Real or true love has nothing to do with need, because it is the love that can set a spirit free. When someone you love dies there is an opportunity for your loved one in spirit to set you free, so you can reclaim the part of yourself that you gave to them. The love returns to you and you become whole again. Yet again, this 'becoming whole' again takes time, but if you journey through your grief with spirit and take care of yourself along the way, you will rediscover your strength, and passion will return to you. That can be deeply healing and blissful.

Over the rainbow

Once you permit yourself to fully experience the loss of a loved one – and to go through all the stages of grief – you will eventually find yourself in a place where you catch glimpses of overwhelming peace and love. I have experienced this bliss on a number of occasions since the death of my mother, and when I feel it I know that she is alive in spirit and watching over me. The last time I experienced the bliss was while I was writing this book. I got a letter from a very brave young woman I have been in touch with for several years because of my books. I knew she had a health condition but did not press for details. She always told me about her moving afterlife experiences, and I always loved hearing from her. This letter was different, though. She told me that her days were numbered, and she wanted to talk about her funeral and get my feedback on what she had planned.

My first reaction was shock, and a feeling that I needed to tell her not to think about her funeral, but to focus on getting better. However, as I crafted a response to her my words felt empty and hollow. I started to cry and as I did I felt a gentle squeeze on my left shoulder. I knew it was my mother in spirit and I asked for her advice on what to say. The response that came into my mind was to not brush aside talk about the funeral plans. I wrote back and gave my advice and recommendations, and as I did I got a feeling of absolute joy and rightness. It was as though a wave of peace and calm gushed over me. It was bliss. As I hit send on my computer I got up and looked out of the window and saw a lovely rainbow – always a sign for me that I am on the right track.

I didn't even know what I was writing at the time, but when I read my response back I had told the woman that it was really important that she choose everything personally. It was important because she was going to be there in spirit, so she needed to make sure it was something she would enjoy, too. She didn't want to be bored at her own funeral! I told her not to get too serious and to include a little humour because heaven loves to laugh. I told her I hoped her time on Earth continued as long as possible, but if it was to end sooner her spiritual adventure would continue on the other side. I said I hoped she would keep in touch with me in this life and the next.

A few days later this lovely lady wrote back to me and thanked me for the introduction to heaven.

Why not me?

Some people seem to be able to receive messages or communications from the other side naturally and easily. I wasn't one of those people, and had to learn the hard way the importance of grieving fully and letting go of preconceptions about how heaven would talk to me, before I began to sense afterlife signs. If you don't feel that sense of spiritual connection yet, I hope you will learn something from my experience. It also might help to know that in spirit there is a very different concept of time, indeed no concept of time at all.

Einstein suggested that time only exists to stop everything happening at once. What he meant here was that the concept of linear time (things happening one after the other in a straight line) is something created by our minds to allow things to happen in an orderly manner – without earthly time there would be chaos. His theory of relativity showed that time is not constant or linear, and that it can be changed or altered by the speed and direction of a moving object. I mention Einstein's theory here to help you get your head around the idea that NDEs suggest that time simply does not exist in heaven. Time is an illusion created to allow us to experience life on Earth. Our eternal spirits exist beyond space and time, and what feels like a lifetime for you may feel like a heartbeat for our loved ones in spirit. The earthly concept of time no longer exists for them, and this may explain why you don't feel you are getting any messages from them.

NDE accounts report that this out-of-time concept and understanding can have a tremendous impact on the way we live our lives on Earth. Once we know that in the perspective of heaven, events on Earth may be happening at blinding speed or occurring simultaneously, but have been

slowed down and ordered in our minds (as we live in a physical rather than a spiritual universe), we begin to understand
that a ninety-year lifespan on Earth is a blink of an eye in
spirit. So perhaps some of us don't feel we have received a
communication because the departed only feel they have
been gone a few moments, or have not left at all.

Having said that, I truly believe it is still possible for us
all to receive gentle messages from above, and reunite with
departed loved ones in our hearts and spirits. Hopefully the
suggestions that follow will help you do just that.

Maintaining contact

Many people ask me if it is possible to talk to departed
loved ones. My answer is always a resounding 'yes', because
even though they have passed to a life in spirit they have
never stopped loving you. The bonds of love in spirit are
unbreakable. They are going on with their eternal spiritual
lives in heaven and it helps them greatly if you do the same
on Earth. As mentioned previously, a certain period of
mourning is essential as you adjust to the loss of a loved one's
physical presence. If that grief is overly prolonged, however,
this can direct their loving energy, attention and concern to
this life rather than to the next, where they belong and can
find their peace and continued spiritual growth – as, yes,
growth continues in heaven, too. In other words, the more
peaceful, happy and loving we are, the more joyful the lives
of our departed loved ones are in spirit.

If visiting a grave or monument helps you feel close to a

loved one, by all means do visit it, but it is not necessary for communication with the other side as it is just the earthly clothes that you are visiting. The spirit, the essence of the person you loved, is free and everywhere.

The power of prayer

The word prayer has strong associations with religion, but any time you feel a sense of connection and communication to the other side, what you are actually doing is praying, just not in the formal or ritual sense. The title of this book is *Heaven Called My Name* and, although some people feel called to a life of devotion, I think that being called isn't about joining a nunnery or monastery, but about living your life in a continuous state of prayer or intimate dialogue with the other side.

The world can often be violent, unfair and cruel, and like many people I often feel despondent or that I can't make a difference – but the more I research the power of prayer, the more I understand that there is something I can do, and that is to pray. Studies (see Appendix 5) show that patients who are prayed for in hospital recover faster than those who aren't. No one knows exactly how this works, but the fact that it can have an impact suggests that prayer or simply sending loving thoughts to someone has incredible power. You may have already felt this yourself when someone told you that you were in their prayers. It feels good, doesn't it?

Try this as a little experiment. For the next few days think about someone you know. If possible, it should be someone you have met but felt distanced from recently, or have even fallen out with. Now, instead of focusing on what you don't enjoy about that person or want to change about them, send them loving thoughts as often as you can. Trust me, this will have a transformative impact on your relationship, and when it does do get in touch and let me know.

I'm not suggesting that prayer will always bring you the desired outcome. Why bad things happen is beyond our comprehension, and some painful experiences are lessons for the soul, but if we pray for ourselves and for others, this can help give us or them the inner courage needed to cope or focus on what truly matters in this life and the next. I'd like to share Judy's story now because it is such a lovely illustration of the healing power of prayer.

Praying hands

My brilliant mum – who has since passed away – told me this story. She was the most honest person anyone could meet. I know it is true.

It was 1972 and my mum had been in hospital for several months. She had been admitted for a simple hysterectomy, but it turned into an infection that drained the life energy out of her body. The doctors didn't know what caused it, but she got weaker and weaker and lost weight rapidly. There's so much talk about hospital-based infections these days, and I suspect she might have fallen victim to one of those, but back then there wasn't as much awareness as there is today. At one point Mum weighed less than 7 stone, and she had always been a well-built woman. She couldn't keep any food down and was placed on drips. This went on for a few more months. Mum lost weight and my dad was told that the doctors thought Mum would die.

My mum was not a woman of faith. In her youth she had been drawn to the Church, but I think she got disillusioned over the years. She loved to collect photographs of religious and spiritual art, though, and her favourite was a painting called the 'Praying hands'. If you haven't seen it, it's an exquisitely drawn picture of a pair of hands raised in prayer. One day when my dad came to visit her, she asked him to bring in that photograph because she said it always comforted her. My dad brought the picture and placed it by her bedside. For the rest of the day my mum and dad stared at it, both of them praying for a miracle, and at one point my dad got down on his hands and knees, and prayed with every fibre of his being.

The next morning the doctors began to make incisions to try and drain the infection. It was their last resort and the chances of success were slim. All through the day the infection poured out of my mum. Everything came out and by the evening she was craving solid food for the first time in four months. She had survived.

I truly believe that the prayers of my mum and dad in the hospital that day worked a miracle. I truly believe that angels are all around us.

Remember, as you have seen throughout this book, spirit can answer you in countless ways, and how, when or where you choose to pray doesn't matter as all you need is love in your heart. You don't need rituals or chants, or to go down on bended knees with hands raised, because heaven will hear your voice whether you speak with your mouth or your heart. Margaret's story illustrates this.

Stan

I've never been religious and have never felt a desire to attend Church, but then my husband had a serious operation in 1991. The hospital told me it was going to be a lengthy process and that it was best if I stayed at home. I prayed with all my heart that the surgeon's hands would be guided from above. I just sat in my front room with a cup of tea and love for Stan in my heart. I could not imagine life without him.

Nearly five hours of waiting and I got the call I had prayed for – Stan was going to make it. I was so happy at the time and didn't think about the power of my silent prayers, but a few days after the surgery, when I met Stan's surgeon, I remembered them clearly. The surgeon told me that the operation had started very badly and they were debating whether to stop the procedure, as they weren't sure of the next best step, but then suddenly, from out of nowhere, he knew the way ahead and found the strength to focus. He even used the words I had silently said in my head: 'It was as if something was guiding my hands.'

I told him about my silent prayers and he just smiled. I didn't press it any further as I didn't want him to think I was saying that he couldn't have done it without some help from above, because he was such a brilliant surgeon, but inside I knew that my prayers had been answered. For the first time in my life, I believed in something. For the first time, I felt a surge of joy and hope.

Stan passed on in 1999, so we got another nine years together. I'm so grateful for that time. It meant the world to me. I miss him deeply, but whenever I feel that he has gone, I sit quietly and think about him, and he is all around me again. Don't ask me how, but I know he hasn't died. I know he is out there somewhere. I don't tell many people about my beliefs, because I don't think they would understand me, but something tells me you will understand.

I know many people get a lot of reassurance from traditional forms of prayer and I am happy for them, but for those of us who are uncomfortable or unfamiliar with formalities, prayer is simply talking to heaven with your heart.

How do you open the lines of communication between yourself and the other side? A good starting point is finding your calm centre.

Find your calm centre

Peace and calm is the place where heaven is most likely to break through. It is hard to hear the gentle voice of heaven when you are rushing from one thing to the next and your head is crowded with a noisy list of to-dos. So, from now on take a few moments, preferably first thing in the morning and again last thing at night, to be silent.

Finding your calm centre is something you can do at any moment, anywhere. It is also surprisingly easy to do as you just need to be silent and start focusing all your attention on what you are doing and thinking. Spending a few quiet moments thinking about all the things in your life you have to be grateful for is another way of achieving this. Taking a few deep breaths from your stomach rather than your chest when you are outdoors can bring calm. Listening to soothing music can bring you inner silence, as can cloud watching and star gazing or walking by the seashore. Reading inspiring and spiritual books, relaxing in a warm bath, drinking hot chocolate, writing in a journal, colouring, singing, dancing, gardening and doing crosswords are other ways to create inner peace. There are endless ways to still your mind and find your calm centre. Simply doing whatever you love takes you to a place of bliss and creates a clearer channel for heaven to speak to you.

In addition to finding your calm centre, an attitude of sincerity and awe, and a genuine desire to talk to heaven, are all divine facilitators. Just getting into the habit of thinking about heaven as often as you can will set things in motion. Then you are ready for the next step, which is simply to start talking.

Start the conversation

If you want to communicate with a departed loved one simply start up the conversation. Talk to heaven. Ask for a sign. It's easy. Talk to them in your mind, then let go and trust a response will come. Don't force anything and in the days ahead gently notice – don't look – for things happening around you. Notice everything. Pay attention to afterlife signs (more about these in Chapter 8) coming to you, perhaps through the appearance of a white feather, the words of a song, an overheard conversation, a thought that suddenly pops into your head, a dream, a passage you read in a book, or a quiet and certain knowing. If, after a few days, you don't think you have received a sign, the chances are that you have, only you simply haven't noticed it. Keep talking to heaven and observing yourself and others, and the world around you. Be patient. Spirit will provide a response when you are ready to hear and accept it.

Each of you will find your own unique way to talk to heaven. For example, Tony got in touch with me to say he hears his departed wife speaking to him when he goes fishing. Lucy tells me her mother whispers to her when it rains. James feels that heaven communicates with him through the laughter of his children, and Belinda feels spirit every day in the notes of her favourite composers. The list of possibilities is endless, but some signs are more frequently reported than others. In the next chapter we take a look at some of them.

For the next few days think of yourself as a spiritual being with a divine purpose, set aside any scepticism and believe that a sign or way ahead will be revealed to you. Set the intention, focus your thoughts and let heaven do the rest. Keep your ears, eyes, mind and heart wide open, and notice patterns and messages that have personal significance for you. Do write to me if this works because it just might. This is exactly what Delphine did, with instant results.

It made me smile

Many years ago, I was reading your book. At that time we lived in a very quiet neighbourhood, where no one was outside after 10 p.m.

I was thrilled to read about angels, rather ready to believe in an afterlife and feeling connected to departed loved ones. I prayed: 'Please, angels, if you are real, give me a sign but make sure it is a clear sign that really rings a bell for me. Thank you.' Literally a few seconds after I had said my prayer, I heard a bell ringing. I ran to the window and there, on the pavement, walked a human being (it was dark, so there was no way to tell more about him or her). While walking by our house, the figure had randomly rung the bell of our bicycle, which was standing outside. This person must have been prompted by the angels to ring the bell and was – probably unknown to him or her – a messenger of the messengers.

I had to laugh at first because there was so much humour in this sign, then I thanked the angels for their resounding answer. As I recall it, this memory still brings a smile to my lips.

If you keep asking and keep noticing, eventually you might hear heaven speaking to you – don't expect the sign to always be profound, because sometimes it will just gently lift your spirits. I love Delphine's story because it shows that heaven has a sense of humour and loves us to smile, so the next time you have a good laugh or smile from your heart, this just might be heaven's way of reaching out to you and signing to you through the language of joy.

Let it go

Keeping yourself open to subtle signs means letting go of any preconceived notions you may have about how heaven speaks to us. You need to understand that there is no right or wrong way to receive a divine communication. You need to understand that the way heaven talks to you is likely to be highly personal and individual. Above all, don't think that you need to be psychic, clairvoyant or a medium to communicate with spirit. I wasted far too many decades worrying that I wasn't psychic, or trying too hard to see and hear heaven in preconceived ways – and all I got was a wall of silence. It was only when I let go of the 'shoulds' and 'oughts' as far as my psychic development was concerned that I began to receive life-changing communications through dreams, feathers, clouds, stunning insights and coincidences.

One way in which I enter into my personal dialogue with heaven today is through a process known as automatic writing or typing. I have found that this is not only a fantastic way for me to connect to the divine within and around me, but also a method of getting in touch with the spirit of my departed mother. What's great about it is that it is a very simple process. It may or may not work for you, but why not give it a try?

All you do is think about your departed loved one or the world of spirit, then just let your hand do the talking. Write or type whatever comes into your head, even if it doesn't make sense at all. Record all your thoughts, feelings, words or pictures. If nothing comes at all, write down the word 'nothing' until it materialises into spiritual communication, which it will. You may find as you write that your handwriting changes or you use words you are unfamiliar with. Don't let any of this frighten you, because fear drowns out heaven's voice – and if at any point you find yourself thinking or writing that this is all your imagination, ask yourself how you know that. If you find yourself doodling circles, half-circles or squiggles, they are heaven's way of breaking through. At the end of the session finish with a loving goodbye. Then, at a later date, read what you have written, and you may be surprised at the insight and guidance you find there.

Anytime, anywhere

You can talk to heaven anytime, anywhere. Don't ever feel that what you have to say is too trivial or that you are not worth heaven's time. You are a miracle. Your DNA is completely unique. There will never be anyone like you ever again on this planet. You deserve every good thing this life and the next have to offer you, because you are one of a kind. There is a divine plan for your life. If you feel inferior to anyone else, what you are actually saying is that the work of heaven is inferior.

It is your fear-based ego that will send you those messages of not being worthy as it attempts to distract you from reconnecting with your spiritual destiny. Notice those fear-based voices, rise above them and let them go. Focus on the voices of divine love within and around you instead, and in time as you enter into a continual dialogue with heaven you will find that your life becomes much happier and calmer.

Finally, while it is certainly true that suffering and grief can be potent catalysts for spiritual awakening, never forget that calm and contentment can do the same and just as effectively. I can't stress this point enough: you don't need to nearly die or be in the depths of despair and grief to hear heaven. Remind yourself that heaven loves you unconditionally, talk as often as you can to heaven with your mind and heart, then relax and trust heaven to respond. The more you enter into this divine dialogue, the more you will feel, hear and see heaven within and all around you.

Spread kindness with your words

Finding a calm centre and starting up a conversation with heaven will set things in motion, but for progress to be made from there and for the connection to grow strong and meaningful, you need to watch your words – by that I mean both what you say and what you think. You can't expect heaven to reveal love and truth to you if you don't speak words of love and truth to yourself and others. Like seeks or attracts like. If you speak words of hate that is what you will attract into your life, but if your words are love centred, heaven has an entry point and a divine dialogue can begin.

It is impossible to always speak the absolute truth, but it is possible to always speak from your heart and with the best interests of yourself and others in mind. Don't beat yourself up if in the past you have said things you regret to others because your emotions got out of control. There is nothing you can do about your past, but there is something you can do about your present, so make the choice right now to be the one in charge of your emotions, and spread only kindness with your words. This is especially important when it comes to the words you say to yourself. Talk to yourself only with loving words from now on, as this will awaken the spirit within you. If words are used that don't have a basis in unconditional love and kindness, the spirit within you simply shuts down, making dialogue with heaven impossible.

In short, heaven can only respond to truthful words spoken from your heart because in heaven there is no other language but truth.

All the difference

When there is a powerful and sincere connection between people on Earth and in heaven, it is possible to form a connection in spirit. Spirits can sometimes return to reassure us or to say goodbye, if it wasn't possible to say goodbye when they died. This is increasingly common in our world today, when many families live and work long distances apart. In some dramatic instances spirits return to warn or guide us, but most of the time they simply want to reassure us that we are not alone and that there is no death – only eternal life. In extremely rare cases spirits may appear as full-blown visions, but it is far more likely that you will hear them whisper to you through gentle afterlife signs, or calling cards. A number of these have already been discussed in previous chapters, but the next chapter covers this topic in greater depth.

For now just hold the thought in your mind that spirits of departed loved ones can call out to you in many ways, and all you need to do is start noticing them. In recent years more and more people have started to talk openly about their experience of communication with the afterlife. This is exciting as the more people talk about eternal life, the more this encourages others to open their minds to the idea, and the more afterlife experiences start to happen – an open mind is an invitation to the world of spirit to manifest itself.

Don't let fear of the unknown shut down your communication with spirit. Think of all the great innovators and inventors of the past and what would have happened if they had feared the unknown. We would still think that the Earth was the centre of the universe. The unknown is where all growth happens. Again, you have a choice here. You can choose the path of security, the known and familiar, or you can head into the unknown. If you want to grow spiritually and find your true meaning, the unknown is where you need to travel. The choice is completely yours. Robert Frost's poem, 'The Road Not Taken', always comes to mind here – it's about a man who remembers the time he stood at a crossroads, and his decision to take the road travelled less frequently 'made all the difference'.

A closed mind that fears the unknown can block the voice of heaven. An open one, which acknowledges the very real possibility that life after death exists, can connect you to departed loved ones in spirit and make 'all the difference'.

The missing link

I have not yet mentioned the work of mediums, or people who claim to have clear lines of communication with those who have died. I would like to touch briefly on the subject because a lot of people write to me saying that they have found comfort after visiting a medium. One person who found tremendous comfort from doing this was Dr Julie Beischel, following her mother's suicide. A decade or so later she changed the direction of her scientific research from pharmaceutical drugs to the investigation of mediums.

The work Dr Beischel is currently doing at the Windbridge Institute in the USA is so intriguing that I have included the full transcript of my interview with her in Appendix 1. Dr Beishel and her team are actually testing mediums scientifically for the first time, and recording the results. The data coming out is promising and may well be the first scientific study to actually prove that communication with the dead isn't just possible, but is happening. In the appendix section you'll also find an interview I carried out with world-famous psychic James van Praagh, so you can gain some insight into the mind and life of a medium. I have included contact details for key websites and organisations that can help you learn about or experience mediumship firsthand.

Although I have merely pointed you in the direction of some amazing people, organisations and research, I want to make it crystal clear that I have never recommended going to a medium or psychic, and don't intend to do so now. This is because I have made it my life's work to stress that we all have the potential to form our own unique and independent or free relationship with spirit, without the need of a priest, psychic, guru, medium or intermediary of any kind. If you aren't hearing spirit, in my opinion you are the missing link.

I truly believe in an individual, personal and direct

connection with departed loved ones, but I also like to keep an open mind and will keenly follow all the exciting new research into mediumship in the years ahead. I know I will also never stop dreaming of a time when establishing communication with the other side, whether via a medium or not, isn't regarded as abnormal or strange any more, but perfectly normal and natural. Perhaps one day doctors may even suggest spiritual therapy as part of a grief-recovery pro-gramme, or they may have scientifically approved mediums working alongside them as grief consultants, so we can all grieve with spirit. This isn't entirely beyond the realms of possibility given the direction of current research.

Do I believe that one day scientists will be able to prove that it is possible to actually talk to heaven? I think they may well do so, but that it is probably years ahead. In the meantime, we have to deal with the here and now – and right now the most important person is you and what you believe. If this book encourages you to trust that you can talk to the other side, and to connect with departed loved ones in a spiritual sense, then I am over the moon. The more of us who start thinking about and talking to heaven, the more we will create a spiritual and peaceful world, one person at a time, starting with *you*.

It's time now to move on to the next chapter, which is all about heaven calling out to us through signs, in ways that are both everyday and magical at the same time. Before that take a few moments to gently ponder these two immortal quotes, and as you do so feel yourself melting into your calm centre – the place where the seeds of eternal life are planted and all conversations with heaven begin.

Death is nothing at all. I have only slipped away into the next room. I am I and you are you. Whatever we were to each other that, we still are.

HENRY SCOTT-HOLLAND

Death is not the end. It is only extinguishing the light before the dawn has come.

RABINDRANATH TAGORE

CHAPTER EIGHT

ANSWERS FROM ABOVE

Perhaps they are not stars in the sky but rather
openings where our loved ones shine down to
let us know they are happy.

ESKIMO LEGEND

Wouldn't it be amazing if we could all hear the voices of departed loved ones clearly, or sense their presence deeply in our minds and hearts? I can't promise that such direct and unmistakable communication will occur for you, for all the reasons given in previous chapters. Far more commonly experienced are the subtle signs that need to be noticed and understood on a personal level, and this chapter is dedicated to them.

By way of explanation of this form of communication, signs, or heavenly calling cards as I often describe them, are deeply personal messages that offer a person absolute reassurance that a departed loved one is close by and alive in spirit, waiting for them. They quite literally can be anything that you can see, hear, feel, sense, touch or just know, which feels like a message intended only for you at exactly the moment you need it.

The best-known calling cards tend to come from nature – a white feather, butterflies, rainbows, clouds, flowers and birds – but signs can also come from the material world, and can include coins, numbers and objects lost and found, as well as internal feelings, words and sensations that can be felt, read or heard at the perfect moment to offer strength and hope.

Perfect timing

It is not so much what the sign is but *when* it appears that makes this feel heavenly. You could dismiss perfect timing like this as purely down to chance. However, even when you put forward arguments like chaos theory (nothing is predictable and everything is random) to explain signs away, there always remains a lingering feeling of awe and a sense that perhaps a sign was something more than that. It is also worth pointing out that in recent years scientists have discovered that there might be patterns to chaos – if you look at the intricate design of a snowflake, for example, or the wonder of DNA, you will understand why. There doesn't seem to be anything random there, just perfection of design where everything has a place and a purpose – and all the people who sent me their stories for this chapter feel the same way about the signs they received. The sign had a perfect purpose, place and meaning. The signs were so well timed and deeply meaningful to them that it was impossible for them to doubt that heaven was calling their name.

From all that I have experienced and researched I firmly believe that nothing in life is ever random, and that we are all interconnected by a higher order and purpose. If even scientists are now tentatively suggesting that the universe may not be entirely random, then stories about afterlife signs do, in their way, add to the growing body of evidence that there is a higher purpose guiding our lives. Sure, the signs you will read about in this chapter could all be explained away logically, but then again there is no conclusive evidence that heaven can't talk to us through the magic of perfect timing. So, until there is, all I ask is that you consider the possibility that there could be great spiritual significance to coincidences – or synchronicity, to use the proper spiritual name.

Turning sorrow into joy

There is a reason why I have left the discussion about afterlife signs so late in this book (even though this is the subject I get by far the most correspondence about). It's because due to the deep personal nature of these signs, they could never become the subject of serious scientific study in the way that near-death experiences have. They are subtle, gentle, symbolic nudges from the other side. However, despite their subtlety, afterlife signs offer countless numbers of people a tremendous amount of comfort, and for this reason they deserve to be discussed.

Losing someone you love is the most dark and painful experience, but time and time again I have seen how reassuring signs from above can heal the pain. Grieving becomes so much easier to deal with when you receive a sign that death is not the end but a brilliant new beginning.

Common signs

There are as many signs as there are individuals on this planet, but certain afterlife signs do seem to be more common than others. I've listed below the most common signs I get sent correspondence about, with sample stories to illustrate them. You may remember a few of these signs from previous chapters, because it is impossible to be clear-cut and logical when categorising spiritual experiences that are undefinable.

Each of the signs discussed is associated not only with the presence of departed loved ones, but also with the presence of spirit, or heaven. Typically the signs appear during times of crisis – but not always. Sometimes they appear for no reason at all. Although the circumstances in which signs manifest always differ, the end result is always the same – comfort and hope that there is more to this life than the eye can see.

Butterflies

In recent years I have received a number of letters from funeral directors about butterflies appearing close to coffins, and how their presence offers a great deal of healing to grieving loved ones. I also get messages about butterflies appearing at significant times in people's lives and how their appearance speaks to them on a deep level. This does not surprise me as butterflies are a universal symbol of spiritual transformation from earth-bound caterpillars into winged creatures that can fly.

Here are two butterfly stories – the first one (Zaneta's) showing how butterflies can offer comfort to those grieving the loss of a loved one, and the second one (Bethan's) revealing that the appearance of a butterfly can remind us that we are never truly alone.

Beautiful people

Last week was the tenth anniversary of my twenty-two-year-old cousin's death. Some family members went over to the cemetery, but I chose to stay at home. I was thinking about my cousin that day, and also about my nan. I went into my garden and there, right in front of me, were two lovely butterflies playing with each other. I see butterflies a lot when I think of these beautiful people who have passed over. This was my sign that they are both happy in heaven.

By my side

I had a difficult last year at university and, as I am quite a shy person, I was very nervous about an upcoming examination requiring me to speak on my own. I was walking up the hill from campus back to my student house worrying about it, when I noticed a pretty blue butterfly fluttering near my left shoulder.

I smiled and thought it would carry on its way as butterflies normally do, but it kept fluttering right beside me as I walked. It was on the side of a busy road so I kept expecting it to be disturbed by the cars and disappear, but the minutes went by and it stayed right by my side. Even when I crossed the road, I was amazed to find that it came with me, staying close to me the whole time. This went on for about ten minutes, and when I neared my house the butterfly gradually drifted away. Theresa, I felt so calm and peaceful and knew that its presence was sent to comfort me and remind me that I'm not really alone.

Birds

When a bird crosses your path or behaves unusually, this can be a sign from above that a loved one is close by, especially if the type of bird has personal significance. Here's a story from Karen to illustrate this.

Close by

My mum died unexpectedly on 8 July 2013, when I was in Australia and she was in South Africa, and I felt so cut off and helpless. I stayed indoors crying that Monday, but on Tuesday night my husband managed to coax me out of the house and took me for a walk along the water to the shops, to try and help me clear my head. He was worried about me, as the tears just continued to flow with no warning whatsoever. I was like a zombie.

While we were walking I felt numb. I put one foot in front of the other and we walked in silence holding hands. All of a sudden a little black-and-white bird (I used to see one similar in my garden in South Africa, which I knew as a wagtail) came out of the tree and started hopping alongside us on the railing. We must have walked about 200 metres with the little bird still following us on the railing (staying about a metre away from us), and eventually we had to cross over and go into a shop. I found it rather strange as it was dark and cold outside, and birds are usually in their nests when the sun has set.

The best was yet to come – we must have been in the shop for about five minutes, and when we came out we crossed over to walk alongside the water again. The little bird came from nowhere and hopped straight over to me. I opened a packet of rye biscuits, put a few crumbs in my hand and crouched down, never expecting the bird to come any closer. It just flitted and skipped straight over and started eating from my hand. We were totally amazed as it continued to hop along the railing next to us, then flitted around in front of us as we made our way home.

Wherever I go I always see this same type of bird close by (within a few metres) and manage to photograph it. This morning I was thinking of my mum and asked for some sort of sign. I was scrolling through small businesses in Perth on the computer while looking for a job, when I came across a medium who does readings. I opened up the site to read her testimonials and lo and behold, there was a picture of my little bird!

I went out this afternoon, and when I got home a copy of your new book was in my letterbox, so I hurried upstairs and sat on the bed. As I took off the wrapper I heard an unusual chirping. I looked out of my bedroom window and there on the railing was the same little bird. I quickly got my camera and the bird stayed long enough for me to take more than twenty photos. I sat there with your book in my hand and thought that Mum was definitely trying to communicate with me.

Books/text

This book could well be your afterlife sign: remember that it found its way to you for a reason. I have had many letters about the intriguing ways people have stumbled across my books without seeking them out, doing so at just the right time to ease their pain – as if they were meant to read them. For example, they've found them on Tube trains or in hospital waiting rooms, or the title just caught their eye when they weren't intending to buy or borrow a book. Sometimes I am deeply humbled to get magical stories like this one sent to me by Lisa, about my books taking on a secret life of their own.

Ruby

There must be many accounts of your books connecting individuals with their loved ones who have passed away. I see my dad's name, Thomas, everywhere, every day almost, and have sometimes wondered why my mum isn't as 'communicative'.

Today I had five minutes to spare in a very hectic schedule and went to one of my favourite places – the book store, metaphysical section. For no particular reason I saw your book. I picked it up off the shelf, opened it randomly and there on page 53 in what seemed like bold type was my mum's name, Ruby. Gobsmacked, I flipped over some more pages. Again randomly, I opened the book on page 73, and this time I saw, actually in bold type, the words 'A little help from Mum'.

Whoa! So cool, I am totally blissed out! Thank you, Theresa, for connecting me. I value such a precious gift.

The second story, from Valerie, is taken from a review of one of my afterlife books posted on Amazon.

It's me

Within a few minutes, after asking my recently deceased husband to show me a sign that he was still around me, I had chosen this book at random. I downloaded it to my Kindle. After turning about five pages in Chapter 1, I found a subheading with just two words, 'It's Me', and they were flashing rapidly on and off. In a state of shock I kept turning back a page and trying it again, and each time the two words flashed several times before coming to a standstill. About sixteen pages after this the same thing happened with another subheading, when two words of another subheading flashed rapidly, and when they came to a standstill they read 'Making Contact'.

I am now wondering if any other readers have experienced the same thing, because my second Kindle Fire does not flash when these two subheadings appear. Does anyone have an explanation as to why these words flash on and off when none of the rest of the text on the page does, or has my husband contacted me? The subheadings are still flashing, but more slowly now, even though I have recharged the battery. However, I have managed to video the phenomenon on both my phone and tablet. I have sent an email to Theresa Cheung to find out if any of her other readers have had a similar experience.

I can't take any credit here. The reason why some people experience a sense of connection after reading my book is nothing to do with the book itself and everything to do with their magical hearts and spirits. You see, something they have read in the book has opened their mind to the idea that consciousness can survive death. Reading other people's stories gives them the courage to consciously or unconsciously believe in spirit, ask for contact and expect to receive it.

It's not just books about the afterlife that can be signs. Any book that inspires or triggers a feeling of connection to spirit can be an arrow to heaven. Or perhaps the sign may be a poem you overhear at a significant time, or an article in a magazine that speaks to you when you are mulling over a problem, or reminds you of something a departed loved one said or did, again at exactly the right time to speak to your heart. I've also had letters sent to me about adverts, logos and slogans that speak personally to some people with just the right message when they need to hear or read it. The message here is to keep your eyes wide open and see what messages in the world around you speak to you. I've even had letters about noticing personally meaningful words on other people's mugs, T-shirts and car number plates, so don't rule out anything. Heaven can be very ingenious.

Clouds

Seeing shapes in clouds is one of my favourite things to do. I know many of you feel the same, because whenever I post a beautiful cloud on my Facebook author page the reaction is very positive. Clouds bring feelings of wonder with their constantly changing shapes, and when one speaks to you personally it can only be seen as a message from heaven, as was the case for Ellen, recounted in her story below.

Cloud watching

I loved my sister dearly and we were very close, but I never got to tell her how much I loved her before she died at the age of nineteen in a freak boating accident. My life has gone on, of course, and I have my own family, but I still think about my sister every day and wonder what she would have done with her life.

I'm writing to you because something awesome happened a few weeks ago when I went to visit her grave. As I put my fingertips on top of the grave, while I was missing her and talking to her softly, I noticed that the sun was fairly low in the sky. I looked up and for a short time a cloud appeared as the outline of a complete angel with large, feathery wings on each side of a tiny body, wearing a floating gown with little feet below it and hands reaching out towards me. It had curly ringlets in its cloud-like hair, and its face was smiling. The image of an angel was crystal clear. Theresa, this was the most blissful and comforting sight to me, and for the first time since my sister's death I had a sense that she was trying to tell me she was with the angels, and that she was happy and fulfilled in heaven.

Coins

Inanimate objects can bring a sense of hope and possibility. I get a number of charming stories about coins appearing in unexpected places, and sometimes the dates on the coins can be significant as they correspond to an anniversary of some kind. This story from Mary is all about the power of a small coin.

Penny dropped

I was reading the section on coins in your new book last night, and it has inspired me to share my experience with you. My mum passed away in February this year. I was distraught with grief, but one day I realised that I must pull myself together and take my little dog Maisy for her morning walk. While walking I was compelled to stand still but didn't know why. I looked down at my feet and in between my wellington boots was a small brown piece of metal. I picked it up and realised that it was a coin.

I wondered who it was from. I cleaned it on my return and realised that it was a 1944 three-penny bit. The year 1944 was my mum's birth year. I realised that the coin was from my mum on the other side, reassuring me that everything would be all right. So in the midst of my grief I actually felt great joy.

Cool breeze

Many people sense the presence of a loved one when a cool, gentle and typically unexpected gust of air touches their cheeks. Sometimes it can even feel like a gentle kiss. Some also feel they can hear a departed loved one whispering words of comfort to them in the wind. Here's a story from Nicola that I received many years ago, but I must include it here because it eloquently sums up the message of this book.

The invisible kiss

At Mum's funeral I was a wreck. Everyone suggested that I see her body, but I made the decision not to as she always told me she wanted me to remember her alive and vibrant. My family pressured me a bit to see her body as they said it helped them see her at peace and healing, but I refused even though they told me I would regret that decision one day.

About an hour or so before Mum's funeral I was lying on my bed crying relentlessly. Mum hated the cold and I couldn't bear thinking of her lying in a cold coffin. I wondered if I should give her one last kiss. Perhaps everyone was right and I needed that closure. Just at the moment when I was reconsidering my decision, I felt a gentle cold breeze on my cheek. All the windows and doors in my bedroom were closed and I can't explain it, but I knew my mother was with me.

After that experience I went to the funeral feeling stronger and calmer, and instead of thinking of Mum alone and cold in her coffin, I made myself remember sunny days and laughter. Towards the end of the funeral I felt a gentle kiss first on my left cheek and then on my right one. I closed my eyes and strong images of Mum smiling and running around came into my mind, just as she would have wanted me to remember her. I knew I had made the right decision, and every time I think of my mother now she is always smiling and running around – alive and vibrant as she wanted to be remembered.

Clocks stopping

There are many well-documented stories about clocks stopping at the exact moment a loved one dies, as if to remind those left behind that time is an artificial construct that only exists on Earth. In heaven there is no time – no past, present or future – just never-ending love, as Debby's story details.

Beyond time

At the time of my sister's death the clock that we had bought together and given to Mum for her birthday some years before stopped working and would not go again, even though it was fully wound and in complete working order.

Mum believed this to be a sign that my sister was in the afterlife and sending us her love. I was not so sure, but when I called Mum on the anniversary of my sister's death, I was shocked to hear from Mum that the clock had started working again just that day. I am sure this was a sign from my sister.

Dreams

See page 86 for information. Dreams are typically one of the first vehicles through which departed loved ones reach out to us from beyond the grave, because they are such a subtle and gentle method of communication, and are least likely to cause us alarm.

Electricals

Lights flickering, and kettles, alarms and electrical equipment behaving strangely, are commonly reported signs that tend to happen at just the right time to bring support. Denise sent this short story to illustrate this, and it is followed by one from John.

Tea bliss

I work with palliative care patients, and your books bring great comfort to those left behind. Only last week I had a client whose wife passed away quite young. The kettle kept going off for days on end for no reason, and she loved her tea! It helped him believe his wife was close by him.

Lighting up

Just before my grandfather died he helped us put up the lights on our Christmas tree. It was a stunning display, but within days the lights around the angel at the top just wouldn't work. We toyed with the idea of getting new lights, but by then the Christmas tree had got so busy with crackers and decorations that it was more trouble than it was worth.

Two days after Christmas, Grandfather was admitted to hospital with a major heart attack, and he died peacefully in his sleep on 4 January. When we got back from the hospital we were all shattered and gathered in the living room to talk about him and remember him. The lights on the tree were not on so I went to switch them on. You guessed it, Theresa — when I did the lights around the angel were working again. It was the most beautiful and healing sign. I can't get over it. I know it was my grandfather talking to us. I just know he has gone to a better place.

Mobile phones

Mobiles can behave irrationally, and doorbells may ring but when you go to answer them there is no one there. See page 60 for a discussion about telephone calls from the departed, and page 56 for a story about a doorbell from heaven.

Feathers

The appearance of a pure white feather for no discernible reason always makes those who believe in heaven smile. Sandy's story is fairly typical of many letters I receive on the subject.

Floating

Seven years ago my grandmother got very ill. She was eighty-six and it soon became clear that she wasn't going to pull through, and doctors gave her a few days, perhaps a week. It was very upsetting for my mother and the rest of our family, as Nanny had always been such a strong and loving woman. The family gathered around, and even my sister, who lives in Canada, flew over. Many tears were shed, then we were all in that horrible situation of waiting. We said our goodbyes but Nanny lingered on and a week stretched into ten days. She was barely conscious but we all stayed with her as often as we could. We were told that hearing is the last sense to go, so we talked to her, read to her and played music to her all the time.

One night my sister and I were sitting in my garden talking, when a single, large white feather floated down in front of our eyes slowly and gracefully, and fell down at my sister's feet. It was getting fairly dark and we couldn't hear or see any birds. The feather was beautiful and glistening white. We stopped talking for a while and were mesmerised by it. A few minutes later the phone rang and my husband came out to say that Nanny had passed away. I'm sure that the feather was her way of saying goodbye.

Anne's story doesn't just feature one feather, but thousands of them.

Feathers from heaven

A couple of months after my beloved sister died, my daughter and I booked to go to London and see the musical *Ghost*. We had seen it before when my sister was still alive and I knew that this time I would find it even more moving and sad, as I was still in the early stages of grieving. We walked up the steps from the Tube into Piccadilly Circus, where the theatre was, and no word of a lie – there were hundreds of thousands of white feathers blowing down the steps and all over Piccadilly Circus! I have never seen so many in my life. When I got home I even googled 'white feathers in Piccadilly Circus', half-expecting to read about a cull of pigeons or something, but there was nothing. I like to think that my sister was literally shouting at me 'I am here, and I am fine and I know about this weekend.'

Feathers are such a commonly reported afterlife sign that some people now see them as unmistakable proof of heaven. This was certainly the case for Pat.

Feathers in my garden

I have always been spiritual, and have had many strange experiences. I came close to angels after the first experience. I went to bed one night and asked for proof of angels. Next morning I opened my eyes and saw something float down from the ceiling. I was curious and got out of bed to have a look, and there was a little fluffy white feather. I couldn't believe my eyes. Wow, this fluffy white feather had floated down from nowhere.

A year or two later, on a bit of a low, I asked for proof again. Well, the angels certainly do have a sense of humour because soon after, there was tons of feathers at the bottom of my path. It looked as though someone had emptied a sack full of feathers at the end of my path. My neighbours all commented, and one asked me what I had been doing to the birds. I knew what the feathers meant, though I didn't say anything, but I had to chuckle. I never asked for proof again.

Flowers

Stories about unusual flowers and other aspects of plants appearing or blooming longer than normal, or returning to bloom after they had withered, are another heart-warming afterlife sign. That sense of warmth comes across enchantingly in Krysia's short story.

Camellia

The first Christmas Day after my mother passed away, I sat on my sofa after my children went to their father's house and cried for my mother. I felt so down and lonely. After a while a sense of calm and warmth filled me. I opened the curtains and looked out at the camellia tree that my mother's ashes are buried under, and to my amazement saw one huge camellia flower. The tree flowers every February, and I know that my mother had sent me a gift on Christmas Day to show me that she was near.

I wrote back to Kitty, whose story is below, saying this was not mere coincidence but mighty coincidence.

Mighty coincidence

I just have to write to you about my experience during a trip visiting my mother's grave a couple of weeks ago in Canada.

I picked up one of your books for my trip back home to Canada two weeks ago. Since my mother passed away twelve years ago, I have started to read books about the other side. While I was reading your book during our two-week stay, I was wondering if she would give me a sign telling me that she was all right, similar to the experience of your readers as described in their stories in your book. During the years that she had gone I had never received any signs from her. I did not feel spiritually connected enough to her, although we were close. Neither of us was what I consider to be a spiritual person, so I thought that getting a sign from her might be too much to ask, and surreal to me.

However, on the fifth day into our trip, our beloved neighbour for the past thirty years showed us something unbelievable. I was about a third of the way into your book at the time. That early morning of 19 August, my sister and I saw the neighbour doing his gardening on the front lawn. He showed us the hydrangeas blooming in his garden, among other flowers. There was one purple hydrangea sticking out of the group of white ones, and he told us that the purple one was growing at the exact spot where he had last talked to my mother the day before she passed away. He'd had the hydrangeas for years, and they had been white all along. He said he had to tell us that and it was a message from heaven.

I got very emotional about the message and started to cry. It was totally unbelievable. I don't consider myself to be spiritual enough to receive a sign, but the message was conveyed to me via our spiritual neighbour. I was very thankful.

If I have not been reading your book at that time, I might not have taken the message so seriously, and dismissed it as mere coincidence.

Lost and found

In some cases an object of great personal significance that has been lost and is suddenly found at the right moment can offer incredible reassurance that a loved one isn't far away. This is what happened to Nick.

Perfect match

My wife promised me before she died that she would send a sign, but I don't think either of us believed it when she said it. She was just trying to comfort me. On the first anniversary of her death I missed her deeply. I needed to keep busy, and had a sudden urge to paint my bedroom. I pulled all the furniture into the centre of the room, and as I pulled out the chest of drawers I noticed something sparkling on the floor. I bent down to pick it up and it was a silver-and-blue earring. I remembered it instantly. It was the gift I had given my wife on our first wedding anniversary. She loved the earrings and wore them many times over the next ten years, but was devastated when she lost one of them. We looked everywhere for days as she knew she had put them on in the morning, but by lunchtime, when she was getting ready to go out, one earring had fallen out.

Eventually, we gave up looking and assumed that one of the dogs had eaten it or something, but here it was twenty-two years later in my hand, on the first anniversary of my wife's death. I can't explain it, as when my wife was doing spring cleaning she would always pull out the furniture to vacuum underneath it. If that wasn't the sign she promised to send me I don't know what is. It gave me a great feeling of comfort and still does, because I have reunited it with the other earring, which my wife kept in her jewellery box. She couldn't bring herself to throw it away and now I know why.

Numbers

The 11.11 phenomenon – when you glance at a clock or watch and it is 11.11, or a text or email is sent at that time – always gives people pause for thought when it happens because of the spiritual significance of the number 11 being the number of heavenly guidance, according to numerologists. This phenomenon is not restricted to the number 11, though. The recurrence or appearance of any number that has personal significance to you can also be a sign from the other side, as suggested in the next two stories, the first from Simon, the second from Linda.

11.11

On page 199 of your book you state, 'Heaven may whisper to you to check your watch and notice that it is 11.11, the symbol of divine love and protection.' Out of sheer curiosity I checked my watch – and guess what? Yes, you got it! It was just coming up to eleven minutes to eleven (on this eleventh month of course). Quite a surprise, but then again, not really. Just thought you may like to know. I will be giving your book to a lifelong friend who has a degenerative illness, and hope that he will find the same or similar symbols of love and protection.

21

A year ago my husband died. It has been a long and hard year to live through as I loved my husband very deeply, but the number 21 helped me cope with my grief. You see, 21 was my husband's favourite number, probably because he was born on that day in September. He used it in his email and other contact names, and whenever it was the twenty-first of the month he always told me it was his lucky day. After his death I began to see the number 21 everywhere. I'd notice the number on clocks, licence plates, till receipts, letters, page numbers, addresses, price tags and so on. Seeing it so often has given me comfort during my grief, and the courage to start moving on with my life again. My husband died, but seeing the number 21 so many times since his death has given me a new spiritual awareness.

Music

I get many stories about the divine inspiration provided by music; during times of grief a song will often be heard playing that has strong associations with a departed loved one. Vincent's story speaks volumes about the spirit-enhancing power of a musical sign.

Deep Purple

Several years ago my beloved son became very ill and the doctors could not work out what was wrong with him. At one point he was flown to Glasgow in an air ambulance and was there for a week. However, on his return home, his symptoms continued and eventually became so severe that I had to rush him to the local hospital. Finally, he was diagnosed with ulcerative colitis and was hospitalised locally. I was with him every day, and one afternoon I went to the hospital cafe while he was sleeping.

The local Gaelic station was playing in the cafe. It usually plays Gaelic and folk music (which I love), but as I sat down to eat my meal 'Black Night' by Deep Purple suddenly began – I'm also a massive fan of DP and of Jon Lord especially, to the point of obsession. I actually began to cry. It was quite unbelievable – in all the times I'd listened to the channel it had never remotely played any 'rock music' let alone 'heavy rock' – and I was there hearing it when it happened! For me, it was surely an unequivocal sign from the other side that my son was going to be all right and for me not to worry. This instinct was proved right because he began to recover his strength from then onwards.

I have often felt that if heaven is somewhere it must be in the notes of great music that lifts the soul. Music has spoken to me in a spiritual way many times in my life. It even did so while I was writing this book.

All in a name

I never liked my name when I was growing up. In my mind it wasn't romantic or trendy. I learned to live with it but in my imagination I was always something far more exciting and exotic, like Isabella or Chloe. This all changed last year when I received an email from the music project Clauin Ri (www.cluainri.com) saying that one of my books had inspired the people involved in it to write healing angel music. They gifted me two of the songs – 'From Lips of Angels' and 'Anam Cara' (meaning soul friend) – and they were bliss for my ears. I was deeply touched and humbled. They also told me their music drew inspiration from my famous namesake, Sister Teresa, and asked if I had been named after her or Mother Teresa, or felt an affinity with either of these two immortal women?

Until that moment I can honestly say that I had never felt any sense of connection to these women, but the album encouraged me to research their lives and spiritual teachings (see Appendix 7), and to discover a new-found respect for my name that had been missing all these years. I knew I could never aspire to their greatness, or share their commitment to a single religious path, but I also knew that from the moment my mother chose my name heaven had been sending me a very clear sign – and that sign was my name. I simply hadn't tuned into it until the musical gift helped me to find the right wavelength.

Noises

Unexplained sounds and noises, such as footsteps, knocking and so on, are sometimes reported in the days after a loved one has passed away. These noises aren't frightening or alarming in any way. They fill a person's heart with a sense of the closeness of spirit – they did so for Eva as recounted in her story below.

Lovely gentleman

After my uncle died, for six days straight I heard him knocking about the house as he used to when he was alive. He won't mind me saying this, but even though he was always smiling, and was a polite, well-spoken gentleman, he could also be clumsy and rather noisy. You definitely knew when he was around. Doors would slam, footsteps would be loud and things would be broken accidentally.

The house still felt as though he was in it after he died, because the noises associated with him continued. One night I was in bed and everyone else was out. I heard his footsteps coming up the stairs. I knew it was him as he had the unusual habit of going up the stairs one, then two at a time, and you could hear that rhythm. The strange thing is that I wasn't scared by any of this, Theresa, because my uncle was someone who just made you smile. I knew there was nothing to be afraid of because in spirit he would be the same lovely gentleman as he was in life. The following night I heard doors slamming and again I was the only person in the house. Then, for the next few days, there were inexplicable breakages in the house, like pictures falling off the wall or glasses falling off tables. I also heard loud footsteps upstairs when I was downstairs in the kitchen when everyone else in the family was eating their breakfast. The noises stopped on the day of his funeral. I hope he has found peace and is making lots of noise in heaven.

Objects moving

Inanimate objects or materials appearing or inexplicably moving can also speak volumes, as illustrated in these next three stories, from Sarah, Mary and Trish, respectively.

Crossword

I lost my wonderful nana in April this year. Since then I have been diagnosed with a rare autoimmune disease, which I am currently having steroid and chemo treatment for.

I have been talking to my nana recently around the house and have had some responses. Yesterday morning my husband and I were having an argument. I went upstairs to finish my make-up and a book on the shelf fell to the floor, and the pen inside it rolled out across the floor. The book was not near enough to the shelf edge for it to fall by itself, and why did it fall at that time?

I didn't feel scared by this as I felt it was my nana. It wasn't until afterwards that I realised that the book was a crossword book that my mum had given me to take to my chemo sessions. I realised that perhaps this was nana's way of saying that the cross words between my husband and I should stop.

I am taking great comfort in this and do not feel scared in any way. The funny thing is that some months before my nana's death, I had actually asked her to send me a message or move things after she passed away. At the time she had laughed at me and I think she thought I was a bit mad, but maybe she is proving to me now that there is more.

Headrest

My husband passed away almost six years ago. In bed one night I kept saying I wanted to see him, and a couple of days later I took my elderly mother for a ride in the car.

This car is only about six weeks old, and had been bought new. On starting off I always check the mirrors to make sure it's clear to move off. I'd only been driving two minutes when I looked in the rear-view mirror and to my shock, saw that the back headrest had been pulled up to the highest position. No one has ever sat in the back seat and no one else has a key. The headrest had been down when I set off. My mother said it was probably up all the time and I hadn't noticed, but if it had been it would have blocked my view to the rear window slightly. I would have noticed. Also, when I first picked up the car I took some photos to send to my son. When I got home I had another look at them, and sure enough the headrest was down. I know it was my husband. I was amazed.

So proud

I have had such weird but wonderful things happen to me since Alan died twelve weeks ago. First his electric guitar fell off the bracket that was screwed into the wall. Then the electric fan would come on by itself each time I sat in my chair in front of it (Alan knew how I suffer from excessive heat in summer). My adjustable bed would shake very gently a few nights on the trot, enough to wake me but not to frighten me. On top of all this, one evening soon after Alan's funeral I sat looking up at the sky and suddenly saw a heart-shaped cloud above me. I was on the phone to my son at the time and told him what I could see.

Orbs

With many people now photographing or recording their lives on their phones for social media, I have noticed a sharp increase in the number of letters and messages about orbs. This email from Tracy is a recent example.

Just amazed

To my amazement, today, as I was recording my son on an Easter egg hunt, there appeared to be orbs around him. I have never seen them before around my son. I was using a Samsung phone and the orbs were small and white. At times they were moving fast. I have kept on replaying what I recorded in amazement. Could it have been a spirit? As you know, I lost a seven-year-old boy five years ago this coming September. Seeing what happened today has excited me a little, as I've read about orbs but never seen them myself before. Would you like to see the recording?

As I type this chapter, above my computer I look at my orb board where I have posted some of the stunning orb photos that have been sent to me over the years. In these photos a distinct ball of bright light can be seen close to a person in the photograph. Typically, the ball of light wasn't present when the photo was taken, and there seems no rational explanation for it, as other photographs don't have the same orbs in them. In her message, Tracy asked me if I would like to see the recording, and whenever I am asked that my reply is always the same. I first give the person contact details of a parapsychologist who would be willing to study material sent to him free of charge to be used as data for his research, but then I give my perspective. Of course, there are always rational explanations – camera malfunction, tricks of the light and so on – but regardless of whether or not there is a rational explanation, for me, the fact that the orbs bring a feeling of connection to the afterlife signifies that they are a sign from heaven.

Rainbows

Rainbows are magical to look at and inspire feelings of awe and wonder – and whenever there is awe and wonder spirit is close by. Judy's story below shows how the appearance of a rainbow at a significant moment can provide comfort and hope like no other.

All the colours

My daughter Bethan died before she was born. She was my first child and my heart was broken. I still think of her every day twenty-two years later, and wonder what she would have done with her life. I was very distressed after she died and didn't take good care of myself. I got so thin that my family was worried I would collapse. I simply lost my appetite for life.

A year after Bethan's death I went to visit her tiny grave and sat there for two hours. It began to rain as I sat there and cried. When the rain stopped I eventually got up to leave, but something felt different. I felt lighter and happier than I had done since her death. I can't explain it, but I felt her around me. I looked up and there in the sky was the most stunningly glorious rainbow I have ever seen. It was huge and seemed to have all the colours. It was pure magic. I gazed at it for ages with my mouth open. I was mesmerised. It felt as though Bethan had painted it in the sky just for me.

When I left the churchyard a couple walked in and I smiled at them. I turned around and wanted to show them the rainbow, but when I did it wasn't there. Theresa, it had just vanished. I know you could easily say this was coincidence and that rainbows can disappear fairly quickly, but for me it was Bethan giving me her blessing and letting me know that she hasn't died. It was a message from heaven just for me.

Wendy's story below also features a rainbow. It is different from Judy's because it shows that rainbows – and indeed all afterlife signs – don't necessarily always appear to remind someone of a departed loved one. Sometimes they can appear to give much-needed spiritual meaning and hope.

Stay longer

This story is special to me because it concerns my daughter-in-law who has terminal cancer. She was diagnosed last Christmas and was given six months to live. She has two little boys and it is heartbreaking to think of her not seeing them grow up. Anyway, she is still with us and we are lucky to have her.

This summer my children and grandchildren went on holiday to Butlin's. My husband and I wanted us all to spend this precious time with each other. My son and daughter-in-law arrived a few days after us and stayed at a site across the road. We went over to see them shortly after they arrived. I sat there watching her play with her children with a big lump in my throat. The boys were so excited, and I could have cried thinking how on earth my daughter-in-law copes, knowing she has this awful illness and that her time with them is limited. It started to rain and we helped to sort out the caravan. We left them to have their tea, and as we drove away from the caravan I just prayed that my daughter-in-law would have longer with her boys. I looked up towards the sky and saw the most beautiful double rainbow. I took a photo of it – it seemed as though it appeared as I asked for help and comfort.

Smells

People sometimes write and tell me about smelling heavenly scents that are either energising or uplifting, like lavender and vanilla, or comforting, like some flowers, when there is no observable source. Here is what happened to Gemma.

Hidden strength

I have been through a difficult relationship, and I also nearly died due to complications following an operation. About a year ago it dawned on me that I have a guardian angel and that heaven must be watching over me.

In the summer months just before leaving that destructive relationship, on two separate occasions when I was at home, once in the kitchen, another time while watching TV in the living room, I smelled a lovely flower scent. The smell could have been that of roses, but as quickly as it appeared it was gone again. There were no flowers nearby or anything that could have caused the smell, which I thought was a little odd, but at the time I didn't think too much of it.

The next time, also in the summer before I left my partner, I was sitting in one of my favourite spots down by the water with a friend. We were chatting and I smelled a citrus, lemon-like scent. I said to my friend that the scent was lovely, and asked if she could smell it, too. She said she couldn't smell anything.

It was then that I remembered the previous, unexplained smell of roses, and I told her about it. When we got to her house we looked on the Internet and came across a reference to the ability to smell someone who is not of this worldly plane. It gave me such a sense of hope, courage and comfort when I needed it the most. Instead of feeling vulnerable and afraid after leaving my partner, I now feel powerful, loved and protected.

Some people may notice a smell that is uniquely associated with a departed loved one, such as their perfume or, as in Amber's story below, paint.

Forget me not

My brother was a handyman and always smelled of fresh paint – even when he wasn't working. Last week I was at home tidying up, when I suddenly smelled fresh paint. My children were in the room at the time doing their homework and I asked them if they could smell it, but they couldn't. I didn't think much of it, but when as I was getting ready for bed that evening, there it was again. I asked my husband if he could smell it but he couldn't. By now it was really making me think of my brother. I started to get emotional. I got even more emotional when my husband reminded me that it was exactly seven years ago today that my brother had died. How could I have forgotten that? I felt so ashamed. It wasn't because I had forgotten him. He was always in my heart. For some reason – and it's unlike me – I had got my days muddled up. However, my brother hadn't and that's why I could smell the paint.

Words

Overhearing a random conversation on TV, on the radio, or in everyday life, with exactly the right advice or message for you to offer guidance, can be incredibly reassuring. Sheila shared this message with me.

Simon says

I'm a twin but my brother died a few hours after he was born. My parents called him Simon. Although I never knew Simon I often think of him and hope he is at peace. Sometimes I miss him very deeply and I can't explain why. Last year something incredible happened, and I would love your thoughts on it. I was in a supermarket feeling extremely low. I'd just had a miscarriage and wondered if I would ever have a healthy baby. At that moment a young girl aged about fourteen walked past me. I overheard her say to her friend or sibling (I'm not sure who it was, as I have never seen her before or since), 'Simon says you should.' The timing was incredible as I was just thinking about whether or not to try for another baby. This felt like heaven giving me an answer. Six months later I got pregnant and I am now the proud mother of a tiny baby boy. My husband had no say in the matter. He is called Simon.

Sheila truly felt heaven spoke to her through the words of an overheard conversation. This has happened to me many times in my life. My mother's name was Joyce and I often hear the word 'joy' repeated around me in conversations when I miss her greatly. Alison wrote to me about her experience of an overheard conversation that gave her (and me when I read her story) goosebumps.

Clever lady

My wonderful mother died last year. It was a calm, sunny day, and I sat down at the kitchen table to write three thank-you letters; one to my mother's doctor, one to the hospital ward and one to the vicar, a family friend. I used my mother's stationary and stamps, knowing this is what she would have wanted. I sent off the letters immediately.

That afternoon I found myself alone, as my student sons were back at university and my husband was sorting out items in my mother's home. Before he set off, he gave our up-and-over garage door a quick coat of paint and left it slightly ajar to dry.

I decided to give the inside of the garage a sort-out myself, and set about clearing the shelves. A few minutes into this, I heard a voice coming from outside. It was a woman's voice in conversation with someone else, although I never heard the other person. I immediately thought it was a Jehovah's Witness, and crouched down behind our table-tennis table as I wasn't in the mood to speak and pretended not to be in. As I listened and peered through the small gap under the garage door, I could see that the woman was standing at my front porch looking at some plants in a pot. The conversation continued, 'Yes, they are beautiful petunias, very beautiful. Yes, I can see she is clever.'

I could not believe my ears because this was a conversation that I'd had with my mother almost every Tuesday and Sunday throughout the summer, when I cared for her and her home. I'm not clever at gardening and only watered and dead-headed her plants, but she thought I was and often told me so, and I recognised that piece of conversation well. The woman then walked down the drive and stood outside the garage door, looking directly at it. The door was still slightly ajar, so all I could see were her feet and legs facing towards me from underneath. She held a small bunch of blue wild flowers by her right side. I was wondering whether or not to reveal myself, but remained quiet. She said, softly, 'Thank you, thank you … yes, that's all, thank you.' With this she turned away and walked back down the road, not stopping anywhere else.

I was left in a fairly shocked state but have since taken much comfort from this event. I cannot explain why I should receive three 'thank yous' from a complete stranger on the day that I sent out three on Mum's behalf, or why the petunia conversation should occur or who the flowers were for. I can only guess that all these signs were meant just for me.

Alive within you

Finally, perhaps the most profound sign of all is departed loved ones suddenly appearing in your thoughts and feelings. Each time you think about them or feel them in your heart they are there, alive within you. Jane sent me this tender story, which illustrates my point to perfection.

Forever

My husband died five years ago. His death wasn't unexpected because he had been ill for a year before, but the shock still hit me hard. The day before his funeral I was exhausted with the crying. My mother told me to get some fresh air as I hadn't ventured out for days. I knew she was right. I forced myself to go out into the garden.

When I was in the garden a sensation of incredible happiness and peace came over me. I felt so light, as if I could float, and I knew I had to go into my husband's shed. It was his favourite place, and the day before he died he told me to go there, but I had felt too upset to do so because it would have been too painful. When I stepped inside the shed I found a giant card on the floor. It had my name on it and was dated sixteen days before my husband died. He had put it there for me.

With shaking hands I opened the envelope. The card had a picture of a red rose, and inside it my husband had written, 'I will no longer see you with my eyes or touch you with my hands, but I will hear you in my mind and feel you in my heart forever.' I have felt him beside me and within me ever since, Theresa, and whenever I miss him I read the card and it is as if he is right beside me.

Opening a window

The most commonly reported signs people write to me about are listed above, but over the years I have been writing about the world of spirit and connecting with departed loved ones, I have learned that a sign can be quite literally anything because it is so personal to the receiver, as this next story from Lisa demonstrates.

Sure, it's Dad

My dad was very artistic and after he died I entered one of his paintings (called 'The Last Snowfall') in a competition. He won Gold. I hoped he was pleased with the outcome in spirit.

Three days later, when I got to work, I noticed that my desk was covered in what I thought was sugar. It looked like the snow that Dad had put in his painting. None of the other three secretaries had white specs on their desks. When I asked one of them what they thought it was, they said it looked like dry paint. More things have happened to confirm that my dad is around. I find coins all the time in all sorts of unusual places. My mum is fairly sceptical about the world of spirit, but when she's upset or worried her bedside lamp comes on. We are sure it's Dad.

In Paula's story below it is not just one sign but a growing collection of signs that convince her she is being watched over by her mother in spirit.

Big heart

Months ago I started to read your books and I find them very interesting. My mum died nearly twenty-five years ago (I was nineteen years old). She was an alcoholic and my parents divorced when I was young. I lived with my mum until I was eighteen years old. Many times life was hard, and I can honestly say that I did not have the best childhood ever. But I survived and my past made me a very strong and independent woman, who is now married to a lovely husband and has three children.

Since moving from my homeland (Italy) to the UK on my own at eighteen, I always thought that my mum, when not under the influence of alcohol, was the best mum ever – she was caring and had a big heart. After she died, many strange, positive things began happening to me. It's only during the last few years that I've become convinced that my mum is behind all of this. I often feel some strange sensation inside, as though someone is guiding me to the right path and decision. For example, when we were looking for a house and a school for my first child, a warm feeling told me that it was the right house and school for us. During a holiday in Australia a few years ago, my husband found £500 in a drawer just before Christmas Day. He said he definitely did not put it there, and the drawer was completely empty when we first moved in.

I strongly believe my mum is looking after me and my family, making up for the old times. Reading your books has given me more belief that angels, loved ones, are definitely around, and I am learning to read the signs. Just after reading your book, I was taking my dog out for a walk. Looking up at the sky I saw a big, perfectly shaped heart, with angel-like wings, and a plane was flying across it, representing the arrow. I stood there looking up for about five minutes. I am absolutely certain it was Mum telling me she loved me.

Mr Grant also received a combination of afterlife signs from his beloved wife Christine. They brought him healing and complete conviction that his wife is alive in spirit within and all around him.

Heavenly records

My wife, Christine, passed away on 12 June 2012. She followed the spiritual path all her life and left her body to medical research.

14 JUNE A very bright rainbow was seen over Camps Bay. I kept hearing the song 'We had joy. We had fun. We had seasons in the sun.'

16 JUNE On waking found the light was on in the kitchen and the sliding door to the terrace was open.

30 JUNE On waking found the second bedroom door closed and light on in passage.

1 JULY Large wall decoration that we were left in 1961 fell off wall.

9 JULY A rainbow appeared in the sky visible from Century City. It was a complete horseshoe, fully visible high in the sky over the city of Cape Town.

13 JULY During the night when I took a throat pastille from one end of my desk, another one fell on the floor. I found it next morning beyond the other end of my desk and behind the leg of the table some 1.8 metres from where it fell.

1 AUGUST While standing in the kitchen at East London the back door slowly opened, then closed again. There was no wind. The air was still.

10 SEPTEMBER Large picture on wall behind my desk fell down in middle of the day.

9 OCTOBER Saw forehead of Christine over my head as I awoke from afternoon nap.

19 OCTOBER Found a 'perfect' pigeon's feather lying 'perfectly' positioned along my path on garden terrace.

23 DECEMBER I meditated and felt Christine saying that was a 'thank you' for going to Silvermine on her birthday with Shelley and cleaning her memorial bench.

31 DECEMBER 2012 Books in bookcase moved and one ended up upside down (a book about European history by Grant and Temperley).

28 OCTOBER 2013 8.30 a.m. There was a loud bang

when I switched on the lights in my bathroom. No lights had blown and the electricity had not cut out.

This is a considerably edited down version of the highly personal signs Mr Grant received over a period of several months. You can see the full record at www.afterlife-exploration.com. For him the build-up of unusual and unexplained events create a powerful case for the continued life of his wife in the afterlife.

Once you have acknowledged one afterlife sign it is often the case that you start to notice others. It is like opening a window. Once you know how to do so, you open it again and again to glimpse the other side, as Pat found in her experience described below.

Beautiful things

So many things have happened for me, some big, some small. The very first was the actual time my dear dad passed away, at 12.05 a.m. on 1 July.

Dad had been taken ill weeks before, and on the evening of 1 July at 12.05 a.m. I was woken by what I thought was my name being called (Pat) very softly, but loudly enough to wake me from sleep. I got up, confused, thinking one of the children had called out. I went to check on them, but they were both sound asleep. When I got back into bed I somehow knew that it was Dad calling me. He had died at 12.05 a.m., as we found out later – and he had called out my name as he passed away. The man in the next bed to him had known us all and told me this later when we met him.

I can think of a lot of other times when I have experienced surreal but beautiful things, some of which are listed below.

- Feeling a soft touch on my shoulder.
- Finding the odd white feather.
- Seeing many rainbows and always feeling something special when I do. Last year I saw a double rainbow – a strong one and a fainter one above it.
- Soon after my dad died, seeing a small glow of light in my bedroom corner, which wasn't moonlight.
- Smelling perfume although no one was in the room.
- Dreaming once, many years ago, that I was being shown around heaven or somewhere very beautiful by my dad.

I do thank you for the books that you write. I'm finding that they are so helpful to me in trying to prove that there is a heaven for us all, and that we do meet our lost loved ones again.

Gifts from above

Subtle and gentle the afterlife signs described in this chapter may be, but I know from personal experience how profoundly life changing and soothing they can be. Over the decades I have come to believe that every moment of our lives we are surrounded by signs from heaven, but we are just too busy and preoccupied in our minds and hearts to notice or recognise them.

Throughout my life I have encountered many signs from my mother in spirit, ranging from dreams to sudden bursts of intuition, and each time they pushed me forwards spiritually, and gave me meaning and guidance. As already noted, I was a late developer spiritually. It took me a while to see the hand of heaven at work in my life, and to read and understand the signs. I sincerely wish I had known what I know now earlier, as it would have saved me a lot of tears, but I hope this book, and in particular this chapter, will help you avoid some of that conflict – it is a book I wish I had read when I was younger. Nothing would make me happier than to know that what you read here has helped you notice, understand and derive comfort from the reassuring signs heaven sends you constantly. And even though in every case the details and circumstances are different, the message is always the same: this life does not end with death, and those you have lost and loved are never far away.

Afterlife signs bring messages from heaven. They are gifts to remind us of our spiritual birthright, to be loving and kind, and to make the world a better place because we have lived in it. Their purpose is to calm and reassure you, because one calm person leads to more calm people and ultimately a more peaceful world – that is why heaven always wants to guide and comfort you. Don't ever feel you don't deserve a sign or are wasting heaven's time asking for one. Nothing is trivial in heaven's eyes, and each one of us is regarded as a totally unique miracle. Also don't feel that you need to be in the depths of despair or close to death to see heaven. While it is true that suffering can be a catalyst, feeling happy and content can also lead to spiritual growth, because when we are at peace and filled with love we are in heaven.

Perhaps there have been moments in your life when you feel close to the truth, or have caught a glimpse of something undefined that you know in your heart is magical. Note that a lot of the people mentioned in this book did not actually see departed loved ones – that something as personally symbolic as a feather, an object lost and found, or a familiar song, was the catalyst for their spiritual transformation. If you look at the world around you and within you with a loving heart, you can catch a glimpse of your own afterlife signs at any moment. Spirit is around you, always. It may be invisible but it is there – you just need to look for it and notice the signs. Search for heaven in a blade of grass, for magic in the breeze and for bliss in a shaft of sunlight. Pay close attention whenever you feel wonder or awe, because when that happens heaven is wrapping its arms around you.

The heart knows heaven first

Afterlife signs won't ever be taken seriously as proof of heaven, but what I've been talking about in this chapter isn't about science or 'proof'. It is about what happens in a person's heart. The heart does not need science to investigate or validate what is going on inside it. It feels and knows – and in all the stories in this chapter, and indeed this book, the people involved felt and knew that they were hearing the voice of heaven or had been touched by it. The mists of materialism, fear and doubt receded, and they glimpsed a profound truth. They discovered that we are eternal spiritual beings having a human experience, not human beings having a spiritual experience.

The role of the heart in your spiritual development and in initiating and maintaining a connection with departed loved ones is so crucial that the next and final chapter is devoted to it.

The kingdom of heaven is a condition of the heart – not something that comes upon the Earth or after death.

FRIEDRICH NEITZSCHE

CHAPTER NINE

THE CALL OF THE HEART

*When you listen to your heart you
are able to open the door.*

PAULO COELHO

An additional ordinary but extraordinary way for heaven to communicate its love to us is through the heartfelt actions or words of other people. On rare occasions this can manifest in the appearance of a mysterious stranger, who arrives in times of need or crisis to offer healing or even to save lives, then seems to mysteriously vanish afterwards.

The third person factor

In all the letters and stories I receive about strangers who save or heal lives, there are usually a number of common factors. They arrive and disappear virtually unseen, and there is something out of this world about their appearance, such as a faraway look or a strange way of dressing. They often have the exact tools or remedy needed in a crisis, and in some cases they even know things, such as names or places, that they can't possible know.

If these strangers are celestial guides then there's no need for further explanation, but if they are humans are they people consciously or unconsciously guided by the voice of heaven? Read the following stories and see if you can decide. The first was reported in the media in July 2015.

A baffling and beautiful rescue

In the early summer of 2015, a mysterious stranger appeared at a terrible crash site in Missouri, USA, prayed for and blessed the victim, nineteen-year-old Katy, after her car had been hit by a drunk driver, then disappeared as mysteriously as he had arrived.

Many witnesses said that the man, dressed in a black shirt and carrying anointment oil, made his way through the security tapes set up around the accident, and tended to the woman trapped in the car. The rescue workers let him get close to Katy and pray for her, as his blessings clearly brought her great peace. His calming presence also brought them courage, as until that point they were unable to get her out and she was fading fast.

To make things even more bewildering, the mystery man does not appear in any of the many crash photos taken at the scene. He stayed until a stronger team of rescue workers arrived. The girl was freed but when the rescue workers wanted to thank the man for the comfort he had given her, he had vanished. Everyone at the rescue scene was deeply touched and moved. Katy's mother called it a miracle.

Liz sent me this story about her encounter with a heaven-sent stranger.

Rescued by a snow angel

It was January 2003 and snow had not been forecast, but as I was working away in my office, a severe snowstorm descended on the UK. When going home for the day everyone had to drive very carefully. I was not dressed for snow and was wearing stiletto heels.

As I got near to my home, I saw that a car had broken down in front of me on part of a hill and was stuck fast. A huge traffic queue was now rapidly forming behind us, and we were all unable to move any further. I got out of the car to help, in my very unsuitable heels, and along with a couple of other drivers tried to push the car, which was stuck in the snow, to get it moving again.

After pushing for some time and getting nowhere, my footing suddenly slipped and I fell flat on my face in the snow. On recovering my dignity, I looked up at the snow-filled sky and in desperation, shouted in my mind, 'Please, help us.' Well, within minutes of my prayer request, right at the back of the queue a great big pick-up truck appeared and started to overtake the now very long queue of trapped cars. The truck pulled up in front of the broken-down car, and a man with long, shaggy blond hair got out. Not speaking a word to anyone, he got a rope and hook from his truck, attached them to the broken-down car, and towed it to safety up the hill and on to even ground. He then unhooked the car and drove off, not saying anything, and simply disappearing.

The problem car drove off from the place it had been towed to, and we all got moving again, getting home safely. On watching the news that night, I could see that there were problems everywhere in the UK. However, because of my prayer, not only for me, but also for others involved, we were rescued by heaven. Wow, what a service!

There is a place here for Belle's tale about a mysterious stranger, or should I say strangers.

Three wise men

My story took place about twenty years ago. I was still at university and had decided to join my mother and two of her friends for a walk in the mountains (I am in Cape Town and the mountains I refer to are near a wine-farm region called Franschoek). Anyway, we stupidly had not checked the weather, and did not have proper maps, warm clothes, food and so on.

We parked our car in the middle of a mountain pass and set off up and over a mountain on what we believed was a circular route. As the afternoon wore on, heavy clouds and rain rolled in. We soon realised we were lost, had no idea which direction we were heading in and were getting cold. Suddenly, three elderly men with German accents appeared in the path in front of us. When we told them about our predicament, they showed us maps and explained which way to go. We thanked them and watched them head off in a direction opposite to ours – and actually wondered where they were going as their path led further into the mountains.

After a couple of hours we finally recognised the path leading back to our car. As we reached the corner in the path where we could get our first glimpse of the car, we all stopped in utter amazement. There were the three German men standing by our car and looking up at us. No other car was in sight. The path took a bend and when we next could see the car, the men had gone – they had literally vanished into thin air.

All four of us witnessed this and we all admitted to getting goosebumps not from the cold, but because we realised that something surreal had just happened to us. There was no physical way those men could have reached our car before us (we subsequently pored over topographical maps to check this), and if it hadn't been for them, we would have been in severe trouble in the mountains. We all agreed we came across angels that day – even my mother, who is highly sceptical about that sort of thing, cannot explain it in any other way.

Michael's story falls into this category of mysterious helpers but is slightly different in that he did not see his rescuer at all.

Where are you?

When I was about ten years old I distinctly remember being saved by a person or presence (I never actually saw a person). I was playing hide and seek with my friends in our house, and thought I would be very clever and hide in the cellar. They would never find me there. I was right – they didn't, but I found something remarkable.

I lost my footing when I was walking down the stairs in the cellar and tumbled to the floor. I heard a crunch and felt a sharp pain in my left arm. Later, I would find out that it was broken. The pain got worse and I tried to get back up the stairs to find help, but couldn't get up as I had twisted my ankle as well. Everything hurt and I howled for help, but no one heard me. I was stuck, and started to get very scared as the cellar was cold, damp and dark. I could smell wine, mud and my fear.

I think I must have been down there for about thirty minutes shivering and crying, when suddenly I felt my hand being held. It gave me so much comfort and the pain stopped. I was content to have someone there beside me and drifted off to sleep. Next thing I remember is being carried upstairs by my dad, and my mum being hysterical. I told them I was absolutely fine and asked who had sat beside me before they arrived. They looked confused and said there was nobody in the cellar when they came down except me. They had searched the house for hours trying to find me until my little brother suggested they look there.

Theresa, I don't know who or what sat beside me when I was frightened and in pain all those years ago, but the memory has never left me and has given me great comfort and a lifelong sense that I am never alone.

This phenomenon of a stranger, supernatural or otherwise, coming to people's aid, then vanishing afterwards without a trace, has been reported so many times that it has even been given a name, The Third Person Factor, from a book by John Geiger about the concept called *The Third Man Factor*. Most of those rescued or comforted are given specific life-saving instructions or help, and even if there is no visual, physical or auditory communication, the feeling of someone being there is so powerful that they no longer feel alone and afraid, and know in their hearts that they will pull through. The experience is often the catalyst for a new-found spirituality. It isn't just individuals who have had these experiences. For example, in Belle's story above, all the climbers saw the mysterious men. Whether this phenomenon is a case of heaven reaching out, or simply of people finding a piece of heaven and externalising it, perhaps it suggests that in times of deep crisis, as Michael's story suggests we are not as alone as we fear.

Sceptics are quick to provide explanations for this mysterious stranger phenomenon. They suggest that the strangers involved may be brave and selfless people, who prefer to leave the scene rather than announce their identity, or that they may result from the brain talking to itself and subconscious suggestion. In my opinion these stories show the hand of heaven at work in one way or another, and illustrate that there are people out there with big hearts and halos, offering us much needed hope. This was certainly the case for Sharon.

Chosen few

I used to think angels came with halos and wings, and were only seen by a chosen few, not ordinary girls who are lost and suffering from a broken heart. I know now that angels can come in the form of people – ordinary people who look like you and me, but with words that could only be sent by heaven, and at the times when we need to hear them, when we are lost and without hope, and the will to go on. I met such an angel.

The meeting took place after a shock break-up with my husband of twenty-seven years. I felt like nothing. I was broken, living was unbearable and I could not see an end to my depressive pain. I was walking home from work and everything was a blur. The only thing that had any clarity was my wish to end my life. I thought about the ways in which I could achieve this terrible end. Then, all of a sudden, a lady of about the same age as my mum, who I had not seen before, grabbed my hand and said, 'Don't worry, you will be all right.' Before I could say more than thank you, she was gone. I know my senses were not as sharp as they had been. The overwhelming and soul-destroying sadness had made me numb and yet feeling the greatest pain I had ever known – but I am absolutely certain that she was an angel. It gave me comfort and hope that I would pull through – and, you know what, I did.

When you read newspapers, switch on the TV news or go online, so many of the things you see, or read or hear about, are depressing. However, if you focus your attention on stories about ordinary people showing extraordinary compassion and appearing at just the right time to save, reassure or heal a person's life, it can renew your faith in human nature. These people seem consciously or unconsciously touched by heaven, but they are merely ordinary people acting with heart and reminding us that heaven isn't just something out there, but something that can exist within each one of us, too.

All about the heart

As I worked on this heart-themed chapter, by some divine coincidence I checked my emails. The first one I read contained this story from Barbara, who suffers from a heart condition. Heaven could not have been less subtle in the message it was sending me.

Barbara's heart

I know angels exist because I had a near-death experience when I was younger, during which I literally watched my heart rate drop a beat at a time. All of a sudden a huge warm feeling came over me and I knew immediately that my time wasn't over. It was a day I will never forget, and a sensation that I can sometimes re-feel in times of need. Having grown up in the hospital environment, I have known close friends to pass away – but I know they are here and that they come back in their own special ways at certain times.

Yesterday I flew home from a holiday. I was sad to leave

but something great happened. I was sitting next to a woman on the plane and we began to speak. I don't know why, but I felt such warmth while speaking to her. She turned out to be a nutritionist for patients with cancer, which I found fascinating, and we spoke a lot about hospitals. I told her about my hospital stays and illness. Midway through our conversation she mentioned that her younger sister had passed away – that her heart had just stopped beating for an unknown reason. We spoke about hospitals and hearts, and about angels and incredible warming experiences that may help us through hard times or give us comfort. Everything was put into perspective for me – we must appreciate all we have. I felt an immediate connection with this woman and we spent the whole five hours speaking about various topics.

I took down the woman's details, and before we got off she gave me a hug, and told me to take care and stay in touch. I find it sad that we can be so closed off sometimes – all it takes is a smile or a simple hello to start something heartfelt and special. We never know who we might meet. Somehow I knew that I had been meant to meet this woman and speak to her.

As I got undressed this morning, I brushed my hand through my hair and a lovely little silver heart fell from nowhere – it fell right onto my dressing table in front of me. I picked it up straightaway to try and see where it had come. I can honestly say that I don't own any jewellery with hearts that small attached to it. I wasn't even wearing jewellery. I don't wear anything in my hair and it definitely didn't come off of my clothes.

When this happened I couldn't help but smile. I stared at

the heart for a good few moments, trying to figure out where on earth it could have come from. I don't know if I saw it as a sign. I just know that it came from somewhere uncontrolled. What happened was something truly beautiful, spiritual and unexpected, so I wanted to share that experience with you.

Hearts mean everything to me.

In the very same week I got another powerful message from above as if heaven again wanted me to include it in this chapter. I was walking my little dog, Arnie, as I usually do in the morning, but for some reason that morning he was being very difficult. I wanted to go along our usual route, but he was determined to take me another way. He kept stopping and starting, so in the end I headed in the opposite direction and he was a lot easier to handle. On the way I walked past a lady and Arnie got very excited and tried to climb up her legs. He had never done this before. I apologised sincerely and jokingly said that she must be a dog lover. She insisted she wasn't, and said that dogs usually made her feel nervous, although she didn't feel nervous at all around mine. Like a proud mum I said he was my angel and truly heaven sent. The woman then said the most striking thing. She told me she used to believe in heaven, but didn't any more since her son had died.

Without thinking I told her that I believed her son was alive in spirit. She shook her head and said she did not feel him around her at all, and didn't believe in life after death. I asked her if she ever had dreams about her son. She told me she had them all the time and I told her that this was him speaking to her in spirit. She paused, but then shook her head again, and asked if that was the case why did she always wake up crying? I told her that her son was trying to reach out to her. The reason why she woke up crying was because her conscious mind wasn't acknowledging and accepting this spiritual connection. The woman gave me a grateful look, then knelt down and stroked Arnie before saying a heartfelt goodbye. I never saw her again but I'm convinced I was meant to meet her that morning, as Arnie has not attempted to lead me in the opposite direction since. I sincerely hope the words spoken without hesitation from my heart brought her relief and her son peace in spirit.

The power of kindness

If you light a lamp for someone it will
also brighten your own path.

BUDDHIST PROVERB

If you still don't think you can hear heaven, start getting in touch with your heart. Let it do the listening and the talking. You really have no idea how your words and actions, however trivial they may appear to you at the time, can impact or inspire others.

There is heavenly potential in all of us and we can all help others feel they have caught a glimpse of heaven. Of course, we can't all save lives in dramatic situations, and many of us won't be in a position to give our time and money to good causes, but we can make a huge difference with simple acts of heartfelt consideration for others. It doesn't have to be much. Simply smiling and saying 'thank you,' or paying a compliment, or holding the door open for a stranger, or just listening when someone needs to talk, can make someone else's day, or even change their life for the better. We really can all reveal glimpses of heaven to each other by reconnecting with our hearts.

Acts of kindness from the heart have a far-reaching impact not only on the people involved, but also on the people who witness them. Observe your response the next time you see a teenager give up his seat on a busy train to an elderly person. You will feel a sense of elation that can for a brief moment make you glad to be alive. Your faith in human nature is renewed once you see the goodness people are capable of when they remember they have a heart. Kindness transcends our feelings of separateness from one another, and reminds us that at a deep spiritual level we are all part of the same consciousness.

So, think about that the next time you perform an act of kindness. There will be a spiritually uplifting effect on you and on the person you help, but perhaps the most life-changing effect will be on those who witness your good deed or hear about it. Such an action will inspire them to do the same, and before long your one single act of kindness will potentially have a ripple effect impacting countless others.

If you still aren't convinced that you can be the beginning of the change you want to see in the world, read this short but perfect story.

On the street I saw a little boy, cold and shivering in a thin pair of shorts and a threadbare shirt. He was begging for food. I got angry and asked my angel: 'Why did you permit this? Why don't you do something about it?' My angel replied, 'I certainly have done something about it – I brought you here.'

As we reach the end of the book, yet again I am having one of those blessed 'aha' clear knowing moments. I have talked about the many and varied ways heaven can talk to us, but I can see clearly now that the simplest and most powerful way to connect with heaven, and feel and honour the presence of departed loved ones, is by speaking and acting from our hearts. If we can do that, and teach our children to do the same, imagine the effect it would have on everyone and everything, and how much easier it would be for us all to believe in the reality of heaven, because we would be seeing heaven all around and within us, all the time.

It is you
The whole theory of the universe is directed unerringly to
one single individual – namely you.

WALT WHITMAN

While we are on the subject of glimpsing heaven on Earth, I want to relate everything that has been said so far in this book directly back to *you*. I'm hoping that all you have read has inspired you or felt familiar in some way. If it has, this is because it is speaking to the divine spark within you.

In this way you become the light – the revelation of heaven on Earth – and as you shine others are reminded of their own potential for divinity and instinctively start to look within themselves for answers. Your inner light inspires them to look for their own higher calling and to be more than they ever believed they could be. It really does all start with the wonder of you.

From this moment on, whenever you want to see heaven, let your fears subside and look in the mirror. Whenever you want to hear heaven call your name, listen to the voice of your heart. It knows what is right and true. It knows the magic, wonder and breathtaking beauty of *you*.

Loving yourself and glimpsing heaven from the inside out is like being brought back into the sunlight and surrounding your heart with the fresh air of eternal life. Your heart feels alive because it has discovered your true purpose in life. It knows you are spirit and that heaven exists both within and all around you. It knows that this life is not the end and we don't die. It knows that consciousness is eternal, and that however much we doubt and feel uncertain, there is always the invisible – full of love, comfort, wisdom and possibility. When we connect to the unseen, the invisible, we understand that nothing is ever ended or lost – not one moment, not one smile, not one tear, not one feather, not yourself and never heaven.

The magic of now

> *How do you connect with the heart? The starting*
> *point is: all you ever have is this moment. So you*
> *look more deeply into this moment.*

ECKHART TOLLE

If you aren't sure how to connect with your heart, look to the present moment for inspiration. Heaven is not something you can only experience when you die. It is the eternal now. This book has focused a lot on the experience of the afterlife, but now I'd like to bring your focus to what is alive within you right now. Perhaps thinking about the other side is taking your energy away from what is heavenly about *this* life.

There is nothing more magical than this life, the eternal life in spirit that you are leading right now, this second, as you read this book. Yesterday has melted away and tomorrow has yet to materialise, so the only way heaven can call out to you is through right *now*. The only thing that is truly real and deserves your complete respect and attention is the magic of the present moment.

The magic of the present moment is the magic of your heart, of being aware that it beats. All the answers are in your heart, and the more you view your life as one eternal present moment, the better you can hear the voice of your heart. How does your heart speak to you? Through feelings, of course, but also through the way it beats. Recent research from the Institute of HeartMath (www.heartmath. org) has revealed that when you experience feelings of love, peace, creativity and joy, your heart beats in a calmer and gentle way. The term coined by HeartMath for this is 'heart coherence', a state of existence when your body and mind are in perfect harmony. Feelings of fear and anger have the opposite effect. So when you connect with your heart through the present moment and experience feelings of love, you are physically, mentally and spiritually at your peak. You are in heaven.

So, find as many ways as you can to connect with your heart in the present moment. Seize the now. Don't think you necessarily need to be doing important or great things. A fulfilled and happy life is often about those precious moments of laughter that fill your heart with joy, rather than about major life changes or events. It is about watching a glorious sunrise or glimpsing the enchantment of a moonlit lake. It is a good conversation or a great song, a comfortable chair or a rainbow peeking through after the rain. It is about seeing your children smile or the warmth of a hug. It is about walking along the seashore, dancing in the rain, or going for a walk or drive without any destination in mind. It is spending time with family, friends or beloved pets, or filling your heart with fond memories of departed loved ones. It is about so many 'insignificant' things, but when you add them all together they make up the magic and beauty of this life. Reintroduce yourself to your inner child and follow your heart wherever it goes. Don't worry that you will lose your way, because the heart is always focused towards the light.

There are countless ways to connect with your heart. Don't feel they all have to be upbeat, because you can also connect with your heart through facing your fears and challenges. Opening your heart to the presence of the divine within and all around you is tremendously empowering. You finally understand that you have the power to experience heaven on Earth. You don't need rituals, mediums, psychics or guides. You just need to listen to heaven calling out to you gently in your heart – the place where all the answers can be found and all the miracles lie.

Start seeing the world around you with the vision of your heart. Close your eyes right now, then open them. See love coming from everyone and everything, most especially yourself. This is the state of bliss, the highest level of spiritual awareness that can be experienced on Earth. Even if you see things that are sad or unfair, notice the love trying to break through. Use your mind and your heart and make a choice to shift your *perception* from one of fear to one of love. See the world with eyes of love. Imagine your life free of conflict, fear, judgement and upset. Imagine yourself happy and living your dreams. Imagine loving yourself just the way you are.

I asked you to imagine all this because it is possible to live in a state of bliss on Earth at any moment – bliss is simply opening your heart and perceiving love wherever you go. It is possible because others before you have chosen that return to love. You don't need to seek love because your heart is love already. You only need to eliminate the barriers of fear and guilt that you have built against it.

Your heart can choose bliss and glimpse heaven on Earth at any moment. Why not make that choice with your heart now, while your heart is still beating?

The miracle of death

> *For those who seek to understand it, death is a highly creative force. The highest spiritual values of life can originate from the thought and study of death.*
>
> ELIZABETH KUBLER ROSS

Knowing that one day your heart and the hearts of people you love will stop beating encourages you to appreciate the present moment and to listen to the wisdom of your heart. Thinking about death has a way of stripping away what is inconsequential and leaving only what truly matters. The miracle of death can teach us so much about how to be truly alive.

I'm not being morbid here, but none of us knows if this day will be our last. I was taught that lesson powerfully two decades ago when a few seconds saved me from certain death in a motorway pile-up in which three people died (*see page 22*). Those three people would have started their day totally unaware that they had so little time left on this amazing planet. As a result, from that day on I have always tried to live each day as if it was my last, with gratitude and no fear of expressing love. Death revealed to me the true meaning of life and how all that truly matters is what goes on in your heart.

The heart in a coherent and peaceful state reflects your spiritual essence and what life is truly like on the other side. So, if you take anything away from this book, let it be to listen intently to the beat of your heart, because that is the call of heaven and departed loved ones in spirit. If you stop listening to your heart, how are you to recognise divine love, compassion and beauty? How are you to hear the voices of loved ones in spirit? Even if you are in pain, tune into your heart for inspiration and guidance – your heart always knows what is right for you.

The more you listen to your heart, the more you will hear angels calling your name, because the power of the heart is greater than the power of death.

If you listen to your heart you will never get lost. It will lead you to heaven.

The way is not in the sky. The way is in the heart.

BUDDHA

Why do we close our eyes when we sleep, when we cry, when we imagine, when we kiss, when we pray? Because the best and most beautiful things in the world cannot be seen with your eyes, or even touched, it must be felt with your heart.

HELEN KELLER

AFTERWORD

NO GOODBYES

There are no goodbyes for us. Wherever you are,
you will always be in my heart.

GHANDI

Thank you for reading this book. I hope it will become a resource you can dip into time and time again for relief and reassurance. Think of it as your message from above, a reminder of the constant loving presence of heaven in your life from the cradle to beyond the grave. Use it for guidance and inspiration whenever you feel the need to remind yourself that those who have crossed over to the other side are never far away, and that this life does not end with death.

Goodbye is a word that heaven does not understand, so as this book draws to a close stay a while longer and read the appendix sections that follow. Don't be put off by the studious-sounding name 'appendix' – I can assure you that what you read there is anything but tedious. I also sincerely hope that the magical journey we have shared together here will continue on with you perhaps reading another of my books, or getting in touch with me directly.

Calling all earth angels

If you have a story or insight you would like to share with a wider audience in my future books, or have a burning question you need answered or insight you want to discuss, please don't hesitate to get in touch with me.

You can contact me via my website www.theresacheung. com and my email angeltalk710@aol.com. You could also write to me care of Piatkus Books (see page 4). I would be honoured to hear from you and will answer every question or discuss any issue personally. Sometimes things get very busy so it may be a while before I reply, but I will do so as soon as I can. Alternatively, for a more immediate response, you may want to comment or message me, and meet fellow spiritual seekers, on my Facebook Theresa Cheung Author page.

Don't feel alone in your quest for the light, or that anything you have to say is not important enough. I welcome and value all your thoughts, questions and stories. Communicating with you is the thing I love most about writing books that explore the reality of heaven.

A world without goodbye is called Heaven.

ANON

APPENDIX 1

THREE INTERVIEWS

Dr Julia Mossbridge

Dr Julia Mossbridge, MA (neuroscience), PhD (communication science and disorders), is visiting scientist and director of the Innovation Lab at the Institute of Noetic Sciences (IONS), founder and research director of the Mossbridge Institute, LLC, visiting scholar in the Psychology Department at Northwestern University, and science director of the Internet start-up Focus@ Will: music to improve concentration. Her major research interest involves understanding how time is perceived by the subconscious and conscious mind, but her passion is to bring soul into science and encourage everyone to discover their own inner wisdom. She is the author of *Unfolding: The Perpetual Science of Your Soul's Work*, and her next book, written with her colleague Imants Barušs, is *Transcendent Mind: Rethinking the Science of Consciousness*.

Working alongside IONS science director and author of *Supernormal*, Dr Dean Radin, Dr Mossbridge belongs to a new generation of scientists who are bridging the gap between science and spirit. I was lucky enough to catch up with this visionary woman in February 2016, and to discuss her groundbreaking research, the work of the Innovation Lab at IONS, and current attitudes among scientists about the paranormal, or events or phenomena that are beyond the scope of normal scientific understanding.

What was the catalyst for your interest in matters paranormal?

I think the term paranormal is a misnomer, as for me there is only psychology. Let me explain. If you went back in time to the Middle Ages and showed people of that period a mobile phone they would say it was paranormal but, of course, it isn't. So, for me, studying the paranormal is the work of trying to understand what science can't currently understand.

Having made that point, I can think of a moment that was a catalyst. I was about eleven and I began to notice that I was having dreams about simple, everyday things, like a friend being off sick from school or homework a teacher would set, but sometimes these simple things happened the next day. I was fascinated by this, and the budding scientist in me wanted a record, so I started to write down my dreams in a journal every morning. I noticed that a lot of the dreams, like falling off a building or arriving at school naked, didn't come true, but others did. I began to recognise what characterised dreams that were precognitive as compared to other dreams. Then I began to think about the nature of time.

I didn't really think I would take it any further, but in my early twenties, when I was in graduate school, I was strongly drawn back to those childhood dream memories and my dream journal. It dawned on me that my scientific interests had always centred around time, or temporal questions in some way, and because every experiment you can imagine involves time, the world of scientific research was an open playing field for me. I also discovered a passion within me for bridging the gap between science and spirit, or the known and the unknown.

Where did this desire to bridge the gap between science and spirit come from?

I think my passion for finding a common ground between the inner and outward life came from my childhood. My mother was a therapist – so all about the inner state. My father was a physicist – so all about the external, about what is observed. As I was growing up I was always caught between those two voices – the external and the internal – and I understood instinctively that they needed to balance, not oppose, each other.

Could you tell me about your main interests now?

My major interests are time and the nature of the conscious and unconscious minds. I guess among non-scientists I am best known for my contribution to the development of the *Choice Compass* app, which is an app to help people learn to get in touch with their internal physical states (in this case, their heartbeats) in order to make better life choices. The research related to that app is ongoing. The more I have worked in science, though, the more I begin to see my role as a scientist who turns the spotlight on what is going on inside a person. If I see scientists coming to conclusions based only on observing external data, I am the voice for also studying the internal world. The reverse is true as well.

Science often lacks soul, which isn't surprising as until recently it has been a very male-dominated profession, and for better or worse, most Western men have been trained to talk about only the 'objective' externals and dismiss the importance of the inner world. The inner world is more the world where women feel at home. Some scientists, both men and women, can be obsessed with getting things right all the time, but in order to progress scientifically we all need to become more comfortable with the unknown.

Do you think this is the reason why there are now more studies on the paranormal or the possibility of life after death than before – because now there are more women scientists than there were?

Well, maybe. It's a theory of mine. I think women in science are opening up the boundaries previously set, and increasingly drawing attention to the importance of soul and spirit in our work. I hope to write a book about the role of women in the development of science at some point – or maybe not just women in particular, but femininity in general. I think there is a whole new generation of scientists out there who refuse to be restricted by the way things were. They are willing to open their minds to studying and valuing the unexplained, and I think a lot of these scientists have more feminine traits than ever before, regardless of their genders.

You must get your fair share of criticism within the world of science?

The results of my research challenge the currently accepted scientific world view. A lot of scientists like to think they are right so, of course, my research is criticised. This does not faze me, though. In fact, it inspires me, as trying to understand what is seemingly not understandable is what created every great scientific leap in history, such as working out that the Earth is round, that the sun and not the Earth is the centre of the solar system, that the subconscious mind exists, and so on.

Can you tell me about the Innovation Lab work at IONS?

The work of the Innovation Lab is currently focused on developing experimental technology to make what science has discovered about the unexplained accessible and easy to incorporate into daily life. We hope to develop IONS apps for mobiles to enable people to experience personal transformation and self-transcendence, and to work with corporations and other organisations. The idea is that our message about consciousness transformation has the potential to become truly global.

Are you developing apps focused on precognitive dreams, given they were such an early interest of yours?

All at idea stage now and not in development, but Dean Radin and I are looking at creating an app to record the dreams of large numbers of people to see if future events can be predicted. I am also toying with the idea of an app that encourages people to record their dreams, then match them up according to similar dream symbols, as discussing similar dreams is a great way to break the ice when you meet someone new.

Is there anything you can say to my readers who have had paranormal experiences and want to understand them better?

Sure. To sit with the unknown is the job of a scientist, and anyone who is on their spiritual journey. There is a desire within not just scientists, but each one of us, to always know the answers, because when we know all the answers we think we will be safe. And if we don't know the answers we think we are not safe. I think it is just the opposite. When you simply let go of the need to always know the answer, you are in fact safe because you accept the truth, which is that you simply can't know everything. The most accurate description of the human experience is to 'not know'. Letting go of the need to understand and always know the answers is spiritually transformative. Unfortunately, we teach science at school as if it is all about knowing the facts, but not knowing is the true state of awareness because as soon as you know something, you have another question.

So, my advice is to relax and enjoy the not knowing as that is the only state when you are truly honest – truly yourself.

What impact would you like your research and the work of the Innovation Lab to have on the future?

I'd like my research and work to encourage more women and people with feminine traits to go into science. I believe that is the way forwards for science, as the nature of the feminine is to turn the spotlight on the importance of the inner world. I would like to see my research help bridge the gap between science and spirit. As for the Innovation Lab, I would like to see the technology we produce doubling the amount of time people spend doing self-transcendent practices (actions that connect us with something beyond ourselves) within the next five years. This is critical, because we know that if people perform self-transcendent practices they actually benefit themselves physically, mentally and emotionally, as well as benefiting others. So we are working towards a world where more and more people are connected with their bodies and their inner wisdom, feeling more clarity, vision and connection, and using these feelings to help others.

How exciting. I think you have the best job in the world. I hope your vision for the future becomes a reality.

Thank you, but it is not just my vision – it is shared by others at IONS, and we are all working hard to make that happen. You are right! I do forget sometimes what a fascinating and rewarding job I have. Thank you for reminding me.

For further information about Dr Mossbridge and the work of IONS, check out www.noetic.org/innovation

For information about Dr Mossbridge's decision-making app, Choice Compass, see www.choicecompass.com

Dr Julie Beischel

Dr Julie Beischel, co-founder and director of research at the Windbridge Institute for Applied Research in Human Potential in Tucson, Arizona, forfeited a potentially lucrative career in the pharmaceutical industry to pursue rigorous scientific research of consciousness with psychic mediums full-time.

Dr Beischel received her doctorate in pharmacology and toxicology from the University of Arizona and is currently a member of the Society for Scientific Exploration and of the science advisory board of the Rhine Research Center. She has had a number of peer-reviewed articles published in scientific journals. Her academic training in several scientific disciplines allows her to apply traditional research methods to the study of consciousness and survival after death.

Dr Beischel now stands as a world leader in mediumship research, and I was lucky enough to catch up with this trailblazing lady in January 2016, just after the publication of her latest book, *Investigating Mediums*, which gathers together all her groundbreaking research to date on mediums at the Windbridge Institute.

What was the catalyst for your decision to investigate mediums?

As long as I can remember science has been my life, but at first it was very much science in the traditional way. I didn't really know much about the work of mediums until I was twenty-four and my mother committed suicide. From that moment on I started to ask serious and profound questions about the exist-ence of an afterlife, and eventually these questions became my primary focus. After I completed my PhD in 2003, I was able to start my research in earnest. It wasn't long before I found out that there was just too much data out there to dismiss, and that it needed to be investigated properly, but science wasn't really addressing it. I knew that this was what I was meant to do, so I didn't pursue a career in the pharmaceutical industry and focused on applying the same scientific method and standards of research to mediumship as are used in drug trials and other fields of research.

Tell me about the research programmes currently taking place at Windbridge?

When my husband and research partner Mark Boccuzzi and I decided to set up our own independent research institution, we knew that the following questions would be our primary focus. What can we do with the potential that exists within our bodies, minds and spirits? Can we heal ourselves and others? Can we affect events and physical reality with our thoughts? Can we know things before they happen? Are we connected to each other? To the planet? And our main ques-tion right now is: can we communicate with loved ones who have passed away?

Why the name Windbridge? Is there any special meaning there?

Bridge, of course, references the role of the medium as an intermediary between Earth and the afterlife, and the word 'wind' suggests something that is real and powerful but cannot be seen. Put the two together and you have a name that sums up what we are trying to do.

Is it possible for you to summarise your mediumship findings to date?

As with most research topics, more work needs to be done, but at present our data, collected under blinded conditions, demonstrates that some mediums can demonstrate anomalous information reception (or AIR). In other words, they have the ability to report accurate and detailed information about a deceased person without any previous knowledge of that person, or about the sitter, the living person wanting to hear from their loved one. Because the medium doesn't interact with the sitter during our research readings, there is no possibility of cold reading. It is possible, of course, that they could be using telepathy to read another person's mind to obtain that information, but for us at the Windbridge Institute that phenomenon is equally compelling and worthy of research.

What is your current focus?

It remains survival research or investigating the possibility of life after death, but we are also very interested in the practical social applications of mediumship readings – specifically how they might be therapeutic for the grieving. In the 1950s the advice the bereaved were given was 'just get over it', but that didn't seem to alleviate any suffering. By the 1980s the 'continuing bonds' model of grief was developed, in which the goal is to recognise that your bond with the person you've lost continues, only in a different form. Our research is directly in line with that model and is focused on examining the potential effects (positive, negative or neither) of readings from credentialed mediums on the bereaved. Anecdotal data implies that consulting a medium can have a positive therapeutic effect, but we'll need funding to perform a larger study on this topic to really prove it.

Investigating the possibility of survival after death must make you a bit of an enigma as far as the scientific community is concerned. How does it regard you?

In the late 1800s a number of researchers did pursue survival research, but because most research being done today in any field is funded by government or private foundation grants, and there are no government and very few private grants supporting survival research, very few researchers can pursue these investigations if they want to be able to pay their rent and eat. Also, I think most scientists are afraid that they will be labelled unscientific if they even consider researching the possibility of life after death. It is tough for me right now because if I announced that I have data which demonstrates that mediums can report accurate information about deceased people with no feedback or prior knowledge of them, I would be viewed in a very negative light, even though I am doing nothing more than reporting my findings. Scientists in other fields do not often find themselves in this position.

So do you believe in life after death?

As a scientist, it is not my job to believe. It is my job to design studies that control for alternative explanations, collect data, and draw conclusions based on that data and the data from other scientists collected on similar topics. Taking into account the data collected to date about mediums, near-death experiences, out-of-body experiences, and so on, I can conclude that the survival of consciousness after physical death ('life after death') is the theory that best explains all of that data.

How are mediums selected and tested in your research?

A journal article I wrote (summarised on our website) explains the complex process, but all of the mediums on our team went through a rigorous, eight-step screening, testing and training procedure, during which they demonstrated that they were able to report accurate and specific information about the deceased under controlled conditions that prevent fraud. They agreed to standards of conduct, including not giving readings unless specifically requested, and volunteered their time for research. We screened our team as part of a specific grant and are no longer screening new mediums.

Do you use data from celebrity mediums?

No – just because a medium has chosen to make a career out of their gift does not make them any more interesting to us, because they are just one medium, which science can dismiss as a fluke. We are interested in collecting data from numerous mediums so it can be used as evidence of a widespread phenomenon or ability.

Individuals don't interest us – it is the combination of all the readings and data that provide the greatest evidence for a scientist. It is the power of witnessing many mediums reporting accurate and specific information about a dead person under strict scientific guidelines.

Do you think that the possibility of survival after death will ever be accepted by mainstream science?

Anything is possible, so perhaps one day – but right now we have a long way to go even though the majority of the public already believes in life after death. In some respects this doesn't concern me as I know that change always happens on the fringes or edges, and never in the mainstream, and right now my primary focus is on how survival research can serve society and ease the grieving process.

How do you respond to criticism from sceptics?

Most sceptics aren't truly sceptics because a sceptic keeps an open mind, but the people who criticise what we do and say all mediums are frauds have closed their mind to any new information. I call them deniers. They are denying that there is all this data out there and refuse to even look at it. It is as though the sky has turned red and everyone can see that, but they keep their eyes and heads down and insist that the sky is blue.

People are having these experiences and science needs to address them. No matter how loudly sceptics scream about how such experiences are impossible, they cannot drown out the people who continue to have them every day. That is why I find what they have to say useless.

In addition, the testing protocol we use at the Windbridge Institute eliminates all the explanations that a sceptic may claim are responsible for a medium's apparent accuracy: fraud, experimenter cueing, information so general that it could apply to anyone, rater bias, and 'cold reading' (a situation in which a medium uses cues from a present sitter to fabricate an 'accurate' reading). The readings take place on the phone between a medium and an experimenter; sitters do not hear the readings as they take place, and they later score blinded transcripts.

However, although sceptics can make our life harder than it need be, by far the biggest obstacle for us is not criticism from sceptics, but funding. Survival of consciousness is not an area of research funded by any government grants or by any but a handful of private foundations. The research we do here at Windbridge is important and socially relevant, but we can't make as much progress as we would like to because we can't afford the necessary equipment and personnel to perform the types and number of studies we'd like to do.

How can people get involved with the Windbridge Institute?

There are a number of simple ways in which people can stay connected with us online at www.windbridge.org/get-involved. People can sign up to volunteer as research sitters at www.wind-bridge.org/participate, find us on Facebook or check out my blog. To keep informed about our current findings, check out our news updates at www.windbridge.org/whats-new, or join our email list at www.windbridge.org/join-email-list.

James Van Praagh

World-renowned medium James Van Praagh, author of *New York Times* bestseller *Talking to Heaven: A Medium's Message of Life after Death*, and co-executive producer of CBS Primetime series *Ghost Whisperer* (which is based on his life), is a natural-born psychic pioneer.

All his life James van Praagh has boldly gone where no medium or psychic has ever gone before. The publication of *Talking to Heaven*, in 1998, was nothing less than ground-breaking. Previous books about the afterlife had tended to be firmly grounded in religion, shrouded in impenetrable esoteric mystery, or tentative/touchy-feely reads for a specialist readership, but *Talking to Heaven* was none of these things. Here was a medium, not linked to any church or faith, assertively and boldly stating in a very simple and matter-of-fact way to the whole world that he had the gift of talking to the dead and bringing back powerful messages of love and hope from the other side. The book touched a deep chord of spiritual longing in the world, and sold well over a million copies. It certainly was an inspiration to me in many ways as a writer and a spiritual being, and I was thrilled when Mr Van Praagh agreed to be interviewed by me.

When did you first realise you were a medium?

I must have been about twenty-four at the time. I remember talking to a girl on the phone and having this powerful feeling that she had a grandmother in spirit and that the grandmother was from Idaho. I was right, then other accurate details came through. It was the beginning of my life as a medium.

Is a medium born or made?

A mixture of both. I think we are all born with psychic powers – we call it intuition – but some of us find it easier to develop their sensitivity than others, a bit like musical ability. All of us can learn to play an instrument but not everyone will become a virtuoso. Certainly for me, once I realised I had mediumistic potential, I made the decision to develop it and went to weekly meetings and meditation groups. I did this for several years, then, as I approached thirty, sensations from the spirit world became stronger and stronger. There was no going back from then onwards. I knew this was my spiritual path.

How does the world of spirit communicate with you? How does it make you feel?

As we are talking about things that are not of this Earth it is hard to describe, but I will try. It is all done with thought and feelings and sensations. When spirits enter our realm it is not always easy for them to adjust to the Earth vibration or mindset. They have to slow down their thought. I have to speed up mine, so we both need to adjust to each other as we blend. Feelings are the first to be sent to me. Then, if it is a good day, I will get personal details like names or what someone was wearing – simple and deeply personal things that the person I am doing a reading for will instinctively recognise. The thoughts and feelings can only be simple because more complex thoughts can't slow down enough to adjust to the Earth mindset.

You need to understand, Theresa, that the spirit world is infinitely more complex than this Earth. Our departed loved ones are on another spiritual level or dimension, and the laws that govern that dimension are different from the laws that govern us here. We are in the physical world and our physical limitations can't fully understand the spiritual dimensions, and spirits come through with hints and pieces of thoughts and feelings that we can understand. I hear these thoughts but it is not like physical hearing. It is like whispers and sounds, and parts of thoughts and feelings. I then communicate those thoughts and feelings as best I can. Most of the time they make sense, but sometimes because of communication problems there will be confusion.

When I'm talking to a spirit my energy levels increase dramatically. It's as though I've drunk too much coffee or eaten too much chocolate. This makes sense because if you are a bridge between this life and the next, the world of spirit has a faster dimension. After a night of readings I can sometimes feel very tired and drained, but I have learned ways to recharge myself again ready for the next reading.

What happens when you pass over? Do we remember everything and everyone?

The process is different for everyone, but when you pass over there is an expansion of consciousness. Our Earth minds are a small part of that consciousness. It's a bit as if before you were a seed and now you are a fully grown plant. When you are a plant you can't really relate to being a seed any more. The physical dimensions are not relative to the spiritual ones. Hope this is making sense to you.

As for memories of Earth in the spirit world, the stronger the emotional connection the stronger the memory in spirit will be, and the stronger the memories will come through to me when I do a reading. Each spirit communicates its memories of Earth to me differently – personalities in spirit are as many and varied as personalities on Earth, and in fact even more so. We are all unique on Earth and we are even more unique in heaven. You do have to remember, though, that spirits are not in Earth time. They are outside time, so asking them what they did a year ago – if they passed away a year ago – may be difficult for them to communicate precisely, because a year ago may feel like another time and place, or even an eternity away.

What is heaven like?

Heaven is made up of what gives us joy. It is created by the thoughts and feelings we had on Earth, so in this way heaven will be different for everyone, as each of us has different thoughts and feelings. That is why I stress in my books the importance of living as positive a life on Earth as possible, and treating people with love and kindness. Every day of our lives here we are creating our lives in heaven. When we pass on we have a life review, and feel everything good and bad we have said and done. We relive our lives outside time. We see how we have treated others and how it made them feel. This could be hell or it could be heaven.

We truly do create our afterlife. There is a great story about a millionaire who died and went to heaven. He was incredibly wealthy but very self-centred, so when he went to heaven and asked where he should reside, he was taken to a hovel. The millionaire was shocked as he said he had expected a mansion, but the angels told him that they could only work with the materials he had given them in his life.

So, you reap what you sow in the afterlife. Be a kind, caring and compassionate person, and heaven will be beautiful fields and flowers. Do the opposite and expect a mud hut.

Do you believe in reincarnation?

Yes, and as I just explained, as you reap so shall you sow, and the life you are living right now will influence the life you are next born into. Each time we have a life on Earth we have to learn lessons for our soul to grow. I think of life on Earth as a soul school. Sometimes we get things right and sometimes we get things wrong. In order to graduate we need to get more things right than wrong. Getting things wrong isn't the end of the world, though, because we learn and grow most from our mistakes, our pain and our problems.

Do you believe in synchronicity?

Again, yes. I always tell people that synchronicity is God's way of remaining anonymous, so pay attention to the signs and messages that are subtly sent your way. I don't think anything that happens to us is random. We need to look for the deeper meanings.

What is the message you want to give to the world?

I have many but, above all, I want people to know that there is
no death. Once you understand that your life transforms in every
way. You lose your fear. You live life to the full. You understand
that you are responsible for your thoughts and feelings, and your
words and deeds. Live your life this way and your life will be
full of meaning.

The spirits on the other side want us to know that we are
loved. When people pass over the first thing they experience is
an expansion of consciousness, and they suddenly become aware
of the love within and all around them that has always existed.
They understand that if they had only known how much love
there was they would not have felt so unfulfilled.

Love changes everything. It is the greatest power. The trouble is that many of us deny ourselves the self-love that is our
birthright. We let other people manipulate us, thinking that if
only they loved us we could be fulfilled. We try to earn their
love, but if we just understood we are love we would realise
that we don't need to do that. We don't need to come from that
weakened position. We have divine love inside us. We have all
that we need inside us. Get in touch with that – find heaven or
God within – and we can find happiness and fulfilment in this
life and the next.

**You are not afraid of discussing the dark side of human
life and nature in your books. What are your opinions on
that?**

Again, this life is very much a school for our spirits to grow and
learn. Problems, pain, suffering, cruelty and injustice are very
much a part of life, and I would be a hypocrite to pretend none
of this exists because it does, so that is why I talk about these

things in my book. I hope what I says helps people cope with or understand the dark side of life better.

Can we all develop our psychic or mediumistic powers?

We can all develop our intuitive powers and I try to teach people to take responsibility for their own self-development, and to get in touch with their inner selves or world. You need to tune out the outside world and tune into the inner world – and the journey begins with trust and letting go of fear and self-doubt.

I do suggest meditation, either in a group or alone, or working with chakra points. One of the best ways to start tuning into your inner world is to pay more attention to your dreams. Before you go to bed ask spirit to send you a sign. If you keep doing this, in time you will get a dream that you will know is more than a dream – it will be a vision, a communication from the other side or heaven talking to you.

To find out more about James, visit www.vanpraagh.com.

THE INSTITUTE OF NOETIC SCIENCES (IONS)

The Institute of Noetic Sciences (IONS)
www.noetic.org
Science-based, non-profit research, education and membership organisation dedicated to consciousness research and educational outreach, and engaging a global learning community in the real-isation of human potential.

http://noetic.org/theresa-cheung
This link takes you to a page specially created by IONS for Theresa Cheung readers and references seven videos in the video library of my Theresa Cheung Author Facebook page, where the science team, led by President Dr Cassandra Vieten, speak directly to my readers. In the videos they talk about their encouraging research into mediumship (Dr Arnaud Delorme), precognition (Dr Julia Mossbridge), channelling (Dr Helane Wahbeh) mind–body heal-ing (Dr Garret Yount), and mind influencing matter (chief scientist Dr Dean Radin.) The aim of the videos is to show my readers that the gap between science and spirit is closing fast.

APPENDIX 3

KEY ORGANISATIONS

The Parapsychological Association
www.parapsych.org
An international professional organisation of scientists and scholars engaged in the scientific study of PSI (or 'psychic') experiences.

The Rhine Research Centre
www.rhine.org
Advances the science of parapsychology, provides education and resources for the public, and fosters a community for individuals with personal and professional interest in PSI.

Forever Family Foundation
www.foreverfamilyfoundation.org
Furthers the understanding of afterlife science through research and education, while providing support and healing for people in grief.

The Windbridge Institute: Applied Research in Human Potential

www.windbridge.org

An independent research organisation investigating the capabilities of our bodies, minds and spirits, and attempting to determine how the resulting information can best serve all living things.

The Institute of Heart Math

www.heartmath.org

Provides free education and training programmes, services, research membership, and tools and technology to transform people's lives by deepening their connection with their own hearts and the hearts of others to encourage a more peaceful future.

Australian Parapsychological Research Association (APRA)

www.parapsychology.org.au

Founded by neuroscientist Vladimir Dubaj, the APRA is a non-profit, Australian-based organisation dedicated to the research of parapsychological phenomena through scientific research and education.

Association for the Scientific Study of Anomalous Phenomena

www.assap.ac.uk

UK-based charity and learned society founded in 1981 to investigate, research and educate on a wide range of anomalous phenomena. It also carries out paranormal investigations and trains members to become accredited investigators.

Koestler Parapsychology Unit (KPU)

www.koestler-parapsychology.psy.ed.ac.uk

Research group based in the Psychology Department of the

University of Edinburgh. Established in 1985, it consists of academics who teach and research various aspects of parapsychology.

The College of Psychic Studies
www.collegeofpsychicstudies.co.uk
Founded in 1884 by a group of eminent scholars and scientists, it is based in Kensington, London, and runs cutting-edge courses in psychic development.

Callum E. Cooper
callum.cooper@northampton.ac.uk
Parapsychologist and author of *Telephone Calls from the Dead* (Tricorn books, 2012) who is based at the University of Nottingham's Centre for the Study of Anomalous Psychological Processes, Fawsley, Park Campus, Northampton, NN2 7AL. Contact details for Callum can also be found on the Afterlife Science section of my website, www.theresacheung.com.

The Arthur Findlay College
www.arthurfindlaycollege.org
The world's foremost college for the advancement of spiritualism and psychic scenes. Based in Essex, in the UK, the college offers advice, courses, talks, information and training for mediums.

Claire Broad Mediumship
Claire Broad is a qualified and highly experienced medium willing to offer advice about mediumship.

APPENDIX 4

BEREAVEMENT SUPPORT

Cruse Bereavement Care
www.cruseorg.uk
Not in any way connected to spirituality or research into the afterlife, Cruse is a nationwide charity that exists to promote the well-being of bereaved people and to help anyone suffering a bereavement to understand their grief and cope with their loss. It offers confidential counselling and support, and advice about practical matters.

Bereavement Advice Centre
www.bereavementadvice.org
Free UK helpline and Web-based information service provided by Simplify, which gives practical information and advice on the many issues that face us after someone dies.

GriefShare
www.griefshare.org
US-based online support group and advice centre.

My Grief Angels

www.mygriefangels.org

A comprehensive list of links to resources and groups to help people cope with the grieving process. The resources are organised by type of loss and there is a section on international resources.

Robin Grey Counselling

www.robingreycounselling.co.uk
robingrey62@gmail.com

Robin Grey is a qualified bereavement counsellor who offers advice about grieving with spirit or developing an ongoing spiritual relationship with departed loved ones.

SPIRITUAL RESEARCH AND READING

Healing at a distance/prayer

Masters, K.S. and Spielmans, G.I., 'Prayer and health: Review, meta-analysis, and research agenda', *Journal of Behavioral Medicine*, 2007 Oct;30(5):447

Radin, D., et al., 'Compassionate intention as a therapeutic intervention by partners of cancer patients: Effects of distant intention on the patients' autonomic nervous system', *Explore: The Journal of Science and Healing* (NY) 2008 Jul–Aug;4(4):235–43

Radin, D., et al., 'Distant healing intention therapies: An overview of the scientific evidence', *Global Advances in Health and Medicine*, 2015 Nov;4(Suppl):67–71

Schlitz, M.J., et al., 'Distant healing of surgical wounds: An exploratory study', *Explore: The Journal of Science and Healing* (NY), 2012 Jul–Aug;8(4):223–30

Survival of consciousness after death

Alexander, E., *Proof of Heaven: A Neurosurgeon's Journey into the Afterlife*, Simon and Schuster, 2012

Beischel, J., *Among Mediums: A Scientist's Quest for Answers*, Windbridge Institute, 2013

Beischel, J., and Schwartz, G.E., 'Anomalous information reception by research mediums demonstrated using a novel triple-blind protocol', *Explore: The Journal of Science and Healing*, 2007 3(1):23–7

Beischel, J., et al,: 'The possible effects on bereavement of assisted after-death communication during readings with psychic mediums: A continuing bonds perspective', *Omega: Journal of Death and Dying*, 2014–1570(2):169–194. doi: 10.2190/OM.70.2.b.

Beischel, J., et al., 'Anomalous information reception by research mediums under blinded conditions II: Replication and extension', *Explore: The Journal of Science and Healing*, Jan 2015 11(2):136–142.

Beischel, J., *Investigating Mediums: A Windbridge Institute Collection*, Blurb, 2015

Cooper, C.E., *Telephone Calls from the Dead*, Tricorn, 2012

Facco, E., and Agrillo, C., 'Near-death experiences between science and prejudice', *Frontiers in Human Neuroscience*, 18 July 2012

Greyson, B., et al., 'Seeing dead people not known to have died: "Peak in Darien" experiences', *Anthropology and Humanism*, Nov. 2010 35(2):159–71

Kelly, E.W. and Arcangel, D., 'An investigation of mediums who claim to give information about deceased persons', *Journal of Nervous and Mental Disease*, 2011 Jan;199(1):11–7

Moody, Raymond, *Life after Life: The Best Selling Original Investigation which Revealed Near-Death Experiences*, Harper, 2015

Moorjani, A., *Dying to be Me*, Hay House, 2014

Nahm, M., et al., 'Terminal lucidity: A review and a case collection', *Archives of Gerontology and Geriatrics*, Jul–Aug 2012 55(1):138–42

Parnia, S., et al., 'Awareness during resuscitation: A prospective study', *PubMed*, Dec. 2014 85(12): 1799–1805

Van Lommel, P., 'Near-death experience, consciousness and the brain: A new concept about the continuity of our consciousness based on recent scientific research on near-death experience in survivors of cardiac arrest', World Futures, *Journal of General Evolution*, 2006 62: 134–52

Van Lommel, P., 'Near-death experiences: The experience of the self as real and not as an illusion', *Annals of the New York Academy of Sciences,* 2011 1234:19–28

Van Lommel, P., 'Nonlocal consciousness: A concept based on scientific research on near-death experiences during cardiac arrest', *Journal of Consciousness Studies*, 2013 20:7–48

Van Lommel, P., *Consciousness Beyond Life: The Science of the Near-Death Experience*, HarperOne, 2010

Precognition

Bem, D., et al., 'Feeling the future: A meta-analysis of 90 experiments on the anomalous anticipation of random future events', *PubMed*, Version 2. F1000Res. Oct 30 2015 [revised Jan 292016];4:1188

Mossbridge, J., et al., *Predictive Physiological Anticipation Preceding Seemingly Unpredictable Stimuli: A Meta-Analysis*, Institute of Noetic Sciences, 2012

Radin, D., *Predicting the Unpredictable: 75 Years of Experimental Evidence*, Institute of Noetic Sciences, November 2011

Science meets spirit

Buruss, I., and Mossbridge, J., *Transcendent Mind: Rethinking the Science of Consciousness*, American Psychological Association, 2016

Carter, C., *Science and Psychic Phenomena: The Fall of the House of Skeptics*, Inner Traditions, 2012

Dossey, L., *One Mind: How Our Individual Mind is Part of a Greater Consciousness and Why it Matters*, Hay House, 2014

Nelson, R., and Bancel, P., 'Effects of mass consciousness: Changes in random data during global events', *Journal of Alternate and Complement Medicine*, 2005 Feb;11(1):85–91

Radin, D, *Supernormal: Science, Yoga, and the Evidence for Extraordinary Psychic Abilities*, Deepak Chopra, 2013

Radin, D. and Schlitz, M.J., 'Gut feelings, intuition, and emotions: An exploratory study', *Journal of Alternate and Complement Medicine*, 2005 Feb;11(1):85-91,

Radin, D., *The Conscious Universe: The Scientific Truth of Psychic Phenomena*, HarperOne, 2009

Schmidt, S., 'Can we help just by good intentions? A meta-analysis of experiments on distant intention effects', *Journal of Alternate and Complement Medicine*, 2012 Jun;18(6):529–33

Sheldrake, R., *The Sense of Being Stared at, and Other Aspects of the Extended Mind*, Cornerstone, 2013

Targ, R., *The Reality of ESP: A Physicist's Proof of Psychic Abilities*, Quest, 2012

Tart, C., *'The End of Materialism: How Evidence of the Paranormal is Bringing Science and Spirit Together*, New Harbinger, 2009

APPENDIX 6

THE HIGHLY SENSITIVE PERSON

Intrigued to discover more about the powerful sense of familiarity I was experiencing from reading afterlife encounter stories sent to me by my readers, I started to compile a list of personality traits. In my psychology research around these key words, the term 'highly sensitive person' kept coming up time and time again. A person born with high sensitivity processes information very deeply and intensely. Given this sensitivity, it may come as no surprise that the incidence of depression or mood disorders in such people is relatively high, because the instinct is to shut down or withdraw when the world overwhelms them. They often wonder why they are different and typically can't cope with life with the resilience that other people have.

The 'highly sensitive' potential lies within us all, but is more developed in some than in others. The term was first used in 1996 by Elaine N. Aron, PhD, who suggested that it may be a genetic trait, as highly sensitive people have a nervous system and brain that processes and reflects information more deeply, and are therefore more highly tuned to feelings and subtleties. I guess you could say they are more aware or observant and can see, hear, think and feel more clearly – perhaps for survival reasons, in that the highly sensitive person would have once alerted a tribe or group of people to danger and led them to safety.

In centuries past, sensitive individuals like this would have been revered members of their communities, and were typically employed as healers, shamans or gurus for their wisdom, healing, empathy and ability to bridge the gap between the invisible and visible world – but in the materialistic world of today respect for people with high sensitivity has waned to non-existent levels. Indeed, many are considered eccentric, head in the clouds, off the wall, anti-social or just plain odd. Constantly feeling that something is wrong with them impacts their self-esteem. Told from a very young age that they are way too sensitive for their own good, many highly sensitive people try unsuccessfully to develop a thick skin, but it is impossible to change their nature as sensitivity is in their DNA. All they can do is learn effective ways to manage it and survive in the world. There are, however, magical traits associated with this kind of personality, such as creativity, imagination, empathy, compassion, finely tuned intuition, a desire for peace and calm, and a deep respect for the beautiful world we live in, and placing a higher value on these traits instead of feeling embarrassed about them or devaluing them is a good starting point.

From the point of view of this book, perhaps the most significant trait sensitive people share is their absolute fascination with and conscious or unconscious connection to the invisible world of spirit and the afterlife. This connection to 'something more' isn't something they could describe or even understand; it is something they just 'feel' and 'know.' They aren't sure how they know, and they may not even have personal proof of it, or consider themselves psychic in any way, but they believe a loving force is at work in the world and that death is not the end. In short, spiritual development, or the belief that there has to be something more to this life, is absolutely fundamental to their well-being.

Seeing clearly at last

For me, researching highly sensitive personalities from both a psychological and a spiritual perspective was mind, heart and spirit opening. I could see me. I could see my struggles, questions and experiences so clearly presented there, and wished I had had access to this kind of information when I was growing up and feeling out of place in a world that did not understand me. Knowing all this would have helped me to overcome my feelings of alienation and find ways to adapt my sensitivity to the world I felt threatened by. Simply knowing I wasn't the only one – and that what I regarded as a weakness or an oddity could in fact be transformed into a strength, and something I should be proud of not embarrassed by – gave me an overwhelming sense of comfort, meaning and reassurance.

It is important for highly sensitive people to develop spiritually, because if they don't they continue to feel like outsiders whose lives lack meaning, purpose and direction. After all, in times past their personality traits and accompanying wisdom and insight about matters invisible were highly valued and sought after. So, it has become my calling to share afterlife stories with as wide a readership as possible, and to encourage more and more sensitive souls to write to me. I don't want anyone who is drawn to the world of spirit, or who has the desire to connect with the afterlife or a deeper meaning in life, to feel as alienated, alone and confused as I was. Without even realising it, I have discovered my calling through my writing, and hopefully along the way encouraged others to discover and embrace who they truly are, rather than feel ashamed of it. In this way the people who send me their stories are all angels calling out my name.

Angels calling

Today, as increasing numbers of people are talking about heaven and believing in the possibility of the survival of consciousness (due to advances in resuscitation techniques and reports of NDEs going mainstream with million-selling books), my greatest wish is that my books, and most especially this one because of the title, will bring an even wider acceptance of those with a sensitive nature who have a strong connection to the unseen world. Instead of feeling that they have to change, or feeling conflicted because they are told they are too shy, or sensitive or head in the clouds, they will know that they are not alone and that they have much of value to offer others. They will use this understanding to trust themselves and discover the confidence to value and evolve their unique gifts, instead of trying to bury or deny them.

I believe that the world has never needed sensitive, kind and loving people more than it does today. Society right now can often be dark, cruel, violent, chaotic and unfair, and there is so much focus on speed, youth, celebrity, money, outward appearance and having more and more material things, that we urgently need sensitive people who know there is a deeper, more meaningful way to be. We need them to help us focus our attention from the visible to the invisible, from what isn't important to what is important, and the need to search within ourselves rather than outside ourselves for true fulfilment. In short, we need *you*.

What I am trying to say here is that you – your sensitivity, love, kindness, connection to the unseen, and belief that there has to be a better way for the world that unites rather than divides people through the power of eternal love – are needed right now more than ever before.

You might find this revelation a bit surprising and wonder how on earth I can be so sure that you are a sensitive soul (or that potential lies within you) with such an important role to play on the world's stage. That's simple to answer: you are reading this book. This is astonishing, really, when you consider the countless other books, magazines, features, newspapers, blogs, websites, videos and so on that are vying for your attention right now. Yet despite all this intense competition you are right here where you should be. I have complete faith that heaven, or the piece of heaven inside you, took you by the hand and heart and led you to this book. You are meant to be reading it.

Whenever you let heaven inspire you in this way you become the message. You become the medium for others to be awakened and inspired. Through you they hear the voice of heaven, and your inner light bypasses their fears and glides gracefully and quietly into their hearts. Then, in time, the voice of spirit will whisper from deep within them and call out their name, just as it is calling yours now.

APPENDIX 7

THE POWER OF A NAME

The idea that our names are intertwined with our destiny goes back to biblical times. When one of my readers asked me last year if I ever drew inspiration from two of my famous spiritual namesakes, Sister Teresa and Mother Teresa, I realised that I had never actually thought about this before. All my life I had never liked my name, but researching the lives of these two women was deeply humbling and revealing. Although I can never, ever aspire to similar piety and greatness, there was so much I could relate to in the lives of these two awesome women.

Teresa of Avila was a Spanish nun, mystic and reformer of the Carmelite order, born in 1515. She was also a spiritual writer and her books, of which *Interior Castle* is the best known, are considered classics in Christian spirituality. Her greatest contribution, however, was in the way she proposed that people could pray. For Teresa, prayer was not a ritual to be confined to one space or time or day, but it could happen spontaneously in many different situations. She was convinced of the value of continuous prayer – in other words, of a life of constant dialogue with God. Although I don't share St Teresa's devotion to one religion, I could not agree more with her teaching about life being a continuous and intimate communication with the divine within and all around us.

Mother Teresa also found great strength in the power of prayer and contemplation. The charitable works and good deeds of this Albanian nun born in 1910 are well documented, but what is less well known is the many doubts and struggles over her religious beliefs she experienced throughout her life – even on occasion feeling 'no presence of God whatsoever', 'neither in her heart nor the Eucharist'. She also frequently experienced deep pain over her lack of faith and, although I can never hope to compare myself to Teresa in her tireless charity work and selfless life, I can certainly relate to her periods of 'spiritual dryness'. Many times in my life I have struggled deeply with doubts and fears, but each time they have been the trigger or catalyst for further spiritual growth, as if heaven was calling out to me through my doubt to question and look deeper within for my own spiritual identity.

Finally respecting my name and by extension myself after years of feeling that it was an uncomfortable fit was transformative. There is a school of thought that believes your soul chooses your name. I don't know about that, but I do believe the sound of a name does carry with it certain energy vibrations, so if you aren't sure of your calling in life one place to look for inspiration and guidance might be your name. Research it and find out everything you can about it. Perhaps it will trigger something in you. As I said, this approach may not work for you, but it is as good a starting point for self-discovery as any. We all have to begin somewhere, so why not start with your name – with who you are.

If you truly don't find anything in your name that resonates or inspires you, just think of love whenever you think of your name. You have an eternity of self-discovery and spiritual inspiration there.

May today there be peace within. May you trust
heaven that you are exactly where you are meant to be.
May you not forget the infinite possibilities that are born of
faith. May you use the gifts that you have received
and pass on the love that has been given to you. May
you be content knowing you are a child of heaven.
Let this presence settle into your bones and allow your
soul the freedom to sing, dance praise and love. It is
there for each and every one of you.

SAINT TERESA OF AVILA

Kind words can be short and easy to speak,
but their echoes are endless.

MOTHER TERESA, SAINT FROM SEPTEMBER 2016